HISTORY OF EARLY STEAMBOAT NAVIGATION

ON THE

MISSOURI RIVER

LIFE AND ADVENTURES

OF

JOSEPH LA BARGE

PIONEER NAVIGATOR AND INDIAN TRADER

FOR FIFTY YEARS IDENTIFIED WITH THE COMMERCE OF THE MISSOURI VALLEY

BY

HIRAM MARTIN CHITTENDEN

Captain Corps of Engineers, U. S. A.

VOL. I & II.

1903

COPYRIGHT 2015 BIG BYTE BOOKS

Discover more lost history from BIG BYTE BOOKS

Contents

PREFACE 7
CHAPTER I. 9
CHAPTER II. 16
CHAPTER III. 21
CHAPTER IV. 27
CHAPTER V. 32
CHAPTER VI. 38
CHAPTER VII. 44
CHAPTER VIII. 52
CHAPTER IX. 62
CHAPTER X. 77
CHAPTER XI. 88
CHAPTER XII. 92
CHAPTER XIII. 100
CHAPTER XIV. 107
CHAPTER XV. 113
CHAPTER XVI. 121
CHAPTER XVII. 128
CHAPTER XVIII. 138
CHAPTER XIX. 141
CHAPTER XX. 152
CHAPTER XXI. 157
CHAPTER XXII. 166
CHAPTER XXIII. 173
CHAPTER XXIV. 179
CHAPTER XXV. 186
CHAPTER XXVI. 197
CHAPTER XXVII. 202
CHAPTER XXVIII. 206
CHAPTER XXX. 218
CHAPTER XXXI. 226
CHAPTER XXXII. 236

CHAPTER XXXIII. 244
CHAPTER XXXIV. 252
CHAPTER XXXV. 258
CHAPTER XXXVI. 263
CHAPTER XXXVII 271
CHAPTER XXXVIII 275

PREFACE

IN the summer of 1896 the author of this work, while engaged in collecting data for a history of the American Fur Trade of the Far West, met the venerable Missouri River pilot, Captain Joseph La Barge, at his home in St. Louis. In the course of several interviews he became deeply impressed with the range and accuracy of the old gentleman's knowledge of early Western history, and asked him if he had ever taken any steps to preserve the record of his adventurous career. He replied that he had often been urged to do so, but that lack of familiarity with that kind of work had hitherto caused him to shrink from it, and he presumed he should die without ever undertaking it. Believing that his memoirs were well worth preserving, as a part of the history of the West, the author proposed to prepare them for publication if he would consent to dictate them. After some hesitation he concluded to try it, and the work was forthwith begun. Full notes were taken in the rough, and a clean copy was then submitted to Captain La Barge for revision. He went through the whole with painstaking care, and the record was left as complete as a memory of extraordinary power could make it. The intention was, at the time, to put the notes into shape for publication at once; but the Spanish-American war interfered with the author's part of the work, and before it could be resumed Captain La Barge died.

This event led to a material change in the plan of the work, and it was decided to make it, not merely a narrative of personal experiences, but a history of steamboat navigation on the Missouri River. Very few people now have any conception of the part which this remarkable business played in the upbuilding of the West. There is no railroad system in the United States to-day whose importance to its tributary country is relatively greater than was that of the Missouri River to the trans-Mississippi territory in the first seventy-five years of the nineteenth century. The business of the fur trade, the intercourse of government agents with the Indians, the campaigns of the army throughout the valley, and the wild rush of gold seekers to the mountains, all depended, in greater or less degree, upon the Missouri River as a line of transportation.

It is not alone from a commercial point of view that the record of this business is an important one. From beginning to end it abounds in thrilling incident, and the life which it fostered was full of picturesque and even tragic details. The circumstances surrounding a voyage up or down the Missouri, whether by canoe, mackinaw, keelboat, or steamboat, were quite out of the line of ordinary experience. No other river in this country has a record to compare with it.

Captain La Barge's life embraced the entire era of active boating business on the river. He saw it all— from the time when the Creole and Canadian voyageurs cordelled their keelboats up the refractory stream to the time when the railroad won its final victory over the steamboat. He was on the first boat that went to the far upper river, and he made the last through voyage from St. Louis to Fort Benton. He typified in his own career the meteoric rise and fall of that peculiar business. He grew up with it, prospered with it, and was ruined with and by it. He saw and shared the wonderful metamorphosis that came over the Missouri Valley in the space of fourscore years, and his reminiscences are a succession of living pictures taken all along the line.

It is hoped that the method adopted, of weaving the story which it is here attempted to relate around the biography of its most distinguished personality, will not detract from its value as historical material. It is not the bare narration of events that gives history its true value, but those intimate pictures of human life in other times that show what people really did and the motives by which they were actuated. To this end, biography, and even fiction, possess distinct advantages over the ordinary method of historical writing.

In the preparation of this work valuable personal aid has been received from many sources, particularly from the Hon. Phil E. Chappelle of Kansas City, Mo.; Messrs. N. P. Langford and J. B. Hubbell of St. Paul, Minn.; Hon. Wilbur F. Sanders of Helena, Mont.; and General Grenville M. Dodge [author of _How We Built the Union Pacific Railway_] of New York City.

CHAPTER I.

CAPTAIN JOSEPH LA BARGE

(When a young man)

HISTORY OF ANCESTRY.

IN the far-reaching operations of the French Government upon the continent of America, by which its western empire at one time embraced fully half of what is now the United States and Canada, two streams of colonization flowed inward from the sea. The course of one was along the valleys of the St. Lawrence River and the Great Lakes to the upper Mississippi and its tributaries. That of the other was along the lower Mississippi northward from the Gulf of Mexico. The two streams met at the mouth of the Missouri, where their blended currents were deflected westward toward the unknown regions of the setting sun. Near this place of meeting there arose, more than a decade before the birth of the American Republic, a village which has now become one of the greatest cities in the western world. Here, in the early days, the Canadians from the north and the Creoles from the south, kindred in language and tradition, mingled in common pursuits and enterprises, and for many years bore an important part in the great movement which proceeded onward from this common starting-point.

Among the well-known families identified with this movement was one whose ancestral line represented both the northern and the southern blood, and was a pure type of their united quality. This was the family of Captain Joseph La Barge, the subject of the present sketch. The father of Captain La Barge was a typical representative of the French peasantry of Quebec. His mother was a Creole descendant of both the Spanish and French elements in the settlement of the Mississippi Valley.

On the paternal side the ancestors of Captain La Barge came from Normandy, France. Robert Labarge was a native of Columbiere in the diocese of Bayonne, and was born in 1633. He came to America early in life and settled in the county of Montmorency, below Quebec, where he was married in 1663. He is said to have been the only person of the name who ever emigrated to America. His descendants are now of the most numerous family in the district of Beauharhois, if not in the entire province of Quebec, where it has held important positions both in Church and State. Its ramifications in the United States have likewise become very extensive. The true spelling of the name was *Laberge,* and this form still prevails in Quebec; but the St. Louis branch of the family has for many years spelled the name in two words, *La Barge.*

Captain La Barge was of the sixth generation from his Norman ancestors. His father, Joseph Marie La Barge, was born at Assumption, Quebec, July 4, 1787. He emigrated to St. Louis about 1808, just as he was arriving of age. He traveled by the usual route, up the Ottawa River and through the intricate system of waterways in northern Ontario which leads to Georgian Bay and to Lake Huron. Thence he went by way of Mackinaw Strait and Lake Michigan to Green Bay, and along the Fox and Wisconsin rivers to the Mississippi, which he descended to St. Louis. He used a single birch-bark canoe all the way, with only eight miles of portaging.

The elder La Barge led a varied career in St. Louis, as did most of the pioneers in those days, when fixed callings were few and men turned their hands to whatever fell in their way. A good deal of information has survived concerning him, and all to his credit.

He was evidently a man of good parts, of strict integrity, loyal in his business relations, and a bold lover of the adventurous life which characterized the early history of this new country.

At the time when the Sac and Fox Indians were giving the government so much trouble, and endangering human life all along the upper Mississippi, La Barge senior was employed in the perilous business of carrying dispatches to Rock Island, having volunteered for this service when others refused to go. He served in the War of 1812, and was present in the battle of the River Raisin, or Frenchtown, January 22, 1813, and was there shot in the hand, losing two fingers. He also received a tomahawk wound on the head, and carried the scar through life. He became naturalized as a result of this service in the army. Although entitled to a pension under the laws of the United States, he never asked for nor received any.

La Barge married in 1813, and some two years afterward acquired a farm at Baden, a small village a few miles north of St. Louis, and now within the limits of that city. His main business here was the manufacture of charcoal, which he hauled to St. Louis for sale. He soon moved to town, where he had gained quite an extensive acquaintance, particularly among the Canadian voyageurs. Here he opened up a boarding-house, which developed into a regular hotel or tavern, with a livery attachment, at that time one of the most important in the city. It was while engaged in this business that he served the English traveler, James Stuart, already referred to.

> *"I can safely recommend him to any traveler, as the best person in his line I have ever met—intelligent, sober, obliging, and never afraid to encounter any difficulty that may occur."*— Three Years in North America, by James Stuart, who traveled in the United States, 1828-30, and employed La Barge to convey him on his journeys in the vicinity of St. Louis and as far east as Vincennes, Ind. He was very anxious to adopt the young child, Joseph La Barge, and take him to England and educate him, but the parents would not consent.

La Barge senior was, to a considerable extent, identified with the early trapping business in the Far West, and has left his name on geographical features in widely separated localities. There is a *La Barge* or *Battle Creek,* a tributary of the Missouri, which took its name from some affair with the Indians in which La Barge bore a part; but the details are apparently lost. The same is true of *La Barge Creek,* a tributary of Green River in Wyoming, which was named before 1830. La Barge was present in General Ashley's disastrous fight with the Aricara Indians on the Missouri River in 1823, and was the man who cut the cable of one of the keelboats so that it might drift out of range of the fire of the Indians.

La Barge senior lived to a good old age, and was sound and healthy to the last. As a remarkable evidence of this, it was long remembered by his acquaintances that he practiced in old age his favorite winter pastime of skating. His death was the result of accident. He had heard that a brother-in-law, Joseph Hortiz, was ill, and he resolved to go to see him. It was a cold wintry day, and Captain La Barge tried to dissuade him, but to no purpose. He slipped on the icy sidewalk at the corner of Olive and Fourth streets, in St. Louis, struck the curb, and received injuries from which he died two days later, January 22, 1860.

Many interesting anecdotes of the elder La Barge have come down to us, some of which are worth relating as illustrating the character of the man in different situations. One of these comes from General Harney, who was long an intimate friend of Captain La Barge. In the later years of General Harney's life', when physical ailments prevented his leaving the house, he used to send for Captain La Barge, if the latter happened to be derelict in his visits, to come and talk over old times. On one of these occasions, not long before his death, he gave the Captain the following story:

"Your father," he said, "was the only man who ever scared me. We were ascending the Missouri River on a keelboat laden with troops and supplies, he in charge of the boat, and I, a lieutenant, on duty with the soldiers. In one place the boat had to round a sharp point, where there was an accumulation of driftwood. The current was very strong, and it required the utmost efforts of the men to stem it. When we reached the most difficult place, the Captain stimulated his men by calling out to them (in the French language), *'Hale fort! Hale fort!* ('Pull hard! Pull hard!'). I didn't understand French, but thought I detected in the Captain's language something like the military command, 'Halt.' As some of the troops were on the line with the voyageurs, and as they might not understand, I thought I could help the Captain by repeating to them his command. This created some confusion, for my men began to slacken while the Captain's were pulling harder than ever. Again he commanded, *'Hale fort!'* and again I called to the men to halt. The situation was extremely critical when the Captain thundered a third time, *'Hale fort!'* in a voice and manner not to be misunderstood. The men all bent to the line and finally extricated the boat from its perilous position. The Captain then came over to where I was standing and told me that if I ever dared interfere again with his management of the boat he would pitch me into the river. I knew he meant what he said, and thereafter confined myself to my military duties."

One fine morning in the early twenties a man called at the house of Mr. La Barge, who met him at the door and asked him what he wanted. The man said: "I applied to you a short time since for employment, having heard that you were hiring men for the Ashley Expedition. I was refused, and I would like to know the reason."

"Simply because you did not suit," replied La Barge.

"I am as good a man as you are or any you have employed, and I take the liberty of telling you so," rejoined the six-footer.

"I want no trouble," replied La Barge, "and therefore will request you to get out, or I will be compelled to put you out."

"Just what I want you to undertake," was the retort. Scarcely were the words out of his mouth when La Barge seized a rawhide riding whip and started for the fellow and laid him about the back and shoulders so vigorously that the man soon gave up the contest and took to his heels.

The next morning a constable came and arrested La Barge on the charge of assault and battery, with directions to bring him at once before Esquire Gamier, Justice of the Peace.

The expeditions of General W. H. Ashley to the Rocky Mountains in quest of beaver fur were very celebrated in those days. They occurred in the years 1822-26.

"Lead the way, and I will follow," said La Barge, taking down his rawhide and starting along with the constable. La Barge told the people he met on the way to come and see the fun. In due course the trial came off and La Barge was fined four dollars. He thanked the Justice, but handed him eight dollars, saying that the fun was cheap at that price, and he would give the fellow another dose. He then seized his whip and started for him, chasing him out into the street, where he gave him a second drubbing, to the great delight of the crowd, who stood around shouting and setting him on.

Another incident, which occurred late in life, exhibits the sterling integrity of the man who could withstand the temptations of wealth rather than do the smallest act of injustice. About the time that the elder La Barge was married he purchased from Joseph Morin, for the sum of twenty-five dollars, a small tract of land on Cedar Street, between Second and Third. Land was then of very little value, and transfers were often made without deed and with no more formality than in exchanging cattle or horses. In this way La Barge traded off his lot on Cedar Street to Chauvin Lebeau for a horse, with which he moved to his Baden farm, only recently purchased. Here, as already narrated, he manufactured charcoal and hauled it to town, where he sold it to Theodore Bosseron and Vilrais Papin, then the principal blacksmiths of the village. Long years afterward, when these transactions were almost forgotten, and the property had become very valuable, a lawyer presented himself to the old gentleman and asked him if he had ever owned any property on Cedar Street. La Barge replied in the affirmative and described its locality. The lawyer then asked him when and how he disposed of it. He could not at first recall, but Mrs. La Barge remembered the circumstances and related them to the lawyer, at the same time remarking to her husband that that was the way they got their horse to set themselves up on the farm with. The lawyer then assured La Barge that the title to this property was still in him, and that he could hold it against all comers, for there was absolutely no record of the conveyance in existence. The old gentleman, with a look of indignation, asked the lawyer if he took him for a thief. "I traded that land," said he, "to Chauvin Lebeau for a horse, which was worth more to me then than the land was. I shall stand by the bargain now. If Chauvin Lebeau's heirs have no title, tell them to come to me and I will make them a deed before I die."

Such are some of the glimpses we still have through the mists of time of the father of Captain La Barge.

On the maternal side he was likewise descended from creditable ancestry. Among the early mechanics in the village of Fort de Chartres, near the mouth of the Ohio River, when to be a mechanic was to be a leading citizen, were Gabriel Dodier and Jean Baptiste Becquet, blacksmiths. The younger of these two men, Becquet, married the daughter of the other. They had three children, the eldest being a daughter, Marguerite Marianne. On the 27th of January, 1780, this daughter was married to Joseph Alvarez Hortiz, who was the son of Frangois Alvarez and Bernada Hortiz, and was born in the town of Lienira, in the Province of Estremadura, Spain, in the year 1753. Alvarez was a private soldier in the military service of Spain, and came to St. Louis after Spanish authority had been established there in 1770. He attained the rank of sergeant, and being a man of some education, was for several years detailed as military attaché to the Governor. He finally became Secretary to the last two Spanish Governors, Trudeau and Delassus, and had charge of the public archives down to 1804. He had nine children, of whom the eighth was a daughter, of the name of Eulalie. This daughter was married to Joseph Marie La Barge in St. Louis, August 13, 1813.

The parents of Captain La Barge thus represented the best traditions of French and Spanish occupancy of the Mississippi Valley. Their marriage took place after their country had become American territory, and their offspring, the subject of our present inquiries, was born an American citizen.

The data for the sketch here given of the ancestry of the La Barge family are mainly derived from letters by Dr. Philemon Laberge, Sheriff of the district of Beauharnois, Quebec, to Captain La Barge. Dr. Laberge had chanced to come across a copy of the St. Louis Republic of January 9,1898, in which there were a biographical sketch and photograph of Captain La Barge. Knowing that there was but one family of the name in America, he set about to trace the relationship, and presently sent to Captain La Barge a complete genealogical table of the family from Robert Laberge down.

The data relating to the maternal line are gleaned from Scharff's "History of St. Louis."

CHAPTER II.

CHILDHOOD AND YOUTH.

JOSEPH *La* BARGE, son of Joseph Marie La Barge and Eulalie Hortiz, was born in St Louis, October 1, 1815. He was the second child in a family of seven children, three boys and four girls, who all grew to adult years. The two brothers were Charles S., who was killed in a steamboat explosion in 1852, and John B., who dropped dead at the wheel in 1885 while making a steamboat landing at Bismarck, N. D.

Soon after the birth of Captain La Barge the parents moved to the newly acquired farm in Baden. There is but one incident relating to the young child while living here that need detain us. Although this place was distant only six miles from where the courthouse of St. Louis now stands, it was at that time unsettled and uncleared, and Indians not infrequently roamed in the vicinity. The Sac and Fox tribes were particularly troublesome, and many were the outrages which they committed upon the isolated settlement. The incident in question occurred one day just before the father had started on his usual trip to town. He was loading his cart at some distance from the garden, where Mrs. La Barge had gone to dig some potatoes to send to her mother in the village. Housewives in those days seldom enjoyed the luxury of nurses, and Mrs. La Barge was obliged to carry her child with her into the garden. Depositing him between the rows of potatoes, she was proceeding with her work, when suddenly the house dog set up a cry of alarm. Looking up, Mrs. La Barge was horrified to see an Indian approaching. She uttered a scream and started for the house, forgetting in the suddenness of her alarm the baby in the garden. Meanwhile the father had heard the dog's bark and his wife's screams, and hastened to see what was the matter. His first question was about the baby, and Mrs. La Barge, more terrified than ever, rushed back to where she had left him. Fortunately the dog had held the Indian at bay, and when the father arrived, gun in hand, he beat a prompt retreat. Captain La Barge's father often reminded him of this incident in after years, predicting that he would always escape harm from the Indians, for they had had their opportunity and had failed. In his many experiences with the

Indians throughout a life spent in their country, he never suffered personal injury at their hands, and came to have faith in his father's prediction.

Captain La Barge was not yet two years old when the first steamboat came to St. Louis, nor four when the first one entered the Missouri River. It is said that his father used to take him to the river bank to see these early boats, and that they always had a great attraction for his youthful fancy. To be a steamboat master was his ambition, and he spent much of his time as a child in drawing boats and making models, and thus unwittingly training himself for his after career.

The boy was a leader among his fellows, and an expert in all youthful games practiced at the time. In contests of skill among the boys of the village each side was anxious to secure Joe La Barge. "He could jump higher," says one authority, "run faster, and swim farther than any other lad in the town."

Among the noteworthy events of Captain La Barge's childhood, the memory of which clung by him even in old age, was the visit of Lafayette to St. Louis in 1825. This venerable patriot, whom, next to Washington, Americans in that day delighted to honor, arrived in St. Louis on board the steamer *Natchez*, at 9 A. M., May 29. He was met at the wharf by a committee of leading citizens, and an address of welcome was made by the Mayor, to which Lafayette responded. He then entered a carriage with the Mayor and Mr. Auguste Chouteau and Stephen Hempstead, a soldier of the Revolution, and was driven to the house of Mr. Pierre Chouteau, Sr., which had been prepared for his reception. He was escorted by a company of light horsemen, and also by a company of uniformed boys, of whom Captain La Barge, then ten years old, was one. The Captain always remembered the venerable appearance of the General and his review of the youthful troop. He shook hands with them, indulged in the pleasant questions which age delights to ask of youth, and doubtless himself took a keen pleasure in the incident, because most of his youthful auditors could reply in his own tongue.

An interesting sequel of Lafayette's visit to St. Louis occurred in that city in 1881, on the occasion of the visit of Lafayette's grandson with General Boulanger and party, who had come to America to attend the centennial celebration of the surrender of Yorktown. Captain La Barge was sent for, to meet the distinguished company at the Merchants' Exchange. When introduced to the members of the party, the grandson of Lafayette came forward, and taking La Barge by both hands, looked at him a moment and said: "You have seen one whom I wish it were my lot to have seen, and that is my revered grandfather." He cordially urged the Captain to come to his home if he should ever visit France, and in other ways showed an almost affectionate interest in this individual who had once, though but a boy, beheld the face of his distinguished ancestor.

Captain La Barge's schooling was necessarily very limited, for the educational facilities of St. Louis in those days were of a truly primitive order. He first went to a schoolmaster of considerable local renown, Jean Baptiste Trudeau, at the latter's private residence on Pine Street, between Main and Second. Here he studied the common branches, all in French. He went for a time to Salmon Giddings, founder of the First Presbyterian Church, in St. Louis, and later to a more pretentious school kept by Elihu H. Shephard, an excellent teacher. At both of these schools instruction was given in English. Captain La Barge's parents foresaw that their native tongue could not long survive in common use, and felt it to be their duty to equip their son, so far as their slender means would permit, with the language of his country. The pupil found the task a tedious one, and was a long while in mastering it. He never forgot the almost insurmountable obstacle he found in the English "th." He used his native language in common intercourse down to nearly 1850, and retained a fluent command of it to his death. He also acquired a very perfect command of English, in which there was no trace of foreign accent, but in which the mellowing influence of the softer tongue had produced a modulation of the voice that was very pleasant to listen to.

In 1819 there was established in Perry County, Mo., a Catholic School, St. Mary's College. Young La Barge was sent there at the age of twelve, and remained three years. On their way to the college himself and father traveled by the steamer *Titscumbia*. It was

Captain La Barge's first ride in a kind of boat with which most of his after life was to be connected. The desire of the young man's parents was to educate their son for the priesthood, and his course at college was shaped somewhat to that end. But the boy did not fall in with their plans, as his tastes ran in a different direction. He did not finish the course, for his career at the school was summarily cut short by a delinquency which is the only one we have to record in a life of more than fourscore years. He became involved in intrigues with young women to an extent which barred him from a further continuation of his course.

Associated with him in this unfortunate episode was Edward Liguest Chouteau, a youth of about the same age as himself. The young men walked to St. Genevieve, on the Mississippi. Chouteau was without funds, and La Barge nearly so, having scarcely the amount of a single steamboat fare to St. Louis. They found the *De Witt Clinton* at the bank on her way up the river. La Barge told the captain of the boat the straight story of their misfortune: that they had only enough money for a single fare to St. Louis, and would have to walk unless they could make some arrangement with him. He laughed, and told them to get on board and he would see them home. This incident, in which the two young men were companions in misfortune, was not forgotten by either, and we shall have occasion to refer to it again in the course of this narrative.

After La Barge left college his father placed him in the office of John Bent, a leading lawyer of St. Louis, and one of the noted Bent brothers. He soon became disgusted with his new situation on account of his preceptor's habit of excessive drink. He then went into a clothing store, and after remaining about a year, left that.

The restless ambition of the young man was now directed toward a kind of life which, in every portion of the country, has filled up the period between discovery and settlement—the business of the fur trade. At this particular time it was the only business carried on in the trans-Mississippi territory beyond the few scattering settlements along the lower Missouri. Large parties of hunters and trappers remained constantly in the wilderness, wandering all over those vast regions in quest of beaver and other fur. Each spring expeditions set out for various points in the Far West from Santa Fe to the British boundary, carrying supplies and recruits and bringing back the furs collected during the previous year. The great bulk of this business was done along the Missouri River, where trading posts were established throughout the entire valley. The annual journeys to these posts were always made by water. In the keelboat days they consumed an entire summer, but after the steamboat came they were completed by the middle of July.

From its very nature this business was one of adventure and excitement, and particularly attractive to those who were fond of an independent and out-of-door life. We can but faintly imagine at this day how strong was the attraction for youth in this wild life.

Now it is considered a great piece of good luck for a boy to get on a common surveying party in the mountains, where he may see something of the wildness of nature, and perhaps catch sight of some surviving specimens of the larger game. In those days a trip to the mountains meant adventure of the genuine sort —absence from civilization, ever-present danger from the Indians, game of all kinds in abundance, and the grandeur and beauty of nature in a region still unknown except to a very few.

Being now at the impressionable age of sixteen, young La Barge became infatuated with the tales of adventure related by those who came back every year from the distant mountains. He told his father that, for the present, his mind was made up. He would join one of the fur-trade expeditions and see something of the Indian country. This decision met a responsive chord in the adventurous nature of the father, who said he had no objection if the mother were willing. The matter was laid before her, and after much entreaty and expostulation, her consent was secured. This was in the year 1831.

CHAPTER III.

ENTERS THE FUR TRADE.

CAPTAIN LA BARGE did not immediately find an opportunity to visit the Indian country. The annual expeditions for the year had all gone. The *Yellowstone* was already far away on her historic first trip up the Missouri for the American Fur Company, and nothing was left for the impatient youth but to await a later opportunity. When the *Yellowstone* returned from her voyage, she was sent down the Mississippi to pass the time until the following spring in the Bayou la Fourche sugar trade. La Barge was engaged as second clerk on this voyage and found himself in constant demand as interpreter during the winter. The people of the Bayou la Fourche district spoke only French, which most of the officers of the boat did not understand. La Barge, who knew both French and English well, was of great use in carrying on the trade.

In the spring of 1832 the *Yellowstone* returned to St. Louis to prepare for her second voyage up the Missouri. This boat had been built as an experiment, to determine if it would be practicable to substitute steamboats for keelboats in the trade of the upper river. In the summer of 1831 she had gone as far as Fort Tecumseh, which stood on the opposite shore from the present capital of South Dakota. It was now proposed to take her as far as the mouth of the *Yellowstone*. The attempt was completely successful, and the voyage has ever since been considered one of the landmarks of the early history of the West.

Although La Barge was only in his seventeenth year he signed a contract binding himself to the service of the American Fur Company, as voyageur, engage, or clerk, for a period of three years, at a salary of seven hundred dollars for the whole time A He did not go as part of the boat's crew, but as an employee of one of the posts. No place was specified -in his engagement, but his assignment was left to the bourgeois of the different posts, who came down to the boat when it arrived, looked over the new engages, and selected such as they thought would suit them. Young La Barge was a promising-looking lad, and did not get above Council Bluffs, where he was taken off and put to work at Cabanne's post, a few miles above the modern city of Omaha.

When the *Yellowstone* returned from Fort Union, John P. Cabanne, the bourgeois in charge of the post, went down to St. Louis and took La Barge with him. While waiting to return to the upper country the young engage took temporary service on the steamboat *Warrior,* Captain Throckmorton, bound for the seat of the Blackhawk, or Sac and Fox, war. She was loaded with government stores for Prairie du Chien, and La Barge went along in some subordinate capacity. It happened that she arrived at the scene of the Battle of Bad Axe just as that decisive conflict was going on. Captain Throckmorton saw a number of Indians trying to make their escape by swimming the river and he fired into them, killing several. They proved to be all women, and the over-zealous captain long had reason to regret his hasty action. After this adventure the *Warrior* returned to St. Louis.

When Cabanne went back to his post at the Council Bluffs young La Barge went with him to commence in earnest his life in the Indian country. His initiation into the business of the fur trade was such as to leave a lasting impression on his mind. He had not been' at Cabanne's post very long when he had a lively experience of the evils of competition in that business, and of the extreme measures to which unrestrained rivalry sometimes led. Narcisse Leclerc, at one time an employee of the American Fur Company, had saved a little means, which certain parties in St. Louis eked out to a respectable sum, and he resolved to go into the trading business on his own and their account. Under the style of the Northwest Fur Company he carried on a prosperous trade in a small way for two or three seasons. The American Fur Company, jealous of all opposition, always treated these petty rivals with the utmost severity, and, if possible, crushed them by sheer force. When it could not do this it bought them out. Leclerc, who was a shrewd fellow, and as unscrupulous as any of the company's agents, had developed staying qualities which caused the company a good deal of uneasiness. He went up the river in the autumn of 1832 with a larger outfit than ever, and the company determined that something must be done to arrest his career. The problem was left for Cabanne to solve, and he was given authority, as a last resort, to offer Leclerc outright a thousand dollars if he would not carry his trade up the river beyond a specified point.

Circumstances, however, threw in Cabanne's way what he considered a better means of dealing with Leclerc. Congress had lately passed a law prohibiting the importation of liquor into the Indian country. Cabanne found out in some way that Leclerc had smuggled a considerable quantity past the military authorities at Leavenworth. Here was his opportunity. He would stop the expedition, and confiscate the property on the ground that Leclerc was violating the law of the land. It did not seem to occur to him that the enforcement of the law is intrusted to duly constituted officials, and that he, not being one of these, could not legally do more than inform against Leclerc. He did not trouble himself about fine distinctions of that sort. Exultantly he wrote to the house in St. Louis: "Have no fear; leave the matter to me, and I will make our incapable adversary bite the dust."

Cabanne laid his plans well for the capture of Leclerc's outfit. As soon as the boat passed his post he organized a party under charge of Peter A. Sarpy, clerk at the post, to go and arrest Leclerc. Sarpy picked out about a dozen men, among whom was the new engage, La Barge. They were all well armed and carried besides a small cannon. Going to a point near old Fort Lisa, where the channel of the river came in close to a high impending bank, Sarpy stationed his men there and awaited Leclerc's arrival. At the proper time, when the voyageurs were cordelling the boat along a sandbar just opposite, scarcely a hundred yards off, he ordered Leclerc's party to surrender or he would "blow everything out of the water." Although Leclerc had some thirty men, they were mostly unarmed, and could make no effective resistance. They surrendered, and the whole outfit returned to Cabanne's post, where the liquor was confiscated and the expedition broken up.

This drastic measure came near proving fatal to the company's business upon the river. Leclerc immediately returned to St. Louis, where he began suit against the company and lodged a criminal complaint against Cabanne. The matter bore a very serious aspect for a time. It was with the utmost difficulty, and with an evident resort to misrepresentation, that the company's license was saved; and doubtless it would have been revoked but for the influence of Senator Thomas H. Benton. As it was, it cost the company a large sum of money, increased the public distrust of this powerful concern, and banished Cabanne, one of its most efficient servants, permanently from the country.

At Cabanne's post La Barge was employed in the various duties of engage, and was frequently sent out to surrounding bands of Indians with small outfits of merchandise to trade for their furs. His most interesting and valuable experience in this line was with the Pawnees, who resided on the Loup Fork of the Platte, about one hundred miles west of the Missouri. They were what are called permanent village Indians; that is, they had fixed villages made of large, strong houses, where they regularly lived; while many of the tribes, like the Sioux, Crows, and Blackfeet, lived onlyin tents, and were always moving from one place to another. The Pawnees, it is true, roved about a great deal on their hunting and war expeditions, but they had a fixed place of abode to which they always returned from their wanderings. Their houses were circular in form and quite large, being sometimes sixty feet in diameter, and, to judge from pictures of them, resembled in appearance, when seen from a distance, a group of oil tanks in a modern petroleum district.

Near to their villages the Pawnees cultivated extensive fields of maize or Indian corn. After the spring planting was over they generally went on long excursions to hunt buffalo, to make war, or to secure wood and other materials for the village. Their cornfields were left to shift for themselves during this period, and their enemies sometimes took advantage of this fact; but on the whole the latter were very cautious about what they did, for they knew that the wily Pawnee would learn who the robbers were and would not fail to exact full retribution. When the corn was ripe the Indians gathered it and remained in their villages a considerable part of the winter. Their business, however, compelled them at this season to make their hunts for robes and furs, which were salable only when taken during the cold weather. When the skins were brought into the villages the squaws took them, scraped them down, rubbed, them with brains or pork, and otherwise manipulated them until they were soft and flexible and ready for the trade.

The custom of the traders was to send over from their posts near the old Council Bluffs one or more clerks, with a few men and the necessary merchandise, to reside in the villages until the trade was over. The clerk generally lived in the lodge of the principal chief, kept his goods there, and also such furs as were received in trade. After the season's business was over the furs were loaded into bullboats, in which they were floated down the Loup and the Platte rivers to the Missouri. Here they were reshipped in large cargoes to St. Louis.

It was on a business of this kind that young La Barge spent his first winter in the Indian country—1832-33. His party consisted of four men, who, with the merchandise, were accommodated in the lodge of the chief Big Axe. Here they settled down to genuine Indian life— not half so uninteresting and repulsive as one might be disposed to think. The business of the trade, the ceremonials, the games and gambling, and the never-failing attractions of the gentler sex, which, one may easily believe, are as potent in the wilderness as in the city, all operated to make the time pass agreeably during the long and severe winters. The huts were very comfortable, and Captain La Barge always remembered them as the coolest habitations in summer and the warmest in winter of any that he had ever occupied. He noted as a remarkable peculiarity that mosquitoes never entered them.

During his winter sojourn among the Pawnees La Barge applied himself assiduously to learning their language. The interpreter would give him words and sentences in Pawnee and he would write them down and learn them. He practically mastered the language in the course of the winter, to the great astonishment of the natives and even of the whites. To the Indians the process of writing was a great curiosity, a "big medicine," and when they saw young La Barge write down something and then read it off, they would put their hands to their mouths in their characteristic manner of expressing wonder.

There were numerous Indian scares during the winter, and Captain La Barge fully expected to see something of Indian warfare before he left the villages, but nothing of the sort actually occurred. In the spring of 1833, before he left for the Missouri. Major John Dougherty, Indian agent residing at Bellevue, about ten miles below the modern city of Omaha, arrived at the villages for the purpose of ransoming a female prisoner of the Crow nation, who had been sentenced to be burned at the stake. He prevailed, through Big Axe, chief of the Pawnee Loups, upon having her given up on payment of the ransom. He then started back with her to Bellevue, accompanied by an escort, until at a safe distance from the villages. When about ten miles on their way they were overtaken by a Pawnee chief, Spotted Horse, who came riding up at a gallop, and when opposite the woman, shot an arrow through her heart.

When the high water of spring arrived the furs were loaded into bullboats and shipped down to the mouth of the Platte. La Barge returned to Cabanne's, and after a short time started for St. Louis with a fleet of mackinaw boats loaded with furs. He reached St. Louis in the latter part of May, 1833.

CHAPTER IV.

CHOLERA ON THE YELLOWSTONE

BEFORE La Barge arrived in St. Louis the company had dispatched two boats to the upper river—the *Yellowstone* and the *Assiniboine*. The voyage of 1833 is particularly noteworthy as the one on which Prince Maximilian of Wied made his celebrated visit to the upper Missouri—a visit which has done more than any other one thing to preserve a true picture of those early times. The *Yellowstone* went only as far as Fort Pierre, whence she returned immediately, and as soon as another cargo could be shipped, started on a trip to Council Bluffs.

Captain La Barge went back up the river on this second trip of the *Yellowstone* to return to his post. It proved to be a most trying and pathetic voyage. The cholera, which was then epidemic throughout the country, broke out with great virulence on the boat, and so many of the crew died that Captain Bennett was forced to stop at the mouth of the Kansas River until he could go back to St. Louis for a crew. His pilot and most of his sub-officers were dead, and he was compelled to leave the boat in care of young La Barge, who thus began his career as a steamboat man on the Missouri. His several voyages had given him considerable knowledge of the art of handling these boats, and he had no misgivings in being left in charge, except the fear that the cholera might take him off. It was a very trying moment. Captain Bennett, when he started back to St. Louis, cried like a child. The terrible power of the disease unstrung everyone's nerves. Victims often died within two hours after being attacked, and no one knew when his turn would come.

Scarcely had Captain Bennett left when a new difficulty arose. The "graybacks," as the scattered population of western Missouri were then called, having learned that the *Yellowstone* had cholera on board, organized themselves into a *pro tempore* State board of health and ordered Captain La Barge to take the boat out of the State, or they would burn her up. The engineer and firemen were dead, so Captain La Barge fired up himself, and, acting as pilot, engineer, and all, succeeded in getting the boat above the mouth of the Kansas and on the west shore of the river, outside the jurisdiction of the State of Missouri.

The *Yellowstone* had a quantity of goods on board consigned to Cyprian Chouteau's trading post, which was located some ten miles up the Kansas River.

Captain Bennett had directed La Barge to turn over these goods to the consignees during his absence. Accordingly, at the first opportunity, he set off alone on foot to find the trading post and tell Mr. Chouteau to come and get his goods. When about a mile from the post he was met by a man who had been stationed there to watch for anyone coming from the Missouri. The news of the cholera was abroad and the lonely post had quarantined itself against the civilized world. The man would not permit La Barge to come nearer, and threatened to shoot him if he persisted. La Barge agreed to stay where he was if the man would return to the post and carry his message to Chouteau. This was done, and Chouteau sent back word to store the goods on the bank and leave them there. It was now too late to return to the boat that night after a fatiguing day's work, and La Barge would have had to go supperless and coverless to sleep but for the kind offices of his old college chum and former companion in misfortune, Edward Liguest Chouteau, who happened to be at the post. Hearing of La Barge's situation, he went to find him. He reached his friend's bivouac about midnight and found him trying to pass the night in some comfort around a large bonfire. He brought something to eat and a large buffalo robe to sleep on, and La Barge got through the remainder of the night very well.

While the *Yellowstone* was lying above the mouth of the Kansas the *Assiniboine* passed down on her return trip. La Barge signaled for assistance, but Captain Pratt would not stop. "It was pretty hard," observed the captain, in narrating this affair. "I never refused to answer a distress signal, even if the boat were engaged in the strongest opposition; but our two boats were in the same trade, bound to assist each other, and yet we were left there alone in the severest straits, with no idea when we should be relieved."

When asked how these grave dangers, which were more or less his portion through life, affected him, Captain La Barge replied that, if in idleness and given time to think about them, they always depressed and in a measure unnerved him; but he was generally actively engaged, and the interest in his work and the responsibility resting upon him caused him to forget the danger. Violence and death were a familiar feature of the life in which he was engaged, and to some extent he became hardened to them. Speaking of the great number of deaths along the river, the Captain shook his head reflectively as he told of the many burials that it had been his lot to make. "There is a spot just below Kansas City—I could point it out now," he said, "where I buried eight cholera victims in one grave. I could easily name a hundred localities along the river where I have buried passengers or crew. I generally sought some elevated ground for this purpose, which the ravages of the river could not reach. The graves were marked, if at all, with wooden head-boards, for there was generally no other material at hand, and if there were, time did not permit the use of it. It will never be known, and cannot now even be conjectured, how many of these forgotten graves there are, but enough to make the shores of the Missouri River one continuous cemetery from its source to its mouth. Were every white man's grave along that stream distinctly marked, the voyageur would never be out of sight of these pathetic reminders of futile contests with the universal enemy. But, alas! no mark remains upon any but a very few, and the names of those who are buried in them are forever wrapped in oblivion."

After a long delay Captain Bennett returned with a crew on the steamboat *Otto,* Captain James Hill, an opposition boat in the service of Sublette & Campbell. This was the year when Sublette & Campbell made such a strong show of competition with the American Fur Company. Sublette himself was on board the *Otto* at the time. As soon as Captain Bennett resumed charge of the *Yellowstone* the boat proceeded on her way and reached Cabanne's post in August.

Cabanne having been expelled from the Indian country, the post had a new bourgeois, Joshua Pilcher, a man of long experience in the Indian country, and former president of the Missouri Fur Company. Late in the month of August Pilcher sent La Barge with a small outfit of goods to the Pawnee villages to buy some buffalo meat. La Barge packed his goods on five horses and set out. He found the Pawnees still absent, and as war parties of their enemies might be lurking around the vacant villages, he thought it prudent to await at a distance the return of the Indians. In the meanwhile his party ran out of provisions, and their situation was becoming serious when La Barge decided to go and get corn enough from the fields to last them until the Pawnees should return. He went with another man, and they soon loaded themselves with ears and returned to camp. This process continued successfully for several days, great pains being taken to levy tribute uniformly throughout the cornfield, so that the Indians might not detect the loss.

They were not skillful enough in this, however, and finally had to pay for the corn.

On the fourth day of their foraging expeditions they were discovered by a small war party of Sioux about a mile off. They took to flight, and tried to infuse some life into their mules, but the stolid animals would not hurry. This was particularly the case with La Barge's mule, which could scarcely be driven into a slow gallop. La Barge saw that at the rate they were going they would surely be cut off, and he told his companion, who had the best mule, to hurry to camp for help, and he would stand the Indians off with his rifle. The companion did not like to do this, but La Barge insisted. He felt comparatively safe for a short time, for he was in a perfectly open plain, where it was impossible for the Indians to approach under cover. Whenever they drew too near he would level his rifle at them and they would venture no further. In the meanwhile he kept moving on toward camp, and soon had the pleasure of seeing his companion riding up at full speed with re-enforcements.

When the Pawnees returned La Barge bought a good supply of meat and took it to Cabanne's. There he found that veteran mountaineer, Etienne Provost, who at that time probably knew the western country better than any other living man. He had just come in for the purpose of guiding Fontenelle and Drips, partners in the American' Fur Company mountain service, and owners of the trading post at Bellevue, to the Bayou Salade (South Park,

Colorado), where they intended to spend the winter trapping beaver. Provost heard of La Barge's adventure and complimented him very warmly upon it. He was now an old man, but he came up to La Barge, took him by both hands, and said to him: "I am glad you did not show the white feather to those rascals. You are the kind of man for this country. I am going to ask Major Pilcher to let you go with me. I have need of such men." La Barge was very anxious to go, filled as he was then with the thirst of youth for adventure. But Major Pilcher needed his services and would not consent. Pilcher was very kind to La Barge, even permitting him to eat at his table—a great concession, for none of the employees were allowed to eat with the bourgeois of the post unless it was so stipulated in their contract of service. Pilcher took a special pride in his young engage, and tried to put opportunities for distinction in his way.

CHAPTER V.
FURTHER SERVICE AT CABANNE'S.

In November, 1833, Pilcher sent La Barge down to a small trading post at the mouth of the Nishnabotna (river where they make canoes), kept by Francis Duroins for the convenience of a local band of Indians. La Barge's misson was to take two twenty-gallon kegs of alcohol to Duroins. He was accompanied by a half-blood Indian, and they made the trip in a canoe. The first night they encamped on Trudeau Island, about two and a half miles above the mouth of the Weeping Water River. This island was named after Zenon Trudeau, a trader, brother of the noted schoolmaster, Joseph Trudeau, and was later called Hurricane Island, from the circumstance of its having been swept by a tornado. It has since been entirely washed away. This was the night of the ever-to-be-remembered meteoric shower of 1833. La Barge was awaked from his sleep by the brilliant light, and, though not apprehensive of any impending calamity, was naturally awe-struck at the extraordinary display. The meteors were flying, as it seemed to him, in all directions, and their number and brilliancy made the night as light as day. The half breed companion was absolutely panic-stricken, and declared that the day of doom was at hand. But he did not forget, in his fright, the divine injunction to "eat and drink, for to-morrow we die." Rolling himself up in his blanket, he besought La Barge to open the keg of alcohol and let him meet his fate as became a man in that wild and lawless country.

As nearly as La Barge could recall, the heavier part of the shower lasted about two hours. A singular incident occurred early in its duration. A deer which had become frightened at the unusual sight came bounding through the undergrowth and plunged directly into camp, coming to a dead halt scarcely six paces from where La Barge was sitting. He seized a shotgun and killed it with a load of buckshot.

In January, 1834, the winter express came up from St. Louis. The express was a matter of great importance in the early fur trade. It was sent from St. Louis every winter to all the posts. Usually an express started downstream from the upper posts before the arrival of that from below. They generally met at Fort Pierre, exchanged dispatches, and each made the return trip from that point. By means of the express an interchange of views was had between the house in St. Louis and the partners in the field; and the latter were able to send down statements of business, requisitions for supplies, with information as to the prospects for the ensuing season's trade at the upper posts, and the condition of snow in the mountains. The carrying of the express was a matter of great danger and hardship. It was generally done in the dead of winter. Between Pierre and St. Louis it was carried on horseback; above Pierre on dogsleds. The packages were put up with the most scrupulous care, and were intrusted only to those in whom the company had absolute confidence. The bearers were not permitted to carry anything else, nor to do errands for others, but were required to attend to the express only. The chief danger on the long journey was from the cold, for at this season the Indians were not dangerous, being generally huddled together in their villages for the winter. The route above Bellevue was along the west shore to opposite Vermillion, where it crossed the river and remained on the east shore the rest of the way until opposite Fort Pierre.

Captain La Barge's father brought up the express from St. Louis in the winter of 1834. He was to return from Cabanne's post, and Pilcher was to provide for its carriage the rest of the way. A few days before his arrival a brutal murder occurred at the post. A half-breed named Pinaud, while in a state of drunkenness, shot and killed a white man named

Blair. Both of the men were hunters for the post. Pilcher immediately put Pinaud in irons, to be held until he could be sent to St. Louis for trial. When the elder La Barge arrived Pilcher asked him if he would undertake to deliver the prisoner to the United States authorities in St. Louis. He agreed to try it. When ready to start he requested Pilcher to remove the irons and put Pinaud on a mule. This astonished Pilcher a good deal, but La Barge explained that the man could ride better with the free use of his limbs, which was also necessary to keep him from freezing to death. He said he could catch him if he undertook to run, for the mule was no match in speed for his horse. He would take the irons and put them on in camp.

The prisoner was delivered in due time to the proper authorities in St. Louis, where he was held for trial. And now ensued one of those miscarriages, or rather travesties, of justice which marked the entire history of the American Fur Company on the Missouri River. Although Pinaud's crime was a cold-blooded and causeless murder, it was nevertheless of vital importance that he be acquitted; otherwise it would bring out the fact that the Company was violating the Federal statutes by selling liquor at its posts. The company therefore took good care that none of the people from the upper country who were conversant with the facts should be in St. Louis when the trial came off. The prosecution, consequently, could produce no witnesses, and the man was acquitted.

Two or three days after the elder La Barge left Cabanne's post for St. Louis Pilcher summoned young La Barge to him and asked him to take the express to Pierre. "There are old voyageurs here whom I can send," he said, "but I can't trust them. I want you to go. What do you say to it?"

"Well, Major," La Barge replied, "I have never been as far above this post in my life, but if you have confidence in me I think I can get through."

"I believe you will," said the Major. "I will trust you, at any rate. Get ready and you shall have the best horse in the post."

In fact Pilcher gave La Barge his own horse, a very fine animal. Captain La Barge made ready and set out alone in a country entirely new to him, uninhabited by white men, and now buried in the embrace of a northern winter. He took a few pounds of hard bread and a few ears of corn to parch, but for the rest subsisted on game. He followed the foot of the bluffs as far as possible, and in due time reached Fort Pierre. Fortunately, the day after his arrival the express from Fort Union came in. Exchanges were made, and after a short rest La Barge set out on his return trip. He reached Cabanne in good time.

The exploit gratified Pilcher highly, and he said to La Barge, "I knew I had made no mistake."

Captain La Barge recalled only two incidents on this trip: He saw one day, what he never saw before nor afterward, although he had heard hunters and Indians relate similar experiences, two dead elk whose horns had become interlocked in fighting, and who had died bound together in that way. While in camp one night, just above Vermillion, he had a good fire of dry cottonwood and willows, and was roasting a prairie chicken in the flame. Happening to look up, he saw four gray wolves only a little way off on the opposite side of the fire, looking steadily at him. He was almost paralyzed at the sight, but nevertheless did not leave his place, but quietly got his gun and pistols convenient for action and sat still and watched his visitors. After looking at him a few minutes, and concluding, apparently, that he was not the kind of game they were after, they withdrew.

In the month of April, 1834, La Barge was sent with a party under one La Chapelle to go to the Pawnees and bring down the bullboats with the winter's trade. They were detained several days at the Pawnee Loup village, waiting for some of the Indians to come in. During this delay a band of horse-stealing Sioux slipped into the village one stormy night, and, opening the corrals, let out some sixty head of horses and got away without waking anybody up. When the theft was discovered the following morning the chief called for volunteers to go in pursuit. Some seventy-five men started, and with them La Barge and a companion named Bercier. La Barge had never had an experience of this sort, and thought the present opportunity a good one. On the second evening after their departure they discovered the thieves and their horses encamped on the Elkhorn River. There were about fifteen of the Indians. The pursuers carefully reconnoitered the position, and next morning at daybreak attacked it, killing eleven of the Indians and capturing all of the horses. The man Bercier, who accompanied La Barge, met death at the hand of another tribe of Indians thirty-one years afterward. In 1865 he went up the Missouri with Captain La Barge to Fort Benton, and was killed by the Blackfeet on the Teton River near that post.

On their way down the Platte from the Pawnees, on this trip, the party were greatly annoyed by rattlesnakes at the camps on shore. If they made camp before dark they carefully scoured the entire neighborhood and killed or drove off these dangerous reptiles. But they often kept on the river as long as they could see, and on such occasions could not take the usual precaution. The snakes were not pugnacious, and sought the camp only because of the warm nestling places they found there. They liked to creep into or under the blankets, and the great danger was that when the occupant of the bed awoke he might step on or otherwise hurt the snakes and cause them to strike before he was conscious of their presence. On one occasion Captain La Barge found two of these snakes under his coat, which he had folded and used for a pillow. In some places they were so numerous as to cause the Indians to move their camps. An instance of this kind occurred at Red Cloud, below what is now Chamberlain, S. D., where the site of the agency had to be changed. As late as 1883, when Captain La Barge was pilot of a boat in the service of a United States surveying party, he took some members of the party to a point near the Bijoux hills, where he remembered having seen long years before a colony of rattlesnakes. Sure enough, there they were, still as thick as in former days. The party killed 130 within a few minutes. Captain La Barge could not recall a single death from a rattlesnake bite in his whole experience on the river. He stated that swine were the best exterminators of these reptiles.

As soon as the robes had been packed into mackinaw boats at the mouth of the Platte, about the middle of May, 1834, La Barge started for St. Louis. This was the last of his service with Pilcher, for before his return the Major had left the post for some more important business in St. Louis. He had taken a great liking to the young engage and undertook to secure him a promotion. He sent down by La Barge a letter of recommendation to Daniel Lamont, one of the partners of the upper Missouri department of the American Fur Company. Captain La Barge knew nothing of the letter at the time. It eventually found its way into the Chouteau archives, where it was discovered by the author of this work and shown to Captain La Barge sixty-two years after it was written. It read as follows:

"NEAR THE BLUFFS, May 16, 1834.

"*Dear Sir:* The bearer of this, Joseph La Barge, wintered with me last winter, and has been faithful, active, and enterprising. He wishes to get a clerkship on the Missouri, but I have not employed him for the reason that I have no use for him, nor do I suppose that Mr. Chouteau will employ him for this post, as I have informed him that there is no use for additional clerks. La Barge writes a tolerably good hand, and if you have any place for him above, I can recommend him as a modest and good young man who has done his duty here (as an engage) very faithfully, and I think him worthy of a better situation." Your friend,

"JOSHUA PILCHER."

CHAPTER VI.
LAST YEAR AT CABANNÉ'S.

After a few weeks' visit among his friends in St. Louis in the spring of 1834 La Barge started back on the steamer *Diana* for Cabanné's post. Pilcher was no longer in charge, having been succeeded by Peter A. Sarpy. During his service under Sarpy La Barge had an adventure which came near cutting off his career on the river almost at its beginning. Late in the fall of the year Sarpy sent him down to Bellevue to take charge of a herd of horses which was being wintered there for the mountain expeditions of Fontenelle and Drips. There were about 150 horses in the herd, and they were kept on the east side of the river in the bottoms, where they subsisted mostly on the bark of young cottonwood trees. This kind of forage was extensively used in those days. It was an excellent food and was liked by the stock. Instances are recorded where they have taken it in preference to grain. Horses throve well upon it, and it is related that Kenneth McKenzie at Fort Union fed it exclusively to his hunting stock.

The method of preparing the bark for forage along the Missouri River was as follows: The trees were cut down and the trunk then cut into short logs three or four feet long. In the winter time the bark was frozen and had to be thawed out before using. To do this the logs were stood up in front of a fire and turned around gradually until the bark was warmed through. It was then peeled off with drawknives and cut up into small pieces, after which it was ready for food. It was very essential that the bark be thawed out when fed, for the sharp edges of the shavings were like knife blades if frozen, and liable to cut the throats and stomachs of the horses. Animals were occasionally lost from this cause. After the logs had been stripped of their bark they were split and piled on the river bank, forming an excellent fuel for the next season's steamboat. Traders at the various posts were under standing instructions to gather up the "horse wood" in their vicinity and pile it on the bank of the river, where it could be reached by the boats.

It was while engaged in this work of caring for horses that La Barge had the adventure just alluded to. It was mid-winter, 1834-35.

The Missouri was frozen deep, and a pathway led from the post at Bellevue across the river on the ice to the east bottoms, where the herd was kept. The path ran between two large airholes through the ice—one just above and the other about a hundred yards below. The weather was extremely cold, and there was every indication of an approaching blizzard. Captain La Barge wrapped himself in a blanket coat, held tight to his body by a belt, and was armed with a rifle, tomahawk, and knife. He experienced no difficulty in crossing to the east shore, for the wind was behind his back. But before he was ready to return the blizzard was on in full force; the wind came from the west obliquely across the river, and the drifting snow completely obliterated the path. La Barge nevertheless felt confident of crossing all right, for the distance was short, and he knew the way so well that he felt as if he could follow it blindfolded. In fact, that was practically his present situation, for the wind drove the snow into his face so violently that it was impossible to look ahead. Getting his bearings as well as he could, he started across on a slow run in face of the blinding storm. It would seem in any case to have been a reckless performance, considering the existence of the airholes near the path; but La Barge was not given to enlarging upon future dangers, and forged boldly ahead. For once his confidence deceived him. All of a sudden he plunged headlong into the river. He instantly realized that he was in one of the air holes— but which one? If the lower one, he was certainly lost, for the swift current had borne him under the ice before he came to the surface. If the upper hole, he might float to the lower. But did the current flow directly from one to the other, and would he be at the top at the critical instant? All these questions and many more flashed through his mind with the rapidity of thought in the presence of imminent peril. He soon rose to the surface and bumped the overlying ice. Sinking and rising again he bumped the ice a second time. The limit of endurance was almost reached, when suddenly his head emerged into the open air. Spreading out his hands, he caught the edge of the ice. He held on until he could draw his knife, which he plunged into the ice far enough to give him something to pull against, and after much severe and perilous exertion he drew himself out. He had stuck to his rifle all the time without realizing the fact, and came out as fully armed as when he went in.

But now a new peril awaited him. The storm was at its height, the cold intense, and his clothing was drenched through. The bath which he had received had not chilled him in the least, for the water was much warmer than the air outside, and his exertion would have kept him warm anyway; but out in the wind the chances were that he would freeze if he did not quickly reach a fire. Hastily recovering his bearings, he set out anew, and had the good fortune to reach the post without any further delay. It is needless to say that the inmates of the post were slow to credit the Captain's story, in spite of the proof afforded by his frozen clothing. Martin Dorion, one of the most respectable of the numerous family of that name, said to La Barge, "Your time hasn't come yet. Your work remains to be done." It was not until after he had changed his clothing and had settled down by a strong fire that the reaction from the terrible strain came; but then for a little while he felt as if he could not keep himself together.

La Barge was an expert swimmer, having practiced the art from childhood. He learned to swim in the old Chouteau pond, which filled the hollow near where the Union Station of St. Louis now stands. It was not an uncommon feat for him in his younger days to leap from a boat when he saw an elk or deer crossing the river, outswim and catch it, hold on to it until its feet touched the bottom, and then kill it as it was ascending the bank.

In the year 1850 La Barge was making a voyage to the upper river on the steamer *St. Ange*. Mrs. La Barge and some other ladies were on board. One day a boy fell overboard from the forecastle. La Barge, who happened to be near, instantly leaped in and seized him, keeping him from the wheel (it was a sidewheel boat), and got him to shore before the boat could get there. A lady sitting on the deck with Mrs.

La Barge asked her if she was not alarmed when her husband leaped overboard. She replied that she was not in the least; that she knew Captain La Barge's qualities as a swimmer too well to doubt his ability to rescue the boy.

In the summer of 1838, when La Barge was serving as pilot on the *Platte,* another incident occurred which illustrated his skill as a swimmer. At a point some twelve miles below Fort Leavenworth one of the guys of the yawl derrick broke, precipitating the yawl into the river. This craft was so essential to the steamboat in navigating the Missouri River that its loss would at any time be irreparable. The alarm was instantly given that the yawl was overboard. Captain La Barge was in his stateroom, but immediately hastened to the stern of the boat, where he met Captain Moore, the master. The latter said he had ordered the steamboat to the shore and would send men down the bank to try to recover the yawl. Captain La Barge replied, "I will get the yawl; send some men down to help me bring it back." So saying, he plunged into the river, overtook the yawl, and brought it to land half a mile below the boat.

In the spring of 1835 Captain La Barge went down, as usual, with the mackinaws to St. Louis. This terminated his three years' engagement with the company. He remained in St. Louis all summer except when absent on short river trips in the vicinity. In the fall he went up the Missouri to the Black Snake Hills (St. Joseph, Mo.), where he engaged for the winter to the trader Robidoux, who was in charge. Nothing of interest transpired, and in the spring he returned to St. Louis.

The next four years of Captain La Barge's life were a practical apprenticeship in the business which he was to follow as a career. They were spent almost entirely on the lower river in the various capacities of clerk, pilot, and master on different boats. Not many events of special note occurred, and the actual voyages made are now somewhat uncertain. But the experience was a useful one, and by the time it was over the Captain had won a reputation as a pilot which thereafter insured him continuous service.

The Captain's first service during this time was as assistant pilot on the steamer *St. Charles,* but the boat was burned at Richmond landing, opposite Lexington, Mo., July 2, 1836. He then engaged as pilot on a new boat, the *Kansas,* and ran in the lower river the rest of the season. In the spring of 1837 he shipped as clerk on the steamboat *Boonville,* but this boat was wrecked on a snag early in

November near the mouth of the Kansas River, and was lost with a full cargo of government freight. In the spring of 1838 he went as pilot on the *Platte,* a boat built during the previous winter, and the first double-engine boat that ever plied the river. He remained on this boat for two years, mainly on the lower river. He made but one trip to the far upper river, and started, in the fall of 1838, for the Bayou la Fourche, to spend the winter in the sugar trade. The boat had gone scarcely thirty miles below St. Louis when she ran upon a snag, which tore an immense hole in the bottom and caused her to sink immediately. In the spring of 1840 the Captain again entered the service of the American Fur Company as pilot of the steamer *Emily,* which was to make a trip to Fort Union. Before the season was over the company assigned him to work on a new steamboat, the *Trapper.* For some reason the Captain did not like this assignment and refused to accept it. This incensed the company, who considered him bound to serve wherever directed. Neither side would yield, and the Captain forthwith left the service of the company.

During these four years of apprenticeship several incidents of interest occurred, some pertaining to the local history of the country and others of a purely personal character. Captain La Barge saw a good deal of the Mormons, who at this time were undergoing those persecutions in western Missouri which finally drove them from the State. They were frequently on the steamboats, and the Captain at one time or another saw nearly all the leaders, including Joseph Smith and his brother Hyrum, Sidney Rigdon, Orson Hyde, and others. Captain La Barge never liked the appearance or demeanor of Smith, and never believed in his sincerity. He thought more of Rigdon, who was a most pleasant talker and who once preached a sermon on his boat. Captain La Barge's knowledge of the Mormons and their doings at this time led them to request him, nearly sixty years afterward (1895), to appear for them and give evidence as to their title to the land in Independence, Mo., on which their temple was built.

Another incident which occurred about this time calls up one of the famous characters of American frontier history—Daniel Boone.

This noted pioneer had passed most of his life in Kentucky, but when settlement began to crowd upon his primeval domain he moved westward and settled in Warren County, near St. Charles, Mo., where he died in 1820. Some years later, by agreement between the governments of Kentucky and Missouri, Boone's remains were moved to the latter State. A committee from the Kentucky Legislature went to Missouri on the occasion of the removal and were taken up the river to Marthasville, where Boone was buried, on the steamer *Kansas*. Captain La Barge, who was serving on the *Kansas* at the time, recalled the circumstances perfectly. Many years later he was invited to go to Frankfort, Ky., to attend an anniversary celebration pertaining to Boone's career, but was not able to accept. La Barge's father knew Boone intimately, and La Barge himself was a warm friend of his son Nathan Boone.

CHAPTER VII.

CAPTAIN LA BARGE IN "OPPOSITION"

The term "opposition" in the early Missouri River fur trade had a definite and specific meaning. It applied to any trading concern, great or small, individual or collective, which was doing business in competition with the American Fur Company. So powerful was this company that it never permitted any other company or trader to occupy the same field with itself except at the cost of ruinous commercial warfare. There were many attempts to compete with it, but all of them ended in failure.

The incident related in the last chapter, which led Captain La Barge to quit the company's service, induced him to try his own luck as an opposition trader; but the result, which quickly developed, was quite like that of his many predecessors and successors in the same line. The Captain had laid by a few thousand dollars, which he put into the venture, and secured additional capital from J. B. Roy and Henry Shaw of St. Louis. The steamer *Thames* was chartered to convey the cargo as far as Council Bluffs, for, owing to the lateness of the season, it was not thought safe to attempt to take the boat further. An outfit of wagons was carried along, and it was expected that they would be able to purchase enough horses and oxen to haul the goods the rest of the way.

It was late in the summer when the boat arrived at Council Bluffs. She was promptly unloaded and turned over to her owners, and the Captain immediately set about organizing his wagon train. October had come before he was finally ready to start. His plan was to reach old Fort Lookout before winter set in. He knew that that post had been abandoned, but he understood that it was still in a good enough state of preservation to winter in. At *L'Eau qui Court* (Niobrara River) he was compelled to abandon his wagons on account of the snow, and build sleds. He traveled the rest of the way on the frozen surface of the river.

Soon after leaving the Niobrara Captain La Barge had a foretaste of what he must expect from the American Fur Company, and found that he must be prepared to contend, not only with the long-established power and unscrupulous methods of that great organization, but with the petty trickery of small traders who were trying to make some headway in the country. At the Niobrara he found Narcisse Leclerc, the same whose expedition he had helped break up at

Council Bluffs eight years before. The Captain knew him well as a man acquainted with the Indians and capable of rendering efficient service, but devoid of good principle and ready for any underhand action that would promote his interest. La Barge found him, with his family, entirely destitute, and, counting on his well-known hostility to the company, he thought that if he were to employ him he might depend on his loyalty. He accordingly engaged him, but later bitterly regretted it.

Soon afterward, when Captain La Barge and Leclerc had passed Handy's old trading post, where Fort Randall later stood, they were met by a party of ten Indians and a white man by the name of Bruyere, who claimed that they were en route from Pierre to Vermillion. Leclerc cautioned La Barge not to believe them, for he was certain that they had been sent down from Pierre to spy out La Barge's movements and break up his expedition if possible. La Barge's experience in the Indian trade, and his strong backing in St. Louis, made his opposition a matter of much importance. It was decided that it must be gotten rid of in some way, by force if that were practicable, and if not, by purchase or competition. The party that had come down the river was evidently sent to find out what could be done.

A parley ensued and La Barge invited Bruyere and his party to go back to Handy's old post and he would give them a feast. This was agreed to, and after reaching the post and fixing camp they were first treated to coffee and hard tack. La Barge then gave Bruyere some liquor, and asked him if he should give the Indians some. Bruyere assented, saying the Indians liked it and he could take care of them. Bruyere's party numbered eleven in all. The Captain resolved to get them all deadly drunk and then set out, leaving some liquor to keep them drunk the longer. As the liquor began to work on Bruyere he became communicative, and openly avowed his mission, which was the same as Leclerc had sagaciously foreseen. "You treat me better than any trader ever treated me before," he said. "I was sent here to do you harm, but now I am for you, and if any Indians attempt to harm you I will defend you."

La Barge then went on to Fort Lookout without any further molestation and took possession of the abandoned buildings, intending to conduct his winter trade there. Shortly afterward he received, by the hands of an Indian, a note from the agent at Pierre, inviting him in the most polite and courteous terms to come to his post, as he had some business to propose, and particularly wanted to have a friendly visit. Here again La Barge's suspicions were aroused. The Indian messenger, who was a brother-in-law of the agent, had come to Fort Lookout totally unarmed, a thing unheard of in the Indian country. He at once inferred that the Indian hoped to allay any fears which La Barge might have of traveling alone with him. La Barge received him kindly, said he would decide in a day or two, and asked him to wait. At the first opportunity the Captain strolled off with his gun, as if on a chicken hunt, and set out on the route by which the Indian had come. He followed the trail several miles, when he found the place where the Indian had cached his gun under a tree top. La Barge confiscated the outfit, took it to camp, and hid it. He then told the Indian that he was ready to go to Pierre, and that they would start the next morning. They accordingly set out at an early hour, intending to accomplish the journey in two days. The distance was something over sixty miles by land, though one hundred by river, for the great bend of the Missouri lay between the two places. When they reached the place where the Indian had cached his gun the latter excused himself for a moment, telling La Barge not to wait. After a while he came up, but showed no signs of what his feelings must have been. He behaved very well all the way. The first night was spent on a sandbar of the river, and Fort Pierre was reached at a good hour on the afternoon of the second day.

The agent could not at first conceal his astonishment at seeing La Barge, but quickly recovered himself, and feigned great pleasure at the meeting, saying he was glad La Barge had gotten through safely— there were so many scoundrels around the country that one's life was in danger, if unprotected. The agent then gave La Barge a good supper, and after it was over insisted that he must sit up all night and talk about things in St. Louis. Jacob Halsey was clerk at the time. They pressed the Captain to join them in their drinks, but without success. The agent then lost his temper, declared that La Barge was "unsociable," and that he was insulting his host by refusing his hospitality. La Barge replied that if it was necessary to get drunk in order to be sociable he would not be sociable.

"I had not been in the Indian country so many years for nothing," said Captain La Barge, when describing this affair. "I knew perfectly well the unscrupulous methods of the company, for I had been an eyewitness of them. They cared not how desperate the measure to arrive at their end if only they could escape detection, and this was a comparatively easy matter. 'Killed by the Indians,' and similar reports, were used to veil deeds which were too black to expose to the world. It was no uncommon thing for servants of the company who had started for St. Louis, with a statement of the amount to their credit, to be heard of no more. Knowing these things, I was confessedly distrustful of my hosts. I knew that they dared do nothing openly, for that would lead to prompt report and investigation; but if I were to join in their revels, and lose my self-control, it would be easy enough to involve me in a fray with an Indian and get rid of me in that way, or get me to sign some agreement drawn up by themselves, which should rob me of my outfit and drive me out of the country. Although a temperance man anyway, I resolved to be particularly so on this occasion, and remain absolutely sober. I knew well enough that a proposition would soon come to buy me out, and I had no intention of losing my ability to drive a good bargain.

"The expected proposition came from the agent on the morning of my second day at Pierre. It was not as liberal as I thought it ought to be, and I rejected it. Next day an express came from Lookout with serious news for me. Leclerc, without the slightest authority, had taken a third of my outfit and had gone to the Yanktonais Indians to trade. This would seriously interfere with my plan, which was to hold my outfit at Lookout until I knew what terms the company would offer. I now felt that the quicker the matter was closed up the better, and knowing the great hazard of attempting to oppose so powerful a company, I accepted the proffered terms. These were that the company should take my entire outfit at an advance of ten per cent, upon the cost to me where it was, while I was to engage myself to the company for a period of three years.

"Even after this arrangement the agent subjected me to new and imminent peril, as if still hoping that he would arrive at his end by a shorter cut. Although he could just as well have instructed his trader on the Little Cheyenne to receive and receipt for the goods in Leclerc's possession, he insisted that I should go to that post and either get the goods or make a personal transfer to the trader there. He refused me any escort, and the only thing that he would do was to lend me a horse and sled. The mission was a particularly perilous one. The Yanktonais were the most dangerous and hostile of all the Sioux tribes. They knew the value of opposition in securing them better terms in trade, and if they were to learn that my mission was to sell out to the company, they would unquestionably undertake to wreak vengeance on me. Notwithstanding the needlessness, as well as the peril, of the trip, I was compelled to go, and accordingly set out.

"The overland distance to the mouth of the Big Cheyenne was about forty miles, and I made it in one day. Here the American Fur Company had a wintering post under charge of a man named Bouis, who had with him as interpreter a very valuable man by the name of Zephyr Rencontre. Zephyr was a good friend of mine and I resolved to practice a little strategy to secure his company to the Little Cheyenne and his assistance there. When I reached the post at the Big Cheyenne, Bouis exclaimed, with a good deal of astonishment, 'What! are you alone?' I replied that I was, but that I had authority to take Zephyr to the Little Cheyenne camp and return. Bouis was somewhat surprised at this, but said that if such were the orders he would go. We set out at once, and as soon as we were well on the way, I laid the whole matter before Zephyr. He advised me by all means not to try to take the goods away, for such an attempt would enrage the Indians. The thing to do was to get an inventory of the goods from Leclerc, transfer it to the trader there, Paschal Cerre, get his receipt, and thus transact the whole business on paper without the knowledge of the Indians. We arrived safely at the post and proceeded at once to our business. Everything went well under Zephyr's management for a time, but the suspicion began to spread among the Indians that I was there either to remove my goods or to sell out, and they began to assume a tone of insolence and bravado. Leclerc was probably responsible for this, for he did not relish at all the turn that things had taken. In the meanwhile I took refuge in the lodge of an Indian who was a friend of Zephyr. The latter said he would dispatch the business with all possible speed. The Indians were feasting from lodge to lodge, and Zephyr said they might try to annoy me at any time, but told me to remain right there, say nothing to them, nor resent their actions if they became troublesome. 'I am looking out for you,' he said, 'and have also some of my Indian friends on guard.' Along in the evening the Indians began to come around, evidently in very bad temper, but none of them entered the tent. They made things very uncomfortable, however, and several times I concluded that all was over. They slashed the tent with their knives, and stuck their guns through and shot into the fire, throwing the coals all over me. They were trying to anger me to the point of resistance, as Zephyr had said they would, and they came near succeeding. I could hardly stand it. It seemed certain that I should be killed, and if I failed to take off one or two of them I should die that much less satisfied. I kept control of myself, however, and presently Zephyr came to me announcing that the business was completed, the inventories receipted, and that when a young Indian should come and tell me to follow I was to get up and go. It was about midnight that the Indian appeared and beckoned me to follow. I left the tent through one of the openings which the Indians had slashed in it, and we immediately struck out at a rapid pace down the Little Cheyenne. After proceeding four or five miles I was joined by Zephyr, and the young Indian was sent back.

"We then started straight across the hills for the mouth of the Big Cheyenne, some forty miles distant. It was very important to get there early the next day, lest we be cut off by the Indians. We ran a good deal of the way, but such was the severity of the weather that we almost froze. The thermometer must have reached thirty degrees below zero. On the open hills the cold was terrible, and the side of my body next to the wind became thoroughly numbed. The journey was not without decided interest, however, for we were treated to one of the most beautiful displays of the Aurora Borealis that I have ever seen.

"We reached the mouth of the Big Cheyenne a little after sunrise, and I immediately got breakfast and set out for Pierre, where I arrived about nightfall. When I reached the fort the agent could hardly believe his eyes. 'What! are you back already?' he said. 'I hardly thought you would succeed in turning those goods over.' I replied that I too was astonished that I had got out of that scrape uninjured. 'How did you manage it?' he asked. 'I took Zephyr along with me.' 'Why, how could Bouis spare him?' 'By your order. Didn't you authorize me to take him?' 'No, I never gave any such authority,' said the agent, as he turned away in anger that he had been so completely outwitted.

"The next day the agent detailed James Kipp, with three or four men and a dozen Indians, to go with me to Lookout and receive the goods at that point. The Indians were wholly unnecessary, and I can explain their being sent only on the theory that the agent had not yet given up the short cut for destroying this new opposition. But Kipp was a different sort of man, and although he was sometimes compelled to do the bidding of others to save himself, he never approved of such desperate measures.

"When we set out Kipp was on horseback and I on foot, and he said, 'Well, let's see who will get to Lookout first.' Bercier and I were the only ones who reached there that night, but I was so badly used up that it was several days before I could walk naturally. Kipp did not get in for two days. The rest of the property was then turned over and the ugly business brought to a close."

Such was Captain La Barge's first experience in opposing the American Fur Company; and if it resulted in a quick collapse the profitable termination to himself, and the extreme opposition of the company, showed that they did not regard his enterprise with an easy eye. The whole affair made them set a higher value on La

Barge's services and treat his opinions and rights thereafter with more consideration.

As soon as the business with the Fur Company was completed La Barge set out for Bellevue, arriving there about April i, 1841. He at once went to the Pawnees, where he used to go seven or eight years before, and brought down the bullboats. He was glad to make this trip, for he always liked the Pawnees. Having arrived at the mouth of the Platte with the bullboats and transferred their cargo, he set out for St. Louis with the mackinaws.

The summer of 1842 was mostly spent on the lower river, without any incident of especial note. This year was marked, however, by a very important event in the life of Captain La Barge. On the 17th of August, 1842, he was married to Pelagie Guerette. His wife's mother's name was Marie Palmer, one of a noted Illinois family of that name. Her father's name was Pierre Guerette, one of the Louisiana French, and he was born in Kaskaskia, Ill. He was a millwright and architect. He built for Auguste Chouteau one of the first grist mills run by water in St. Louis. The mill was located at the old dam which extended from Chouteau Avenue to Market Street, in the vicinity of Ninth Street. Pelagie Guerette was born January 10, 1825, and was therefore nearly ten years Captain La Barge's junior. He had known her from childhood. She was a beautiful woman, and although not robust in health, reared a family of five boys and two girls, to adult years. She was a very sensible, noble woman, and a constant help to her husband during their married life of nearly sixty years.

CHAPTER VIII.

THE MISSOURI RIVER.

We have now followed the career of Captain La Barge through the various experiences of youth and early manhood until he is finally settled in the business of his subsequent life—the navigation of the Missouri River. It is therefore a proper time to consider the nature of that business, its features of peculiar interest, and its relation to the growth of the western country. This is the more important because it is a phase in the development of that country which has permanently passed away, and in the general mind is already buried in oblivion. Yet for fully a hundred years the history of the Missouri River was the history of the country through which it flowed. Its importance no one to-day can comprehend. Now the railroad has made accessible almost every section of the country. Then there were no railroads to speak of west of the Mississippi, nor, for that matter, any other roads worthy of mention. The river was the great, and almost the only, highway of travel and commerce.

Everything was done with reference to it. Commercial posts and military garrisons were established; expeditions were undertaken, and all business operations were carried on with careful reference to this mighty stream, which descended from the distant mountains to the very heart of the continent and thence to the sea, whence the road was open to every quarter of the globe. But now its influence upon the growth of the western country has ceased to exist. The mighty river, which was once alive with steamboats and other craft, from the Great Falls to its mouth, cannot boast a single regular packet. In the most absolute sense its glory has departed, and not a trace is left to remind the modern observer of its former greatness. In the following descriptions, therefore, we hope to be serving the true purpose of history, in gathering together for preservation some interesting features of a type of our frontier life which has long since run its appointed course.

Of all the rivers on the globe the longest is the Missouri-Mississippi. On the summit of the Rocky Mountains, above the upper Red Rock Lake, some forty miles west of the Yellowstone

National Park, and directly on the boundary between the States of Montana and Idaho, Jefferson Fork of the Missouri, finds its source. From this point, by a continuous water course to the Gulf of Mexico, the distance is

4221 miles. The river is formed by the confluence of three fine mountain streams which unite at a point about fifty miles south of Helena, Mont. They were named by their discoverers, Lewis and Clark, the Jefferson, Madison, and Gallatin rivers, in honor of the national administration which set on foot the expedition of these explorers. Two of these streams rise in the Yellowstone National Park, and the other, as we have seen, a little distance to the westward.

Of the many tributaries of the Missouri the most important is the Yellowstone, which rivals in size the main stream and joins it nearly eight hundred miles below the Three Forks. Like the Missouri it finds its source in and around that now famous region, where Nature has lavished without stint her most marvelous handiwork, and which the government of the United States has set apart for the common enjoyment of the people. Both the Missouri and the Yellowstone rivers, in the upper portions of their course, flow over immense cascades and rapids which have become well known among the cataracts of the globe. The Great Falls of the Missouri are located near the modern city of the same name. They comprise several cataracts and rapids, the highest perpendicular distance being 87 feet, and the total fall over 500 feet. The falls of the Yellowstone are within the National Park, the highest perpendicular distance being 310 feet, and the total descent from Yellowstone Lake to below the first canon near Livingston, Mont., being about 3200 feet.

Upon emerging from the foothills of the mountains, both streams begin to assume that peculiar character which distinguishes them throughout the rest of their course to the sea. They flow through alluvial bottoms, built up of the detritus from the highlands and mountains, until the present bed of the river is in most places fifty to a hundred feet above the original bed in the solid rock. The usual characteristics of an alluvial river are here found in their highest development—a muddy current, freshly formed islands, sandbars innumerable, an unstable channel, and a shifting bed which is never in the same place for two years in succession.

Among the most striking phenomena of a river like the Missouri is the constant change that is going on in the location of its channel. This seems to be in some places a periodical matter. The forces of the river get to working on particular lines and push their devastations for many years in one general direction. Being finally arrested by some insurmountable obstacle, or turned, it may be, by trifling causes, they work in another direction, and invade lands which have enjoyed long immunity, and upon which the cottonwood, walnut, and cedar have attained mature growth.

The river, in its unrestrained rambles from bluff to bluff, performs some curious freaks. It develops the most remarkable bends, varying in length from one to thirty miles, with distances across the necks but a small fraction of those around. In time these narrow necks are cut in two, and the river abandons its old course, which soon fills up near the extremities of the bends and leaves crescent-shaped lakes in the middle. This process is a never-ending one, and the channel distances along the river are in a state of never-ending change. There is one bend in the upper river, known from the earliest times as the Great Bend, which was not formed in the way just described. The course of the river here is comparatively permanent, and is evidently the same as that of the original stream bed. The distance around is nearly thirty miles, while that across is only a mile and a half. It was a regular custom with travelers, when the Indians were not too dangerous, to leave the boats at the beginning of this bend and walk across, going on board on the other side.

The existence of so many bends increased the length of the channel, but this drawback was more than offset by the reduction of the slope which made the current less strong and enabled steamboats to overcome it with greater ease. The river is like a great spiral stairway leading from the ocean to the mountains. A steamboat at Fort Benton is 2565 feet—two and one-half times the height of the Eiffel tower in Paris—above the level of the sea; yet so gentle is the slope nearly all the way that, in placid weather, the water surface resembles that of a lake. This wonderful evening-up of the slope of the river by the extreme sinuosity of its course is a fact not only interesting as a natural phenomenon, but of the utmost importance in the behavior and use of the stream.

Not only does the general course of the river have these larger windings, but in periods of low water they are multiplied many fold. When a large proportion of the river bed between its banks becomes exposed, as it does in the low-water season, the stream flows back and forth across this bed until its length is largely increased over that at high water. Here again is to be seen the wisdom of nature's methods. In periods of high water, when it is important to move the floods rapidly down the valley, the river straightens out, shortens its length, increases its slope, and accelerates its velocity of flow.

Of the immense carrying power and potential energy of this stream it is difficult to form an adequate conception. It yearly carries into the Mississippi 550,000,000 tons of earth, which has been brought an average distance of not less than 500 miles. The work thus represented is equivalent to 275,000,000,000 mile-tons, or tons carried one mile. The railroads of the United States carried in the year 1901 141,000,000,000 mile-tons of freight.

That such an exercise of power should leave its impress deep upon the country through which the river flows is not to be wondered at. Every year thousands of acres of rich bottom lands are destroyed. Forests, meadows, cultivated fields, farmhouses, and villages fall before its tremendous onslaught, and the changes that have been wrought in the topography of the valley during the past one hundred years almost defy belief. To one familiar with its history, the many crescent-shaped lakes and curvilinear benches show where the river once flowed and where it may flow again. In recent years the government has seriously undertaken to set metes and bounds to the migratory habits of the stream; but it has found a most refractory subject to deal with. Even with the expenditure of vast sums of money in the construction of the most powerful dikes and improved bank protection known to engineering, it can never feel certain that its prisoner will not break its bonds at any moment and escape.

A curious illustration of the great changes which have taken place along the Missouri Valley occurred a few years ago. In 1896 a farmer was digging a well near the mouth of Grand River, Mo., several miles from the present channel of the Missouri. A Bible was found in the excavation, and on its cover was the name *Naomi*. The book was sent to Captain La Barge to see if he could suggest any explanation of its presence where it was found. The Captain recalled perfectly the fact that the steamer *Naomi* was wrecked at that precise spot fifty-six years before. In those days the missionaries always left Bibles on board the various boats, attached by chains to the tables or other parts of the cabin, and lettered with the names of the boats to which they belonged.

As with most of our Western streams the principal arboreal growths along the banks of the Missouri are the willow and cottonwood. The willow matures very rapidly, and well-grown forests are constantly met with in places where the river flowed but two or three years before. The cottonwood requires more time to mature, but this is afforded by those longer cycles of change in which the river passes back and forth across the bottoms. On many of the islands along the central portion of the river there were formerly extensive growths of cedar. The walnut and other trees abound to a less extent. Every year great numbers of trees that line the river bank are undermined and fall into the stream. They are borne along by the current until they become anchored in the bottom, where they remain with one end sticking up and pointing downstream, sometimes above and sometimes below the surface. These trunks or branches have always been the most formidable dangers to navigation of the river. They are called snags or sawyers, though sometimes, from the ripple or break in the surface of the water, "breaks." It is, in fact, only by the appearance of these breaks that a submerged snag can be discovered by the pilot; and fortunately, in a rapid current, like that of the Missouri, a snag will cause such a break if it is near enough to the surface to touch the bottom of a boat. These snags were the terror of the pilot, as well they might be. The record of steamboat wrecks on the Missouri, and it is an appalling one, shows that about seventy per cent, were due to this cause.

A large portion of the river is in a latitude where it freezes over every winter. During the ice period it is indeed effectually enchained. The banks are safe for a season, and the water itself becomes comparatively clear. But as soon as the breezes of spring soften the ice the river resumes its customary wanderings, with renewed vigor after its long rest. By way of celebration of its release from its icy prison it frequently gives exhibitions of power that far surpass all its other manifestations. When the ice "breaks" and begins to "run," it is liable to strand like a steamboat on the shallow bars. Other ice following, and finding the way obstructed, piles up on that before it. Gradually, sometimes, and sometimes rapidly, the accumulation spreads, cutting off the channel of the river, until, as often happens, it forms a veritable dam across the entire stream. These ice "gorges" develop a power that nothing can withstand, and the amount of property destroyed by them in the history of the river has been very great. There is almost nothing that can be done to break them. Dynamite explosions are resorted to, but the ice piles up so rapidly and in such vast quantities that the most powerful blast seems harmless. In the face of this appalling danger man is forced to stand a helpless spectator until the river itself accumulates sufficient force to burst through the dam. It has more than once happened that, before the dam has given way, the river has cut an entirely new channel.

The moving of the ice, even when not accompanied by serious blockades, is always an impressive sight. Usually the warm weather loosens it from the shore before it begins to move, and even disintegrates it, so that it is unsafe to cross upon. The softer it becomes before it begins to run the less danger is there of its gorging. After the movement begins it continues for several days, until the vast quantities of ice stored in the river above have floated by, or melted away. During the height of the movement the crushing of innumerable ice cakes upon each other produces a continuous roar which can be heard for a long distance from the river.

To the lonely dwellers of the valley in the early times the annual "break-up" of the ice was the most welcome event of the year, for it was the knell of the long and tedious winter, and the certain harbinger of approaching spring.

The river has two regular floods every year, one usually in April and the other in June. The first flood is short, sharp, and often very destructive. The second flood is of longer duration and carries an immensely greater quantity of water, but does less damage than the first. The April flood is due to the spring freshets along the immediate valley as the snow melts off and the first rains come. The June rise comes primarily from the melting snows in the mountains. The great and exceptional floods, however, are not due to these regular causes, but to periods of long and excessive precipitation in the lower portions of the valley.

The slope of the river in the lower half of its course is less than a foot to the mile, and the velocity of its current varies from two to ten miles per hour, depending upon the stage of the water.

From an aesthetic point of view, the Missouri River has an unenviable reputation. People who never see it except in crossing railroad bridges, from which they look down into a mass of muddy, eddying water, are liable to compare it unfavorably with other important streams. But to him who is fortunate enough to travel upon it, and study it in all its phases, it is not only an attractive stream, but one of great scenic beauty. As seen in its more placid periods, near morning or evening, when the slanting rays of the sun show the water mainly by reflection, robbing it of its muddy tinge, and replacing it by a crimson hue or silver glimmer that stretches away toward the horizon, cut off again and again by the bends of the river,, but ever and anon reappearing until lost in the distance, there are few scenes in nature that appeal more strongly to the eye of the artist.

Again, in its less peaceful moods, when the persistent prairie winds blow day after day without ceasing, there is a peculiar attractiveness about the weird scene. In all directions, as far as the eye can reach, the air is filled with clouds of sand, drifting along the naked bars, and changing their forms almost as rapidly as does the water those in the bed of the river. The willows and cottonwoods bend complainingly before the blast. The river is lashed into foam, and often becomes so tempestuous that rowboats cannot live in it, while larger craft, making a virtue of necessity, lie moored to the shore until the wind has abated its fury.

Perhaps the most frightful scenes on the river are the violent summer storms of thunder, hail, and rain, with the characteristic tornado tendencies so common in the central prairies. When these black storms gather, and the incessant lightning seems to bind the clouds to the earth, and the rolling and agitated vapors disclose the terrible play of the winds, the river man discreetly makes for shore, and loses no time in gaining the shelter of some friendly bank. The fury of these storms as they break into the valley, pouring down wind and rain with terrific violence, until the river yields up clouds of spray like the vortex of Niagara, forms one of the wildest and most sublime manifestations of the forces of nature. It cannot be truly enjoyed by an eyewitness, because of the element of danger which is present, but the impression produced upon one who is fortunate enough to pass safely through it remains ineffaceable in the memory. These storms generally come from the southwest, and it was a well-recognized rule on the river in boating days to tie up for the night on the southwest, or right shore of the river, so as to be under cover of a bank if a storm should come before day. Accidents from these storms were numerous. Boats were often torn from their moorings and driven upon the bars, where they were as good as lost. Smokestacks, hurricane deck, and pilot-house were frequently carried away and windows destroyed by the hail.

The condition of the weather had an influence upon the business of navigating the river which was of the highest importance, yet would never occur to one unless his attention were directed to it. The excessively uneven and broken condition of the bed of the river, filled as it was with ever-shifting sand-drifts or bars, sometimes called reefs by the river men, produced an appearance upon the surface of the water which was almost the only guide in tracing out the sinuous channel. The experienced pilot could tell from this appearance, not only where snags and other hidden obstructions were, but the outlines of submerged sandbars, and the position of the deepest water. Anything, like wind or rain or a slanting sun, which disturbed this normal appearance, disturbed the serenity of the pilot's mind. Wind was less troublesome than rain, for it ruffled the deep water more than the shallow, and thus left some indication of the locality of each. Rain, on the other hand, reduced everything to a common appearance. The sun, when below forty-five degrees from the horizon, was exceedingly troublesome on account of the reflection from the water whenever the boat was sailing toward it.

Captain La Barge records a curious fact in regard to the appearance of the Mississippi and Missouri rivers as seen by night. He found the Missouri much easier to "read," and always experienced a feeling of relief when he left the main stream and entered its great tributary. The Mississippi seemed black in the night, and this appearance aggravated the darkness. The Missouri, on the other hand, had a distinct whitish tinge, and it seemed, as he entered the stream, as if a faint light had been struck up along its surface.

Such are some of the more striking physical characteristics of this very remarkable stream. It is not surprising that, in the early times, when it first came to be known, it produced a profound impression on the minds of explorers and drew from them expressions of wonder and awe. Marquette and Joliet, who discovered the river in 1673, were floating down the Mississippi in a comparatively clear current, when they came to a point where a mighty volume of water poured itself into the Mississippi from the west shore, carrying trees, stumps, and drift of all descriptions. It filled them with amazement, as it has every person since who has stood at the confluence of these two mighty streams, particularly when the Missouri is bringing down the great floods of spring.

We do not know when the Missouri was first entered by white men, but probably about the year 1700. The French had made sufficient progress along its course in the early years of the eighteenth century to alarm the Spaniards, who, in the year 1720, sent an expedition to destroy the Missouri Indians, the allies of the French. This expedition was itself destroyed by the Missouris, but the event caused the French to build a post some two hundred miles up the river on an island opposite the village of the Missouris. This was Fort Orleans, and was, so far as we know, the first structure erected by white men along the course of the stream.

The name of the river comes from the tribe of Indians just mentioned, who once dwelt at its mouth, but were driven from this position by the Illinois Indians. The word means "dwelling near the mouth of the river," and has no reference to the muddy quality of the water.

The fact that the Missouri River is longer than the entire Mississippi, and more than twice as long as that portion of the latter stream above the mouth of the Missouri, has led to the frequent observation that the name which applies to the lower course of the Mississippi should apply also to the tributary. But this would evidently not be a fitting nomenclature. The Mississippi is the trunk stream, receiving the drainage from the Alleghenies on the east and the Rockies on the west. It divides the continent into approximately symmetrical portions. This division has entered into the very life of our national development, and is so natural and convenient that the stream itself from north to south is appropriately known by a single name. The Missouri is the great tributary from the mountains on the west, as the Ohio is from the mountains on the east. The characteristics of the Missouri are so peculiarly its own that a separate name is more befitting than one divided between itself and another and very different stream.

During the eighteenth century the French gradually extended their knowledge of the river. It is not likely that the voyageurs had ascended as far as to the Mandan villages, a short distance above the modem capital of North Dakota, when, in 1738-43, De la Verendrye crossed over from the north and struck the river at that point. But it is quite certain that at the time of the founding of St. Louis, 1764, the river was well known for a thousand miles above its mouth. From that time knowledge of it increased more rapidly, and when Lewis and Clark went up the river in 1804, they found that white men had preceded them almost to the mouth of the Yellowstone.

CHAPTER IX.

KINDS OF BOATS USED ON THE MISSOURI.

The swift and turbulent character of the Missouri River led to exaggerated accounts by the early explorers of the difficulty of navigating it. Such navigation was at first considered wholly out of the question except in the simplest craft. Tradition says that Gregoire Zerald Sarpy was the first to introduce keelboats on the river, but the date of this essay is not very definitely fixed. It would seem that the French must have used large boats at the time they were established at Fort Orleans. In any event the advent of the keelboat on the Missouri in connection with the fur trade could not have been long after the founding of St. Louis, and probably antedated it. Gradually these boats made their way to points farther and farther up the river, until in 1805 they were taken by Lewis and Clark to the head of navigation. A similar experience was gone through with in the case of the steamboat. It was at first thought impossible for such boats to navigate the river at all, but in 1819 the attempt was made, and the *Independence* entered the Missouri on either the 16th or 17th of May, and ascended the river two hundred miles. The *Western Engineer*, a government boat, went as far as the old Council Bluffs in the same year. From that time on steamboats remained on the river, making farther and farther advances toward the head of navigation, which was finally reached forty years after the first boat entered the river.

The principal craft which have been used on the Missouri and its tributaries are the canoe, mackinaw, bullboat, keelboat, and steamboat. The yawl, a very important boat, was not much used for independent navigation, but rather as an appurtenance to the steamboats.

The *canoe* was the simplest and most generally used of all the river craft. It was the wooden canoe, or "dugout," and not the bark canoe which was so much used where the proper material could be found. The Missouri River canoe was generally made from the logs of the cottonwood, though frequently from the walnut, and occasionally from cedar. The cottonwood in the river bottoms attained immense size, ample for the largest canoes, for these boats rarely exceeded thirty feet in length and three and one-half in width. The ordinary length was between fifteen and twenty feet. A suitable tree having been found, it was felled and a proper length of the trunk was cut out. The exterior was straightened with the broad-ax, and reduced to a round log shorn of all roughness and irregularity. The top was then hewn off, so as to leave about two-thirds of the log. The ends were given a regular canoe model, and were sometimes turned up on bow and stern with extra pieces for purpose of ornament. The log was then carefully scooped out from the flat surface so as to leave a thin shell about two inches thick at the bottom and one at the rim. To support the sides and give strength to the craft the timber was left in place at points from four to six feet apart, making solid partitions or bulkheads. A good-sized canoe was easily built by four men in as many days. They had tools especially adapted to the work, the most important being the *tille ronde,* or the round adz.

These log canoes made excellent craft, strong, light, and easily managed. A full crew generally consisted of three men, two to propel and one to steer. The paddle (French *aviron*) was always used. A mast was occasionally placed in the center and rigged with a square sail, but this could be used only with an aft wind, for fear of capsizing the canoe.

Sometimes these boats were made with a square stem, and were then called pirogues; but this name was more frequently used where two such boats were rigidly united in parallel positions a few feet apart and completely floored over. On the floor was placed the cargo, which was protected from the weather by the use of skins. Oars were provided in the bow for rowing and a single oar in the stern between the boats for steering. Sails could be used with a quartering wind on these boats without danger of upsetting. Dube's ferry, on the Mississippi, one of the earliest ferries of St. Louis, used a boat of this kind.

The principal use of the canoe was for the local business of the larger river posts. Often, however, they were used in making trips to St. Louis, even from the remotest navigable points of the main stream or its tributaries. Many such a journey has been made with a single voyageur running the gantlet of hostile tribes all the way from the mountains to the Mississippi. A common use of the canoe was for sending express messages down the river, and there are several records of their having been used to transport freight. An example of this last use was the shipment of bear's oil, which was extensively used in St. Louis as a substitute for lard in the early days when swine were scarce and black bears plentiful. The oil was extremely penetrating, and would rapidly filter through skin receptacles. Barrels or casks not being available, the center apartment of the canoe was filled with the oil and tightly covered with a skin fastened to the sides of the boat. Honey was also transported in this way. In those days bee trees were exceedingly plentiful in the Missouri bottoms, and large quantities of honey were taken from them.

The *mackinaw boat,* as the name implies, was an imported design, having already been used on the Eastern lakes and rivers. It was made entirely of timber, and before nails were carried up the river all the parts were fastened with wooden pins. The bottom was flat, and was made of boards about one and a half inches thick. On these rested cross-timbers, to which, and to the bottom, were fastened the inclined knees that supported the sides. The boats were sometimes made as large as fifty feet long and twelve feet beam. The plan was that of an acute ellipse, and the gunwale rose about two feet from, the center of the boat toward both bow and stem. The keel showed a rake of about thirty inches from the bow or stern to the bottom. The hold had a depth of about five feet at the two ends of the boat, and about three and one half at the center.

The central portion of the boat was partitioned off from the bow and stern by two water-tight bulkheads or partitions. Between these the cargo was loaded, and piled up to a height of three or four feet above the gunwale and given a rounded form. Over the cargo lodge skins were drawn tight and fastened with cleats to the sides and gunwales of the boat, so as to make practically a water-tight compartment. In the bow were seats for the oarsmen, and in the stern an elevated perch for the steersman, from which he could see over the cargo in front, and give directions to the crew in the bow or study the river ahead.

The crew of the boat ordinarily consisted of five men, four at the oars and one at the rudder. The latter had charge of the boat, and was called the *patron*. Only experienced, courageous, and reliable men were chosen for this responsible work.

These boats were only used in downstream navigation, and the labor of handling them was not arduous. The men found ample time for song and gossip, and every hour or so, after a vigorous pull, would take advantage of a good stretch of river to rest their oars *(laisser alter)* and take a smoke *(fumer la pipe)*. Then they would let fall their oars *(tomber les rames)* and bend to their work for another hour. They ran from fifteen to eighteen hours per day and made from 75 to 150 miles. The boats carried about fifteen tons of freight, and the cost per day was about two dollars. Transportation by mackinaw boat was therefore inexpensive.

These boats were cheaply made, and were intended only for a single trip down to St. Louis, where they were sold for four or five dollars apiece. After the advent of the steamboat the mackinaws were frequently carried back to the upper rivers on the annual boat, for even steam did not absorb the peculiar field of usefulness of these craft. They were quite safe and were preferred to the keelboat for downstream navigation.

The lumber for the mackinaws was manufactured where the boats were built, or rather the latter were built where suitable timber could be found. There being no sawmills, the boards had to be sawed by hand, and for this purpose the logs were rolled upon a scaffold high enough for a man to work underneath. They were first hewed square, and were then sawed by two men, one standing above and the other below. At all important posts there was a *chantier* (French for boatyard) located where timber was to be had. Here all woodwork was done. The Fort Pierre chantier, always called the navy yard, was some fifteen miles above the post, and was a very active place. The Fort Union chantier was twenty-five miles above the post, while that at Fort Benton was three miles below at the mouth of Chantier (now Shonkin) Creek. At all these workyards skilled artisans were employed.

The *bullboat* of the fur traders, in distinction from (After Maximilian) the tubs which were used by some of the Missouri River tribes, was an outgrowth of the conditions of navigation on such streams as the Platte, Niobrara, and Cheyenne. The excessive shallowness of these streams precluded the use of any craft drawing more than nine or ten inches. The bullboat was probably the lightest draft vessel ever constructed for its size, and was admirably fitted for its peculiar use. It was commonly about thirty feet long by twelve wide and twenty inches deep.

The frame of the bullboat was constructed by laying stout willow poles, three or four inches in diameter, lengthwise of the boat, and across these similar poles,, the two layers being firmly lashed together with rawhide. The side frames were made of willow twigs about an inch and a half in diameter at the larger end and six to seven feet long. The smaller ends were lashed to the cross-poles, and about two feet of the larger ends were then bent up to a vertical position. Along the tops of the vertical portions and on the inside was lashed a stout pole like those forming the bottom of the framework. To this gunwale were lashed cross-poles, at intervals of four or five feet, to keep the sides from spreading. No nails or pins were used for fastenings, but rawhide lashings only. The frame so constructed was exceedingly strong, and its flexible quality, by which it withstood the continuous wrenching to which it was subjected, was an important element of strength.

The framework, being completed, was then covered with a continuous sheet of rawhide formed by sewing together square pieces as large as could be cut from a single buffalo hide. Only the skins of buffalo bulls were used for this purpose (whence the name of the boat), for they were the strongest and best able to resist abrasion from rubbing on the bottom of the river. The pieces were sewed together with buffalo sinew. Before this work was done the hides were carefully dressed by the Indians so as to be free of hair and perfectly flexible. When the covering was all sewed together it was thoroughly soaked and then placed over the framework and the sides and ends made fast to the gunwale of the boat. The hides would then dry and shrink until they were drawn as tight as a drumhead.

The final operation in the work was to pitch the seams. The material used was a mixture of buffalo tallow and ashes, and it was carefully rubbed into all seams or cracks until the whole covering was watertight.

The boat so built was very light, and could be easily turned over by two men. When in the water and ready for its cargo, a layer of loose poles was laid lengthwise on the bottom so as to keep the cargo five or six inches from the bottom and protect it from any water that might leak in. The cargo nearly always consisted of furs, securely packed in bales about thirty inches long, fifteen inches wide, and eighteen inches deep. They were placed one bale deep over the bottom of the boat, leaving space in bow and stern for the pole men. The bales were always laid flatwise, so that if the water should reach them it would injure only the bottom skins and not all, as it would if they were set edgewise. The cargo rarely exceeded six thousand pounds.

The boat was handled by means of poles, and the crew generally consisted of two men. The draft of the boat, when placed in the water in the morning, was about four inches, but the boat hide becoming soaked during the day, and possibly some water leaking in, it would probably be as much as six or eight inches by night. Every evening when camp was made the boat was unloaded, brought up on the bank, and placed in an inclined position, bottom side up, to dry. In this position it served as a shelter for both cargo and crew. In the morning the seams were repitched, and any incipient rents or abrasions were carefully patched. The boat was then launched and reloaded and the voyage resumed.

Low water, even on the Platte, was generally preferred to high water for bullboat navigation, because in high water the current was too strong. Every little while the boat would glide into deep pockets, where the poles could not touch bottom, and it was then necessary to drift with the current until a shallower stretch would give the men control again. Sometimes in those wide and shallow expanses, which give the Platte such a pretentious appearance in high water, the wind would play vexatious pranks with the bullboat navigators. A strong prairie gale blowing steadily from one direction during the day would drift most of the water to the leeward side of the stream. The boat would naturally follow the same shore, and the night camp would be made there. If, as often happened, the wind changed before re-embarkation, the river would very likely be wafted to the other side of its broad bed, and the crew would find themselves with half a mile of sandbar between them and the water.

Bullboat navigation, as here described, was most frequently resorted to in bringing the trade of the Pawnees on the Loup Fork of the Platte to the Missouri, but it was likewise extensively used on the Cheyenne and Niobrara and other tributaries. There were some very extensive bullboat voyages. A good many were made from Laramie River to the mouth of the Platte, but generally it was impossible to find enough water to make a continuous voyage. In 1825 General Ashley loaded one hundred and twenty-five packs of beaver into bullboats at the head of navigation on the Bighorn River, with the intention of conveying them in that way to St. Louis. But at the mouth of the Yellowstone he met General Atkinson, who offered him the use of his keelboats for the rest of the journey. In 1833 the Rocky Mountain Fur Company, Captain Bonneville and Nathaniel J. Wyeth, embarked all their furs, the product of a year's hunt, in bullboats on the Bighorn River, and together went downstream to the mouth of the Yellowstone. Sometimes these boats were actually given names, and we have a record of the bullboat *Antoim,* in which a free trapper, Johnson Gardner, shipped his furs from the "Crossings of the Yellowstone" to Fort Union in 1832.

The boats just described were quite different from the hemispherical tubs used so extensively by the Mandans and other tribes of the upper Missouri. These little boats had a circular rim or gunwale, and the willow supports passed from one side entirely under the boat to the other. The frame was generally small enough to be covered with a single hide, and was designed to carry ordinarily but one person. A fleet of these boats, numbering a hundred or so, was one of the most singular sights ever witnessed on the river. The squaws often used them, on occasions of buffalo hunts above the village, to transport the meat downstream. In fact the women rather than the men were the navigators of this picturesque little craft.

We now come to the *keelboat,* the representative river craft of ante-steamboat days. It was in this boat that the merchandise for the trade was transported to the far upper river, and it was used on all important military or exploring expeditions. It was a good-sized boat, sixty to seventy feet long, and built on a regular model, with a keel running from bow to stern. It had fifteen to eighteen feet breadth of beam and three or four feet depth of hold. Its ordinary draft was from twenty to thirty inches. It was built in accordance with the practice of approved shipcraft, and was a good, stanch vessel. Keelboats were generally built in Pittsburgh at a cost of two to three thousand dollars.

For carrying freight the keelboat was fitted with what was called a cargo box, which occupied the entire body of the boat excepting about twelve feet at each end. It rose some four or five feet above the deck. Along each side of the cargo box was a narrow walk about fifteen inches wide, called the *passe avant,* the purpose of which will be explained further on. On special occasions when these boats were used for passenger traffic, as on expeditions of discovery or exploration, they were fitted up with cabins, and made very comfortable passenger boats.

For purposes of propulsion the boat was equipped with nearly all the power appliances known to navigation except steam. The cordelle was the main reliance. This consisted of a line nearly a thousand feet long, fastened to the top of a mast which rose from the center of the boat to a height of about thirty feet. The boat was pulled along with this line by men on shore. In order to hold the boat from swinging around the mast, the line was connected with the bow by means of a "bridle," a short auxiliary line fastened to a loop in the bow and to a ring through which the cordelle passed. The bridle prevented the boat from swinging under the force of the wind or current when the speed was not great enough to accomplish this purpose by means of the rudder. The object in having so long a line was to lessen the tendency to draw the boat toward the shore; and the object in having it fastened to the top of the mast was to keep it from dragging, and to enable it to clear the brush along the bank.

It took from twenty to forty men to cordelle the keelboat along average stretches of the river, and the work was always one of great difficulty. There was no established towpath, and the changing conditions of the river prevented the development of such a path except along k few stable stretches. It was frequently necessary to send men ahead to clear the most troublesome obstructions away. In some places, where it was impossible to walk and work at the same time, a few men would carry the end of the line beyond the obstruction and make it fast, while the rest would get on board and pull the boat up by drawing in the line. This operation was called warping.

When the boat was being cordelled there stood at the bow, ilear where the bridle was attached, an individual called in French a *bosseman* (boatswain's mate), whose duty it was to watch for snags and other obstructions, and to help steer the boat by holding it off the bank with a pole. There was selected for this place a man of great physical strength, prompt decision, and thorough knowledge of the river. The patron, or master of the boat, stood at the rudder, which was manipulated by means of a long lever from the rear end of the cargo box. This position gave him an elevated point of view, from which he could overlook everything.

There were many places where the keelboat could not be cordelled at all, as along sandbars where the water was too shallow for the boat to get near the shore, or the alluvium too soft for the men to walk in. At such times it was necessary to resort to the pole, as it was called. This was a turned piece of ash wood regularly manufactured at St. Louis. On one end was a ball or knob to rest in the hollow of the shoulder, for the voyageur to push against; and on the other was a wooden shoe or socket. In propelling the boat with these poles eight or ten voyageurs ranged themselves along each side, near the bow, facing aft, pole in hand, one in front of the other, as close together as they could walk. The whole operation was under the direction of the patron. At his command *"A bas les perches"* (down with the poles), the voyageurs would thrust the lower ends into the river close to the boat and place the ball ends against their shoulders, so that the poles should be well inclined downstream. They would all push together, forcing the boat ahead, as they walked along the *passe avant* toward the stern, until the foremost man had gone as far as he could. The patron then gave the command *"Levee les perches"* (raise the poles), upon which they would be withdrawn from the mud, and the men would walk quickly back to the bow and repeat the operation. All steering was done while the poles were up, for the boat could not change direction while the men were pushing. It was always essential to give the boat sufficient momentum at each push to keep her going while the men were changing position. The *passe avant* had cleats nailed to it to keep the feet from slipping, and the men, when pushing hard, sometimes leaned over far enough to catch hold of the cleats with their hands, thus fairly crawling on all-fours.

In some places where the water was too deep for the poles and where cordelling was impracticable, oars were resorted to. There were five or six of these on each side of the bow. They often furnished assistance also when the boat was being cordelled.

A great reliance in propelling the keelboat, strange as it may seem considering the nature of Missouri River navigation, was the wind. A mast was rigged, with a square sail spreading about one hundred square feet of canvas, which often gave sufficient power to propel the boat against the swift current of the river. Unless the direction of the wind were altogether wrong the sinuous course of the stream would every now and then give an aft or quartering breeze. In some places the wind seemed to follow the bends, blowing up or down the river clear around. Thus Brackenridge relates that when Manuel Lisa's boat, in June, 1811, was going around the Great Bend below Fort Pierre, where in the course of thirty miles the river flows toward every point of the compass, an aft wind was experienced all the way, and the entire circuit was made under sail. Some idea of sailing speed up the Missouri under favorable conditions may be gleaned from the fact that, on the day of passing the Great Bend, Lisa's boat made seventy-five miles, a portion of the distance being made at night by the light of the moon. And on another occasion on the same trip Brackenridge records that "we had an extraordinary run of forty-five leagues from sun to sun."

Thus, by means of the cordelle and pole, the oar and sail, the sturdy keelboat worked and worried its way up the turbulent Missouri in the early days. It was a slow and laborious process at best. A good idea of its maximum accomplishment under rather unfavorable conditions is furnished by Manuel Lisa's voyage, already referred to. It was made with an exceptionally fine boat, a picked crew, and the most untiring and energetic commander that ever ascended the Missouri. There was especial necessity for rapid progress, for it was of the greatest importance to overtake the Astorian expedition, which was a long distance ahead, before it should reach the dangerous Sioux country. The difficulties from wind and storm were greater than the average, and the rate of progress was not increased by any fortuitous aids. Lisa left St. Charles, 28 miles above the mouth of the Missouri, April 2, 1811. He overtook Hunt at 1132 miles, on the morning of June 11. He therefore made about 1100 miles in sixty-one days, or about 18 miles per day. This, however, was better than the average. A keelboat trip to the upper river was practically an entire summer's operation.

Above the mouth of the James or Dakota River keelboating was easier than below, because the natural obstacles of all sorts were less; but everywhere it was a very laborious process. Captain La Barge often remarked that it would be wholly impossible in this day to get men to undergo such exertions as were required of the keelboat crews. They worked early and late, in water and out, and often to the very limit of endurance. Their food was of the plainest description, consisting mainly of pork, lyed corn, and navy beans. From this allowance, slender as it was, meat was cut off as soon as the game country was reached. The cooking was done at the night camp for the following day. On top of the cargo box there was sometimes placed a cooking stove, in a shallow box filled with ashes or gravel to protect the roof from fire. The men's baggage was stored in the front of the cargo box, where there was also a place for anyone to lie down who might fall sick. It was, however, a very poor place to be sick in. There were no medicines, no physicians, no nurses or attendants, and nothing but the coarsest food. The prospect itself was enough to frighten everyone into keeping well.

The hired laborers who did the work on these river expeditions were called voyageurs, and were generally of French descent. They were an interesting class of people, and presented a phase of pioneer life on the Missouri which has become wholly extinct. They were a very hard-working class, obedient, cheerful, light-hearted, and contented. It was a marvel to see them, after a hard day's work, dance and sing around the evening campfire as if just awakened from a refreshing sleep. The St. Louis Creoles were regarded as more desirable boatmen than the French Canadians. The American hunter was not so useful in river work as the French voyageur, but was far more valuable for land work and in situations involving danger or requiring the display of physical courage.

Washington Irving, whose love of the romance of early Western history was ardent and sincere, beheld with unfriendly eye the introduction of the *steamboat* upon the Missouri. He lamented the "march of mechanical invention," which was "fast dispelling the wildness and romance of our lakes and rivers," and "driving everything poetical before it." However well-founded this fear may have been in the general case, we are inclined to think that the exact reverse was true of the Missouri River steamboat. This remarkable craft introduced romantic features of which the old keelboat and its Creole crew never dreamed. The incidents of a single steamboat voyage from St. Louis to Fort Union would make an entertaining chapter in any book of adventure. As to impressiveness of appearance, certainly no craft on our Western waters, if upon any waters of the globe, displayed more majesty and beauty, or filled the mind with more interesting reflections, than these picturesque vessels of the early days in the boundless prairies of the West. The very surroundings lent a peculiar attraction to the scene. In every direction the broad and treeless plains extended without water enough anywhere in sight even to suggest a boat. Winding through these plains was a deep valley several miles broad, with a ribbon of verdure running through it along the sinuous course of the river.

Everything was still as wild and unsettled as before the advent of the white man, and there was little or nothing to suggest the civilization of the outside world. In the midst of this virgin wildness a noble steamboat appears, its handsome form standing high above the water in fine outline against the verdure of the shore; its lofty chimneys pouring forth clouds of smoke in an atmosphere unused to such intrusion, and its progress against the impetuous current exhibiting an extraordinary display of power. Altogether it formed one of the most notable scenes ever witnessed upon the waters of America. Naturally enough the wild Indian viewed with feelings of awe this great "fire canoe," whose power to "walk on the water" had subdued the intractable current to its own will. It is said to have been the advent of the steamboat which finally turned the scale of the Indian's favor toward the Americans as against the British.

In truth, the Missouri River steamboat was a most attractive-looking craft. Unlike an ocean vessel, which is in large part buried beneath the waves, the river boat drew only three or four feet of water, and was therefore almost entirely above the surface. This gave it a great apparent size compared with its actual dimensions and tonnage. Its architectural design was pleasing to the eye. Its successive decks, surmounted by the texas and pilot-house, all painted a clear, even white, made it look like a veritable floating palace as it moved majestically among the groves of cottonwood and willow, or through the parched plains of the ashen-colored sage brush.

The criticism has been made that the river steamboat is one of the few modern mechanical contrivances which have shown no particular development, but remain to-day as they were long ago. The criticism is a mistaken one. If comparison be made between the first river steamboats and the best of to-day it will be found that progress in this development is quite up to that in other lines, and it is doubtful if any other machine is more perfectly adapted to its peculiar work. In very recent years there has naturally been but little development, for the steamboat business on Western rivers has largely passed away.

The earlier boats were usually of the sidewheel pattern, with only one engine, and an immense flywheel to keep it from stopping on the dead point. Unlike the modern boat, most of the accommodations for freight and passengers were abaft of the wheels. The stages for getting on and off were located there. The forward part was mainly taken up with machinery. The men's cabins were in the hold. The shape of the boat was ill adapted to its work. It had a model keel, which gave it fully six feet draft with half of the load which has since been carried on three feet.

Far different from this early boat was that used in the later years of business on the Missouri. The first-class modem river steamboat was about 220 feet

The first Yellowstone, built in the winter of 1830-31, is a good example of the original river boat. It was 130 feet long, 19 feet beam, 6 feet hold: beautiful model; side wheels; single engine; flywheel; cabin aft of shaft; ladies' cabin in stern hold; boiler decks open; no hurricane roof; pilot-house elevated; two smokestacks; one rudder; 6-foot wheel bucket; 18-foot wheel; stages aft; draft, light, 4 feet; loaded to 75 tons, 5 feet.

In the river boats the main or forecastle deck was the first above the water, and the one covering the hold; the boiler deck was the second one, just over the boilers, covered by the hurricane roof; the hurricane deck was the third deck. Upon this were situated the texas and the pilot-house. long and 35 feet wide, and would carry 500 tons. It was built with a flat bottom, so that it would draw, say, thirty inches light and fifty loaded. It was propelled by a stem-wheel, a most excellent arrangement, which had become practicable through the invention of the balanced rudder: that is, a rudder with a part of the blade on each side of the rudder post. There were two engines of long stroke, one on each side of the boat, communicating directly with the wheel shaft and thus avoiding all loss from the friction of gearing. A proper distribution of the weight required that the boilers be placed well forward. This left a large space between them and the engine room, which was well aft.

The forecastle was equipped with steam capstans and huge spars, which served a purpose similar to that of the poles on a keelboat in pushing the boat over sandbars. Steam hoisting apparatus was used, and in the hold were light tramway cars to convey the freight from the hatchway to its place of deposit. Enormous stages, swung from derricks on either side of the bow, facilitated communication with the high banks of the river. The quarters of the crew and steerage passengers were on the boiler deck. On top of the hurricane deck was the texas—a suite of rooms for the officers of the boat. Above the texas stood the pilot-house, high over the river—a very important consideration, for the more directly the pilot could look down the better he could see the channel. The hurricane deck, and particularly the pilot-house, were favorite resorts for the passengers.

High above all towered the lofty smokestacks, carrying the sparks from the wood fire well away from the roof of the boat and giving a strong draft to the furnace. Between the two chimneys the name of the company generally appeared in large initial letters, legible for a long distance. One or more flags displayed their colors to the breeze, and a light armament, consisting of one or two small cannon, answered the double purpose of firing salutes and terrifying Indians who became too defiant.

A noted steamboat that ran on the lower river during a portion of the fifties was the Felix X. Aubrey. Between the smokestacks was the figure of a man riding at full speed on horseback. The reference was to a horseback ride, very celebrated in its day, from Santa Fe to Westport, where Kansas City now stands. In the year 1853 Felix X. Aubrey made this ride in five days and thirteen hours. The distance was 775 miles.

CHAPTER X.

STEAMBOAT NAVIGATION ON THE MISSOURI RIVER.

The Missouri River pilot was beyond question the most skillful representative of his profession. In no other kind of navigation were the qualities of quick perception, intuitive grasp of a situation, nerve to act boldly and promptly, coolness and judgment in times of danger, so important and so constantly in demand. Navigation on the ocean was child's play in comparison. The Missouri represented in the highest degree the peculiar dangers characteristic of alluvial streams. Its current was swift, its channel full of snags, its surface nearly always ruffled by the prairie gale, and never for five minutes in succession in a condition which would permit the pilot to take his hand from the wheel or the engineer to let go of the throttle. The elaborate system of communication between the pilot-house and the engine room was always in service, and the tinkle of signal bells in the engineer's ear was almost continuous. The position of pilot was responsible and exacting, and called for a high order of ability. And so it resulted that the better class of pilots were men of high standing and character, in whose care business men unhesitatingly intrusted their property and the lives of their families.

The ever-shifting condition of the river channel caused the pilot to seek all available information as to its latest position. When other boats were met there was an eager swapping of notes, for it was a common practice in later years for pilots to assist each other by keeping notes of the condition of the river over which they passed f The pilots thus came to know the river by heart from its mouth to the head of navigation. The extraordinary knowledge of its topography and nomenclature which Captain La Barge retained to the end of his life was almost incredible. There was not a bend or rapid, a bed of snags, or other

"Of all the variable things in creation the most uncertain are the action of a jury, the state of woman's mind, and the condition of the Missouri River."—Sioux City Register, March 28, 1868.

As an example of primitive lighthouse or fog-signal work, the story is told of a steamboat captain who always made a certain crossing on the lower river, if at night, by the aid of the bark of a dog belonging to a farmhouse directly in line with the course of the boat. The dog came out on the bank whenever boats were approaching, and saluted them vigorously until they had passed. The captain ran by this bark with the most implicit confidence. But unhappily the dog did change his position—once—and the captain ran by its bark no more, for the next morning his own bark was a hopeless wreck upon a neighboring sandbar. feature in all of its twenty-six hundred miles that was not as familiar to him as the rooms of his own house.

The most serious problem with which the Missouri navigator had to deal was that of procuring fuel. Wood alone was used, and this was obtained from the growths on the banks of the river. Cottonwood was the main reliance, because of its greater abundance, but it was not a first-class firewood. If green, it was next to impossible to maintain steam with it except by the aid of rosin. It was often found impracticable to carry the boat from one established wooding place to another, and it was then necessary to gather drift logs, or anything else that could be found. Whenever a trading post was abandoned its palisades and buildings quickly found their way into the steamboat furnaces, to the great, though transient, delight of the crew.

In the earlier years the fuel was cut by the crew itself as the boat proceeded on her voyage. But as the traffic became more regular, wood yards were established, either by the boat-owners or by others who cut wood for sale. The Indians themselves found the business a profitable one, and finally refused to let the whites cut wood at all. The sale of their wood thus became a source of considerable revenue to them. In later years, during the Sioux hostilities, the wooding of boats was a most perilous matter. Crews were attacked at the landings and only the most vigilant precaution prevented great loss of life at such times. To reduce this danger as much as possible, Captain La Barge equipped one of his boats with a sawmill, and took along a yoke of oxen. When he had to have wood he swung out a large stage, drove the team ashore, and dragged several logs on board with the utmost speed. As soon as this was done the boat proceeded on her way and the crew then sawed up the wood i

The "wooding" of a boat was an interesting performance. The moment the boat touched the bank for this purpose the mate called out "woodpile," and every available man leaped ashore, loaded himself with wood, and hastened back to the boat. In an incredibly short time the work was done and the boat was again on her way.

Steamboat hours were as long as the light of day would permit. It was not customary to run at night, unless there was ample moonlight and the business was extremely urgent. But every hour of daylight was improved. In the higher latitudes morning and evening twilight almost touched hands across the few hours of intervening darkness. Three o'clock A. M. was a common hour of starting, and 9 P. M. of stopping. The crew were divided into four watches, so that they could take turns in getting sleep during the day.

The early morning run was liable to be the most successful of the day, unless it were the late evening run. At both times the wind was generally low enough to form no serious drawback. The landscape likewise appeared at its best, and the sight of sunrise or sunset on the river was one to be remembered. The water was comparatively calm at those hours, particularly in the early morning. Later in the day the wind generally began to rise, and the pilot always viewed as an evil omen the first cloud of sand that he saw drifting over the valley. If the wind increased beyond a certain point he was compelled to make for the shore and wait for it to subside. The area of the boat exposed to the wind was so great that in narrow channels it was impossible to keep within them, and it was often necessary to lie at the bank for several hours. This enforced idleness was generally improved in cutting wood for present and future needs.

The danger from snags was always present and sometimes very great, and the passage of these obstructions was a matter of anxious solicitude on the part of both officers and passengers. Less dangerous, but not less annoying, was the passage of shallow bars where there was not sufficient depth to float the boat.

This usually occurred at the "crossings," or places where the channel, after having followed one side of the river-bed for a distance, crossed over to the other. In these places the channel generally split up into chutes, none of which might have the required depth of water. The pilot's first step would be to select the most promising channel. If this failed, he retreated and tried another. Always at such times one of the deck hands was kept at the bow on the forecastle sounding the channel—a function most interesting and novel to one who had never witnessed it. On the shallow Missouri a pole was used instead of a lead line. A deck hand seized this pole and thrust it into the water every five seconds, at the same time calling out the depth in a drawling, sing-song voice. The Canadian boatmen would generally preface these calls with a snatch from some of their native songs, winding up with the required information as a sort of refrain. So novel was the performance to the uninitiated that an expert sounder would attract around him an audience of listeners.

In case no channel was found by direct trial with the boat, the pilot sent the mate out in a yawl, or more generally went himself, and carefully sounded the entire river over the shallow portion. Having determined where the deepest water lay, he returned to the boat, and if the obstacle were not too great, at once proceeded to move the boat over it. Steaming in the proper direction, as determined from the sounding, he would run the boat as far as she would go. The crew then lowered the huge spars on either side, set them in the sand with the lower ends pointing downstream so that a pull on the lines would both lift the boat and crowd it ahead; then hauled taut the lines, threw them around the capstans, and proceeded to "walk" the boat over the bar. The process was often long and laborious, and instances were not uncommon where one or two days were consumed in this way. An occasional resource, which always puzzled the uninitiated, was to set the wheel going with a reverse motion, as if trying to back the boat. The object of this was to dam the river up slightly and relieve as much as possible the pressure on the bar. The water was sometimes backed in this way up to a height of four inches, and this meant a great deal. The backward power of the wheel was so much less than the forward power of the spars that it was not considered at all. This was one of the scientific aspects of Missouri River navigation.

The few rapids on the river which were too steep for the boat to stem unaided were usually passed by the method of warping. As soon as the boat reached the foot of a rapid she made for the shore. The moment her prow touched the bank a dozen men leaped out and started on the run up along the water's edge. The foremost carried a pick and spade and a few stakes, the second a stick of timber a little smaller than a railroad tie, and the rest at proper intervals a strong line which was rapidly uncoiled from the boat. Having arrived well beyond the head of the rapid the men proceeded to plant a "dead man": that is, they dug a trench three or four feet deep in the hard prairie soil, large enough to receive the stick of timber, and with the long dimension at right angles to the river. The timber was then buried and firmly staked down, and the line fastened to it at its middle, while the crew on the boat threw their end of the line around the capstan, which was then slowly wound in under the power of steam. The operation was a very slow one, though less so as a general thing than sparring over sandbars.

Occasionally the pilots encountered genuine whirlpools of such magnitude that steamboats could not cross them. In 1867 the *Bishop* was swamped in an eddy caused by a new cut-off on the river. The boat was caught at the point where the swift current of the cut-off entered the old channel. At about the same timer the *Miner* narrowly escaped disaster in a violent eddy not far below Sioux City, Ia. The whirl of the water was so swift that the center of the eddy was nearly twelve feet below its circumference. The boat was trying to pull itself by with a line when it was caught by the eddy, swung out into the stream, whirled violently around and careened over until the river flowed right across the lower deck. Wood and all other movable material were swept off, and two men were drowned. Only the mate's presence of mind in slacking off the line saved the boat.

One of the most formidable perils of Missouri navigation during the period from 1860 to 1876 was the hostility of the Indians. The Sioux tribes in particular terrorized the boatmen all along the valley from the Niobrara to Milk River. Many were their actual attacks and many were the lives lost. It became necessary on some voyages to barricade the decks and staterooms, and the most careful vigilance night and day was required in order to avoid disaster.

An exciting and often dangerous pastime indulged in by the river boats was racing. This was particularly true of the period about 1858, when the boating business was rather overdone and there was great competition in the trade. Racing on the Missouri was very risky in any case, owing to the uncertainty of the channel and the abundance of snags; but the chief danger arose from the temptation to raise the steam pressure above a safe limit. Of all classes of steamboat disasters, the most dreadful were those caused by boiler explosions. There were six of these wrecks in the history of the river, although it is not known that they were all caused by racing. In 1842 the *Edna* was destroyed at the mouth of the Missouri, and forty-two German emigrants were killed. The most terrible accident was that of the *Saluda,* April 9, 1852, at Lexington, Mo. The boat was a sidewheeler, with two large boilers, and was on her way up the river with a load of merchandise and many Mormon passengers. The river was very high and the current so strong that the boat could not round the point just above town. After waiting several days without any improvement of the situation, the captain, Francis F. Belt, ordered another trial. Going into the engine room, he inquired how much steam was being carried. The engineer replied that he was carrying every pound that the boilers could stand. The captain recklessly ordered more steam to be made, and declared with an oath that he would round the bend or blow the boat to pieces. He then went above, rang the bell, and ordered the lines cast off. The boat swung into the stream; the engines made but one or two revolutions when the boilers burst with a terrific explosion that blew the boat into splinters and scattered them far and wide. Nearly all the officers were killed, among them the pilot, Charles La Barge, Captain La Barge's brother, and the second pilot, Louis Guerette, Mrs. La Barge's brother. It is said that over one hundred bodies were found. Several, children who escaped, but had lost their parents, were adopted by the people of Lexington and grew up to be citizens of Missouri instead of Mormon residents of the future State of Utah. The bell of this boat was blown out on the bank while yet it was ringing under the hand of Captain Belt. It was purchased with other wreckage by a resident of Lexington, who sold it to the Christian Church in Savannah, Mo., where it has done duty for the past fifty years.

After the time when the boats began to carry passengers in considerable numbers, much more attention was paid to the table fare than in the days when the passenger list was made up almost entirely of men going to service with the fur companies. In those days pork, lyed corn, and navy beans made up the substance of the bill of fare. It was always a rule, when in the Indian country, to rely on game for meat. For this purpose hunters were regularly employed on the various boats, selected for their skill, and never called upon for any other work. The hunter's custom was to leave the boat about midnight, some three or four hours before she was to start, and to scour the bank of the river, keeping well ahead. Whenever any animal was killed it was hung up in some conspicuous place, and was brought in by the steamboat yawl as the boat came along.

Captain La Barge had many of these hunters in his employ during his career. Henry Chatillon, the same who appears in Francis Parkman's "Oregon Trail," was one. He was a fine man, an excellent hunter, and sensible and gentlemanly in all his relations. The Captain's favorite hunter, however, was Louis Dauphin, who was more fearless than Chatillon and equally skillful as a hunter. He had a very long career on the Missouri River. He seemed to delight in danger, and was never afraid of the Indians; but his lack of prudence at last cost him his life, and he was killed by the Sioux near the mouth of Milk River in 1865.

Such are some of the peculiar features of Missouri River navigation as it existed fifty years ago. To bring back more of the reality of what has now become only a reminiscence, let us follow one of these steamboats on a typical voyage up the river. The principal event on the annual trip was the embarkation at St. Louis. The cargo consisted of a heterogeneous assortment of goods, designed for the Indian trade and for the equipment of hunting and trapping parties. It frequently included also the government annuities for the various tribes, and stores for the Indian agencies and military posts. The passengers composed an even more heterogeneous mixture than the cargo itself. There were, first, the regular boat crew, numbering from thirty to forty. Very likely there were several Indians returning home from St. Louis, or even from Washington. Then there were recruits for the various trading companies, consisting of hunters, trappers, voyageurs, and mountaineers, and possibly a company of soldiers for some military service. Nearly always there were passengers distinguished for wealth or scientific attainment, who were making the journey for pleasure or research. Government exploring parties generally traveled by boat to the initial point of their expeditions. In all there were from one hundred to two hundred people on board, with sufficient variety to insure vivacity and interest, however monotonous the journey might otherwise be.

The departure from port was always attended with more or less carousing and revelry, particularly in the keelboat and early steamboat days, when a trip up the river might mean years of absence. The kind of farewell that captured the fancy of the average voyageur was a general debauch, which often disqualified him from being ready when the hour of departure arrived. Sometimes these delinquents who failed to appear hied themselves across the country to St. Charles, and joined the boat there. In order to protect itself from loss, the American Fur Company made all its payments to the men conditional upon a certain amount of service. It made an allowance of clothing and blankets, but never delivered them until the men were on board and out of port. Wages were never advanced except to trusted employees.

As the boat swung out into the stream a running salute of musketry was kept up by the mountaineers and others until it was out of hearing. The roll was then called, and the engages were given their parcels of clothing. Next began the work of putting the boat deck in order for the trip. The bales of goods, which were strewn about in disorderly heaps, were carefully stowed away, and before night the boat was reduced to the appearance which it would wear during the remainder of the trip.

There still remained to be settled a final preliminary to a successful and harmonious voyage—the championship for physical prowess among the engages on the boat. As in a herd of cattle, so here, someone must be recognized as the strongest—able to whip anybody else in open contest. The crew being largely strangers to each other in starting, there were more or less friction and bickering until a settlement by fist force was reached. Usually the contest would settle down to a small number in a short time. It was a favorite pastime with that veteran mountaineer, Etienne Provost, who was often sent up in charge of recruits, to compel an early settlement which would determine all blustering and quarreling. He would form a ring on the forecastle and compel every braggart to make good his claims before the assembled passengers and crew. One after another would succumb, until one man would emerge from the contest victorious over all the others. He would then be awarded the championship, and receive a red belt in token thereof.

Captain La Barge recalled an interesting incident of this kind in which he himself had a hand. It was on the *Robert Campbell,* in 1863. He had on board a large quota of Irish engages, in fact they were mostly of this nationality; but there was one well-built, quiet, rawboned American, whose full name he had forgotten, but who was commonly known as Yankee Jack. In modern slang, the Irishmen "had it in" for this Yankee, and made his life as uncomfortable as possible. Two men in particular made it a point to harass and annoy him in every conceivable way, until the Captain finally asked Jack why he did not resent their conduct. Jack, who had a higher respect for authority than his persecutors, had not felt at liberty to take the matter up on the boat, but now told the Captain that, if he would permit it, he would settle the matter once for all very promptly. The Captain told him to go ahead, and himself arranged the preliminaries, and told the Irishmen that they would have to stand up and "take their medicine." With a good deal of contempt for the Yankee they made ready for the fray. A place was cleared on the deck and one of the men stepped out before Yankee Jack, and the battle began; but before the Irishman knew "where he was at" he lay sprawling upon the floor totally *hors de combat.* The next man stepped up and was led to the slaughter with as little ceremony as the other. For the rest of the voyage the Yankee was unmolested.

While the officers and crew were kept alert and active the livelong day in getting their boat up the troublesome stream, the passengers whiled away their time as best they could. Games of all practicable sorts were indulged in. It was a common pastime to stand on the forecastle or boiler deck and shoot at geese and ducks on the river. Now and then the sight of deer and other animals enlivened the moment, and occasionally the appearance of Indians on the bank caused a flutter of excitement. To relieve the tedium of the voyage it was a common thing, when there was no danger from the Indians, to land at the beginning of extensive bends, and ramble across the country to the other side, rejoining the boat when it came along.

The pilot-house was the favorite resort on the boat when the condition of navigation would permit the passengers to be there. The pilot was always an interesting personage to get acquainted with. When in the proper mood and sailing along some easy stretch of river, he would unloosen his tongue and entertain his listeners with tales of *his* adventurous experiences, in reality the accumulated stories of many years, but as new to the tenderfoot as if told for the first time. Here he would point out a dry sand waste where the channel ran the year before and where now a fine crop of willows was shooting vigorously upward. The high bank yonder, with a grove of cottonwoods close to the water's edge, was where the boat was attacked by Indians a few years before and two of the crew killed. The holes where bullets tore through the pilot-house were still visible as tragic reminders of a hairbreadth escape. A little further on was where the boat once had to stop to let a herd of buffalo cross the river, for it would not do to try to run through the herd lest their huge bodies become entangled in the wheels and cripple it altogether. Sometimes these delays amounted to several hours. In another place the Captain would point out the grave of some Indian chief reposing in the arms of a tree, where it had been placed by his people years before, and the sight would suggest many thrilling experiences, and even tragedies, which marked the intercourse of these primitive people with the navigators of the river. The recital of these traditions appealed to the imagination of the traveler, and helped allay the monotony of the voyage. If the landscape might often be likened to the "uniform view of the vacant ocean," there were nevertheless a thousand features on every trip which the most interesting ocean voyage lacks.

Among the important events of every voyage were the arrivals at the various trading posts. To the occupants of these remote stations, buried in the depths of the wilderness, shut out for months from any glimpse of the world outside, the coming of the annual boat was an event of even greater interest than to the passengers themselves. Generally the person in charge of the post, with some of the employees, would drop down the river two or three days' ride and meet the boat. When she drew near the post, salutes would be exchanged, the colors displayed, and the passengers would throng the deck to greet the crowd which lined the bank. The exigencies of navigation never left much time for celebration and conviviality. The exchange of cargo was carried on with the utmost dispatch, and the moment the business was completed the boat proceeded on her way.

These are some of the typical features of steamboat life as it used to exist on the Missouri River. In later years, when the gold discoveries in Montana gave the business such an astonishing impetus, other features of interest developed. The business was always a romantic one, and will stand in American frontier history as one of its most picturesque and delightful memories.

CHAPTER XI.

THE STEAMBOAT IN THE FUR TRADE.

The most important early use of steamboats upon the Missouri River was in connection with the fur trade, for this was the principal business conducted along the valley in the first half of the nineteenth century. Steamboats had entered the river in 1819, but that early experiment had not been very successful and had led to no regular traffic as late as 1830. The American Fur Company, which monopolized the fur trade of the Missouri Valley, continued to send its annual cargoes of merchandise up the river in keelboats. The great difficulty, heavy cost, and extreme delay by this method of transportation were a serious handicap upon the business. It took an entire summer to reach the far upper posts and not infrequently ice closed the river before this could be done. A large crew was required for a comparatively small cargo, and it was necessary to bring them all back in order not to have more men in the field than were needed.

The practicability of commercial steamboating on the Missouri River had begun to be recognized about 1829. In the summer of that year the W. D. Duncan *commenced a regular packet trade to Fort Leavenworth.*

It was from considerations of this character that the use of steamboats was determined upon in the summer of 1830, and from that time the true history of Missouri River navigation begins. The American Fur Company then had its headquarters in New York. John Jacob Astor was the real head of the company, although his son, William B. Astor, was its president. The Western Department of the Company was established in St. Louis and managed by the firm of Bernard Pratte & Company. Pierre Chouteau, Jr., writing for the firm, August 30, 1830, to the house in New York, thus describes the beginning of this new undertaking:

"Since the loss of our keelboat and the arrival of Mr. McKenzie, we have been contemplating the project of building a small steamboat for the trade of the upper Missouri. We believe that the navigation will be much safer in going up, and possibly also in coming down, than it is by keelboat. The only serious drawback will be the danger of breakage of some important pieces of machinery, which it would be difficult and perhaps impossible to repair on the spot. However, after consultation with some of the ablest steamboat captains, we think that by having spare parts and a good blacksmith outfit on board, we may be able to overcome this difficulty. I imagine that there will always be a little risk to run, but I also believe that, if we succeed, it will be a great advantage to our business. The expenses we are annually put to in the purchase of keelboats and supplies, and in advances to engages before their departure, are enormous, and have to be repeated every year. With the steamboat we could keep all our men in the Indian country, where we could pay the greater part of their wages in merchandise instead of making the large outlay of cash which we are now constantly required to do. The boat would make the voyage to the upper river every spring. By starting from here [St. Louis] at the beginning of April with the full season's outfit of merchandise, it would probably be back early in June, and bring with it a portion of the peltries. The finer furs could still be brought down in the ordinary way.

The merchandise would all reach its destination before ice closed in the fall, which we now sometimes fail to do, to our great loss. Furthermore, by having boats on hand at the trading posts, we can always bring down the returns in case of accident to the steamboat. After the return of the latter from the annual trip it can be used in freighting on the lower river during the balance of the season. Such a boat as we require we think will cost in Cincinnati or Marietta about $7000, but as we shall want a number of duplicate parts and extras the cost may amount to $8000.

"Our plan, promising as it seems to us, has its difficulties, and we submit it to you for approval before taking definite action. We beg you to think it over and reply as soon as possible, for, in case of your approval, we have no time to lose in getting the work under way, if the boat is to be ready by spring."

Such is the clear statement of the origin of a business which thirty years later assumed enormous proportions. The house in New York gave its approval, the boat was built, and was named, most appropriately, the *Yellowstone,* and in the spring of 1831 started on its first voyage for the far upper river.

The boat did not get as far as was expected on this trip. A little above the mouth of the Niobrara River it was stopped for a time by low water. Pierre Chouteau, Jr., who, with McKenzie, was the soul of the enterprise, was a passenger. Burning with impatience at the delay, he sent to Fort Tecumseh for lighters to take off a portion of the cargo. Every day he got out upon the high bluffs overlooking the river and paced up and down, watching for the desired assistance and praying for a rise in the river. The bluffs have ever since been known as the Chouteau Bluffs.

At last three boats came down and relieved the steamer of enough of her cargo to enable her to reach Fort Tecumseh, where Fort Pierre, S. D., now stands. No attempt was made to go farther, and in a short time she returned to St. Louis.

In spite of the failure to reach the mouth of the Yellowstone the experiment was considered enough of a success to justify its repetition. Accordingly, in the spring of 1832, the *Yellowstone* set out again, and this time reached Fort Union. The voyage was highly successful, and the return trip was made at the rate of a hundred miles a day. Pierre Chouteau, Jr., was again a passenger. Since the previous year Fort Tecumseh had been rebuilt in a situation less exposed to the ravages of the river, and was ready for occupancy when the *Yellowstone* arrived on her upward trip. It was at that time christened *Fort Pierre,* in honor of the distinguished visitor and member of the' company. George Catlin, the painter of Indian scenes and portraits, was also a passenger, and his writings and sketches have added to the celebrity of the voyage.

The success of the second experiment in navigating the Missouri gave great satisfaction to the company and to the public in general, for it had never been considered possible to take steamboats so far. It added seventeen hundred miles to the internal navigable waters of the United States, with every prospect that this would be extended to the very foothills of the Rocky Mountains. The voyage created great interest both in this country and in Europe, and John Jacob Astor, who was in France at the time, wrote home that nearly all the public journals of the Continent had made mention of it. Ramsay Crooks, general agent of the company in New York, thus expressed his pleasure to the house in St. Louis at the great success which they had achieved:

"I congratulate you most cordially on your perseverance and ultimate success in reaching the Yellowstone by *steam,* and the future historian of the Missouri will preserve for you the honorable and enviable distinction of having accomplished an object of immense importance, by exhibiting the practicability of conquering the obstructions of the Missouri, considered till almost the present day insurmountable to steamboats, even among those best acquainted with their capabilities. You have brought the Falls of the Missouri as near, comparatively, as was the River Platte in my younger days."

The experiment thus inaugurated grew into a regular business. The American Fur Company sent up one or more boats every spring, as long as it continued in the business. In the spring of 1833 it sent up two boats, the *Yellowstone* and the *Assiniboine.* It was this year that Maximilian, Prince of Wied, went up and spent several months at Forts McKenzie, Clark, and Union. The *Assiniboine* went above Fort Union for some distance, thus making another advance toward the head of navigation. It was caught in this advanced situation by low water, and was compelled to remain there all winter.

A most interesting and valuable relic of these early steamboat days has survived in the form of a journal, or logbook, covering the voyages from 1841 to 1847 inclusive. It is all in French except that for the year 1847. It is very complete, and exhibits in the clearest detail the manner of life which existed on the Missouri River steamboat in those early days. Captain La Barge was pilot on some of these voyages, and we shall now note a few of the interesting incidents with which he was connected, for they furnish a living picture of a condition of things which has long since ceased to exist.

CHAPTER XII.

VOYAGE OF 1843.

The voyage of 1843 known in more complete detail than any other in the history of the river. There are two complete journals of it—the Sire logbook, just referred to, and the published journal of the great naturalist, Audubon, who was one of the passengers. Captain La Barge himself gave the present author his full recollections of the trip. There were in all about one hundred passengers, besides some Indians returning to their country from a visit to St Louis. The passenger list included the usual picturesque variety, but its most conspicuous and noteworthy feature was, of course, the presence of Audubon and his party of scientists. Captain Joseph Sire was master of the boat and Captain La Barge pilot.

The *Omega* left St. Louis April 25, 1843. Along the lower course of the river the voyage was more than ordinarily difficult. The waters were high and the bottoms were badly overflowed, making shore excursions very unpleasant. The current was strong and the winds so severe and constant that the boat had to lie at the bank for several hours nearly every day. These delays were improved by the boat crew in procuring wood, and by the scientists in studying the country.

No incident worthy of particular mention occurred until the boat reached Bellevue, a few miles below the modern site of Omaha, Neb. The importation of liquor into the Indian country was prohibited under the severest penalties, and inspectors were stationed at Leavenworth and Bellevue to examine all cargoes bound up the river. Now it so happened that liquor was the one article above all others that the traders considered indispensable to their business, and they never failed to smuggle it through in some way or other. In the earlier years there was only one place at which the cargoes going up the river were inspected, and that was Fort Leavenworth. Later, when an Indian agency was established at Bellevue, that place also became a point of detention. At this particular time it was the *bete noire* of the American Fur Company traders. The military authorities at Fort Leavenworth, from long experience in the country and intimate knowledge of conditions prevailing there, exercised their office as inspectors with reasonable judgment and discretion. They understood very well that the small competing traders would smuggle liquor past them in spite of all they could do, and that to deprive the only responsible company on the river of its means of maintaining itself was simply to debauch the trade with the Indians to a reckless and demoralizing rivalry among a horde of irresponsible traders. They were therefore very lenient in their inspections, and the company rarely had any difficulty in getting past them.

Not so, however, with some of the newly appointed Indian agents. It was about this time that the Indian Department tried the experiment of assigning clergymen to the agencies—an example of good intentions but bad judgment. These new agents showed more zeal than discretion in their work, and although they put the traders to a great deal of trouble, it is doubtful if they lessened by a single drop the amount of liquor carried into the country.

On the occasion of the voyage of 1843 the agent at Bellevue happened to be absent from his station when the boat arrived. Elated at this unexpected good fortune, Captain Sire lost no time in putting off the freight destined for this point and in getting on his way. He pursued his voyage until nine o'clock that evening, and doubtless felicitated himself that he was out of danger. But it appears that the agent had delegated the function of inspector during his absence to the commander of the United States troops in the vicinity. The boat left her mooring at daylight next morning, but had scarcely gotten under way when a couple of rifle shots were fired across her bow. She brought to at once and made for the shore. There Captain Sire found a lieutenant in charge of a few dragoons, who had come from his camp four miles distant. The young officer came on board and presented to Captain Sire a polite note from Captain Burgwin, commander of the camp, stating that his orders required him to inspect the boat before letting her proceed.

This was like a dash of cold water to the buoyant spirits of Captain Sire, and none the less so to Audubon, to whom, as well as to the company, the loss of the liquid portion of the cargo would have been irreparable. The naturalist had a permit from the government to carry with him a quantity of liquor for the use of himself and party, and upon showing his credentials to the young officer he was, to use his own words, "immediately settled comfortably." But in the moment of his good fortune he did not forget his companions who were not yet "settled comfortably." He understood that time was required to prepare for the approaching function, and he could at least help to secure this time by delaying inspection as long as possible. He accordingly expressed a desire to visit the camp, and the lieutenant detailed a dragoon to accompany him. The great naturalist rode four miles to call upon an obscure army officer whom he knew he could see in a short time by waiting at the boat. The officer was overwhelmed at the honor of the visit, and when Audubon offered to present his credentials he politely and gallantly replied that his name was too well known throughout the United States to require any letters. Audubon says of the occasion: "I was on excellent and friendly terms in less time than it has taken me to write this account of our meeting." Between his entertaining conversation and the shooting of some birds he contrived to detain the Captain for a good two hours before they returned to the boat.

The time had not been wasted by Captain Sire and his loyal crew. The shallow hold of the steamboat of those days was divided lengthwise into two compartments by a partition or bulkhead running the full length of the boat. A narrow-gauge tramway extended down each side of the hold its entire length, the two sides connecting with each other by a curve which passed under the hatchway in the forecastle. Small cars received the cargo let down through the hatchway, and carried it to its place in the hold or brought it out again when the boat was being unloaded. A car could pass from the stem of the boat on one side of the hold around the curve in the bow and to the stern of the boat on the other side. There being no windows in the hold, everything was buried in blackness a few feet from the hatchway. Workmen were lighted to their labors by means of candles.

During the absence of Audubon the crew had loaded all the liquor upon the cars, and had run them down on one side of the hold far enough from the hatchway to be entirely concealed in the darkness. They were carefully instructed in the part they had to play in the approaching comedy, and very likely were put through a preliminary rehearsal or two.

When Captain Burgwin arrived in Audubon's company, he was received most hospitably and treated to a luncheon, in which was included, as a matter of course, a generous portion from the private store embraced in Audubon's "credentials." By this time the young Captain was in most excellent temper and was quite disposed to forego the inspection altogether. But the virtuous Sire would not have it so. "I insisted, as it were," says the worthy navigator in his log of May 10, "that he make the strictest possible search, but upon the condition that he would do the same with other traders."

A proposition so eminently fair was at once agreed to by the inspector, whose mellow faculties were now in a most accommodating condition. The shrewd steamboat master, who never forgot to be sober when his company's interests were at stake, escorted the officer down the hatchway, and together they groped their way along the hold by the light of a not too brilliant candle. It may be imagined with what zeal the scrupulous Captain thrust the ineffectual flame into every nook and corner, and even insisted that the inspector move a box or bale now and then to assure himself that everything was all right.

Arrived at the foot of the hold, they passed through an opening and started back on the other side. The officer was doubtless too much absorbed with the effects of his recent collation to notice the glimmer of light under the hatchway at the other end of the boat, where a miniature train with its suspicious cargo was creeping stealthily around the curve and disappearing toward the side which they had just left. The party finished their inspection, and everything was found quite as it should be. With many protestations of good will the clever hosts and their delighted guest parted company, and the good Captain Sire went on his way rejoicing. But woe to the luckless craft of some rival trader which should happen along with no Audubon in the cabin and no tramway in the hold.

The ordeal of inspection being over, the boat proceeded on her way with no further drawbacks than those arising from the various hindrances to navigation. One of the disagreeable features of the trip above the mouth of the Big Sioux River was the vast number of dead buffalo that were encountered. They had been drowned on the upper river at the time of the spring break-up in attempting to cross the ice after it became too weak. Their bodies had then floated downstream and had lodged all along the river on sandbars, islands, or the low shores. Some time having elapsed since they were drowned, their flesh was now in a condition that rendered the air almost insupportable.

An incident which caused considerable excitement, but luckily no misfortune, occurred at Handy's Point (where Fort Randall later stood) on the 22d of May. A band of eight or ten Santee Indians, apparently angered because the boat would not stop for them, opened fire upon it from the bank. The bullets tore through the cabins and pilot-house, but by the greatest good luck no one was hurt. A Scotchman who was

The above description of this inspection is from "The American Fur Trade of the Far West," by the present author. asleep in his bunk was awakened and terribly frightened by one of the bullets which entered his berth, passing through his pantaloons, and flattening itself against a trunk. Audubon saved two of the spent bullets as relics. He was himself standing near one of the chimneys and saw a bullet splash in the water just in front of the boat. Considering the large number of people on board, the escape of everyone was almost miraculous.

Captain La Barge was at the wheel at the time. In the pilot-house with him was a French negro from Louisiana named Jacques Desire, always known as Black Dave. He was an excellent pilot and was on board with a crew to return with the steamboat *Trapper,* which had been left up the river the previous autumn on account of low water. When the bullet crashed through the pilot-house Black Dave walked quietly out and took shelter behind one of the smokestacks, where he remained until the boat was well away from the scene of the attack. Captain La Barge asked him why he did not remain in the pilot-house, so as to be ready to take the wheel in case he himself were disabled. Dave replied that it was not the fear of bullets that drove him away, but that his eyesight was all he had to make his living by, and he was afraid of its getting injured by the flying glass.

As may readily be understood, a feature of first importance on this trip was the presence of so distinguished a passenger as the naturalist Audubon. The impression which the celebrated scientist made upon the crew and those who were entertaining him was quite unfavorable. He was very reserved, and when he did hold intercourse with members of the crew it was generally in an overbearing manner which alienated their good will. It thus resulted that his hunters rendered him inefficient service, and his journal is full of complaints at their failure to keep their promises. Certain personal habits aggravated this defect, and altogether he was not a popular traveler with the crew.

Captain La Barge mentions several instances of his ill treatment, one of which concerned himself, and is here given in his own words, as he once prepared them for publication in the *Missouri Republican:*

"On one occasion he [Audubon] asked me if I had ever seen any black squirrels during my voyages on the upper Missouri River. My answer was that I had often killed them. 'Do you know what a black squirrel is?' he asked. I replied that I knew what I called a black squirrel, and would try to get him one at the first opportunity. A few days later we were wind-bound. Seeing that we would be compelled to remain tied to the bank most of the day I took my gun and started around to look for a black squirrel. I was fortunate. I ran across a very fine one and shot him. He proved to be a fine large buck. I brought him aboard. The first person I met was Mr. Bell, taxidermist of the Audubon party, who remarked, after examining the squirrel, that it was certainly a very fine specimen. He called Mr. Audubon's attention to it, who examined the animal carefully, and then said to me: *'That* is what you call a black squirrel, is it? I expected as much. It *is* very strange that people born and raised in a country do not know the names of the animals and birds which it produces/ After the squirrel had been thus criticised for some time, I remarked that I would take it down to the cook and have it baked for dinner. 'No, no!' said Mr. Audubon, 'Mr. Bell will take care of it'; and then walked off.

"Some few days after this one of his assistants called to me to show me a painting that Mr. Audubon had finished that morning. This was after dinner, as Mr. Audubon had always to retire to his stateroom after that meal and have his long afternoon nap. The assistant took advantage of this opportunity to show me some of the drawings which Mr. Audubon was opposed to our seeing. On entering the room I saw the drawing of the squirrel just finished, and certainly I never saw anything representing life so strikingly.

The assistant then told me that Mr. Audubon had remarked that it was the best specimen of a black squirrel that he had ever painted."

The crew soon lost a good deal of the deference and respect which were justly due to individuals of such scientific attainments as were those of the Audubon party; and it is to be feared that they played pranks on them now and then which they would have avoided with people of more congenial manner. Etienne Provost was serving as guide to the party. No one in that day knew the Western country better than he, and he was quite astonished when Mr. Prou, Audubon's botanist, said to him one day that he could tell the name of any plant in that country from the leaf and stalk, even if he had never seen it growing. "You may think so," said Provost, "but I will undertake to prove that you are mistaken; for I know a plant that grows in this country whose name you will not be able to tell, even with the aid of your books." Soon afterward the boat landed to take on wood near the mouth of the Cheyenne River. A band of Indians had spent the previous winter near by and had dropped some of their corn on the ground. This was now well sprouted and the tender blades were just shooting up. Provost carefully cut the ground around a spear of the corn so as not to disturb the roots or the kernel, which was still attached thereto. He deftly concealed everything except one leaf and then showed it to Mr. Prou. The eager scientist was looking for some test of a formidable character, and anything like corn did not even occur to him. It is doubtful if he realized at the time that corn was grown in that country. He racked his brain for a plant that he could identify with the specimen. He grew nervous under the scrutiny of the on-lookers that had gathered around him. Taking his book, he searched back and forth, but to no purpose. It was indeed a new species, and he finally acknowledged himself beaten. Provost then, with provoking gravity, pulled away the dirt around the roots and finally disclosed to the astonished scientist—a kernel of *corn*.

Above Omaha the boat made its way with more than usual speed and good luck to its destination. It reached Fort Pierre May 31 and Fort Union at sundown June 12. It left Fort Union June 14, reached Pierre June 21, and St. Louis June 29. The time consumed was forty-nine days from St. Louis to Fort Union and seventeen days returning. Mr. Audubon and party remained at Fort Union until autumn, returning in a mackinaw boat.

CHAPTER XIII.

VOYAGE OF 1844.

IN the winter of 1843-44 the American Fur Company built a new boat, the *Nimrod*, designed to correct certain defects in the *Omega*, and in this boat the voyage of 1844 was made. As in the previous year, Captains Sire and La Barge were master and pilot. It was in the spring and summer of this year that occurred the great flood of 1844. This appears to have been the greatest flood in the lower Missouri and central Mississippi ever known before or since. The entire bottoms in the vicinity of St. Louis were covered with water to a width of several miles. The flood had the curious effect of completely filling up the old bed of the river, so that, when it subsided, the river had to cut out a new channel, and it was many years before the channel was restored to its condition before the flood. The high water lasted far into the summer. When Captain La Barge returned from his trip to Fort Union he ran his boat up Washington Avenue to Commercial Alley, where he made her fast through a window in J. E. Walsh's warehouse at the corner of those streets. This great flood was mostly from the lower country, and scarcely at all from the mountains. When the *Nimrod* reached the Omaha villages, a short distance below the modern site of Sioux City, Ia., she found the water so low that she was compelled to wait several days for a rise. This fact is a noteworthy one, as another refutation of the popular idea that floods in the Mississippi have their origin in the melting snows of the Rocky Mountains. As a matter of fact they always come from the heavy rains of the lower country.

The *Nimrod* passenger list, like that of the *Omega* the year before, included some notable names. Among these were the Comte d'Otrante, son of the famous Fouche of France, and another Frenchman, the Comte de Peindry. D'Otrante was much liked by the crew. He was an accomplished gentleman, very wealthy, and had with him a retinue of servants who had been reared with him upon the ancestral domain in France. He was making the present journey solely for the purpose of pleasure. De Peindry was a different sort of man. He and D'Otrante met by accident on this trip and had little to do with each other. It was noted that De Peindry treated his compatriot with great deference and respect as being his superior. He was silent and impenetrable, and spent much of his time hunting. When leaving the boat on these hunts he would give directions not to wait for him if he did not return. He was repeatedly cautioned that the boat could not wait for him, but his invariable reply was: "Do not wait; I will turn up; if I do not, it is no matter." He caused a great deal of uneasiness on several occasions by not getting back in time, and Captain Sire in his journal comments severely upon his conduct. He was said to be a noted duelist, who, for some unknown cause, had been compelled to leave Paris. He was very much of an enigma to the passengers of the *Nimrod*. In 1845 he went to California, whence the report came a few years later that he had been assassinated.

In passing the Indian agency at Bellevue this year it was necessary to indulge in some more sharp practice to get the annual cargo of alcohol past that point. The new Indian agent at Bellevue was an ex-Methodist minister of the name of Joseph Miller—as zealous in his new role of liquor inspector as he had ever been in the regular practice of his profession. It was his boast that no liquor could pass his agency. He rummaged every boat from stem to stern, broke open the packages, overturned the piles of merchandise, and with a long, slender, pointed rod pierced the bales of blankets and clothing, lest kegs of alcohol might be rolled up within. The persistent clergyman put the experienced agents of the company to their wit's ends, and it was with great difficulty that they succeeded in eluding his scrutiny.

The urgency of the problem, however, produced its own solution. Captain Sire had the alcohol all packed in barrels of flour. But he knew that even this device would not alone be enough, for the energetic agent would very likely have the barrels burst open. The Captain therefore had them all marked as if consigned to Peter A. Sarpy, the Company's agent at Bellevue, and they were labeled in large letters "P. A. S." The moment the nose of the boat touched the landing at Bellevue, the Captain, as was his custom, ordered the freight for that point placed on shore, and the barrels were promptly bowled out upon the bank and carried into the warehouse. The agent, never suspecting this freight, went on board, and after a most rigid search, found nothing wrong. The boat was permitted to proceed, but, contrary to its usual haste in getting away as soon as the loading and unloading were complete, it remained the rest of the day, and gave out that it would not sail until the following morning. The extraordinarily good character of the boat on this occasion, and the unusually long delay in departing, roused the suspicions of the agent, who stationed a man to watch the boat and to whistle if he saw anything wrong.

Everything remained quiet until some time after midnight, except that a full head of steam was kept up in the boilers. Presently there was great activity on the boat, although with an ominous silence about it all. The pilot, Captain La Barge, was quietly engineering the reloading of the barrels. He had spread tarpaulins on the deck and gang plank to deaden the noise, and the full crew of the boat were hurrying the barrels back in a most lively fashion. "What does this mean?" one of the deckhands asked of another. "We unloaded these barrels yesterday." "Why, don't you see?" was the brilliant reply of another, "they're marked 'P. A. S.'; they've got to pass." The work was quickly over and every barrel was on board, when the agent's sleepy guard awoke to the fact that something was going on. He uttered his signal, and the agent made haste to turn out and see what was the matter. La Barge and Captain Sire, who knew full well what the whistle meant, did not linger to make explanations. Captain La Barge seized an ax and cut the line. "Get aboard, men!" he shouted; "the line has parted!" The boat instantly dropped back into the current and then stood out into the river under her own steam. She was already out of reach of the bank when the reverend inspector appeared and wanted to know why they were off so early. It was about 3 A. M. "Oh, the line parted," replied Captain La Barge, "and it was so near time to start that it was not worth while to tie up again."

This was a little too much for the agent, who could not understand how it happened that the boat was so thoroughly prepared for such an accident, with steam up, pilot at the wheel, crew at their places, and all at so early an hour. Next day he found that the barrels consigned to Sarpy were gone, and saw how completely he had been duped. Mortified and indignant, he reported the company to the authorities, and a long train of difficulties ensued, with ineffectual threats of canceling the company's license, f Meanwhile the alcohol found its intended destination in the stomachs of the Indians, and the company reaped the enormous profit which traffic in that article always yielded.

As already noted, when the *Nimrod* arrived at the site of the Omaha villages, the river was so low that she could not proceed for several days. A crew was kept constantly busy with the yawl, sounding the channel to detect any favorable changes in its shifting bed. On one of these sounding excursions, when about five miles from the boat, and under a high cut bank, La Barge was surprised and captured by a Pawnee war party on their way to steal horses from the Yanktonais. When the Captain heard them speak Pawnee he felt safe, and at once opened conversation with them in their own tongue. Although he knew none of the Indians personally, he succeeded in inducing them to come to the boat and partake of a feast. Thus the Captain's knowledge of the Pawnee language, acquired in the villages of that tribe ten years before, stood him in excellent stead. These Indians might not have killed him, belonging as they did to a friendly tribe; but war parties, even of friendly Indians, were lawless and desperate, and they would no doubt have handled the little boat crew pretty roughly.

Among the crew of the *Nimrod* there were two ocean sailors, good men, but with no river experience, who had engaged for the trip to see the interior of the country. They were employed principally in handling the rigging. One Sunday morning, May 19, while the boat was still at the Omaha villages, they set off together with a single gun to try their luck hunting. They failed to return that day and likewise the next, when general uneasiness began to be felt about them. Parties were sent after them in all directions, guns were fired, and everything done to find them, but to no purpose; and the boat proceeded on her way without them. The general opinion was that they had been killed by some vagrant war party of Indians. Some two weeks later, as the boat was setting out one morning, a trader by the name of Kensler was seen coming down the river with a small boatload of furs. La Barge ran his boat to shore and hailed the trader, who promptly hove to and came on board. La Barge explained the circumstance of these two men having been lost, gave Kensler some provisions for them, and asked him to stop at the woodpile, where the boat had laid up so long, and see if he could find any traces of the men. He did so, and actually found them there. They had converted the woodpile into a rude fortress, with one opening on the river just large enough to enable them to get out for water. They were almost starved to death, being reduced to mere skeletons, scarcely able to crawl back and forth to the river. Kensler took them to P. A. Sarpy's trading post at Bellevue, where the *Nimrod* found them on her way back and took them to St. Louis. They gave La Barge the following story: On the first day of their hunt they became confused and lost, and after much wandering came to the bank of the river. But they were utterly unable to conjecture whether they were above or below the steamboat, and in this dilemma resolved to build a raft and float down the river. If above the boat they would, of course, come to where it was; if below, they would land after having proven the fact, and return on foot. As a matter of fact they were below the boat, and after drifting some thirty miles concluded to start back. They were considering the question of landing when their raft ran upon a snag, broke to pieces, precipitated them into the water, and lost them their gun. They swam ashore and walked up the river bank until they reached the place where the boat had been. They resolved to stay there and wait for someone to come along. They disposed the woodpile so as to make a rough fort, and gathered into their fortress all remnants of camp refuse left by the *Nimrod* which could sustain life. Here they waited for several weeks, and had about given themselves up as lost when they were rescued in the manner already related.

The fare provided by the company for its steamboat crew was exceedingly plain and scanty. The men got very tired of it, and as they were much delayed by low water in getting into the buffalo country, La Barge told them that the first buffalo they came in sight of they should have, even if he had to lie to half a day to get it. La Barge had as first mate an excellent man, John Durack, who had served in the English navy, and had made his way to New Orleans and thence to St. Louis. He had been on the river before, but had never been engaged in a buffalo hunt, and the Captain thought this a good opportunity to initiate him. When the boat reached the vicinity of Handy's post four buffalo bulls were seen swimming the river. "Man the yawl, John," said La Barge. "I will go with you and we will have a buffalo before we get back." The Captain gave orders to the men on the boat to shoot the buffaloes, and he would then lasso one of the wounded ones and drag it to the boat. He put Durack in the bow with a line while he took the rudder. The men on the steamboat fired and wounded two of the buffaloes. To get to the wounded ones the boat had to pass close to the two uninjured ones. The Captain supposed that Durack fully understood the programme, but the mate was not "up to buffalo," and to La Barge's consternation slipped the noose over the head of one of the uninjured animals. Too late Captain La Barge shouted to him not to do this—that he did not want to anchor to a live buffalo.

"Oh," replied Durack, "he's as good as any." The buffalo kept straight on his course. The men backed their oars, but to no purpose; they could not stop him. Finally his feet touched bottom and up the bank he went with the boat and its helpless crew after (him. They might indeed have taken a boat ride over the bare prairie had not the stem of the yawl given way, being wrenched entirely out of the boat and carried off by the terrified animal. There stood the sorry crew, shipwrecked on a sandbar across the river from the steamboat—and with no buffalo. A whole day was consumed in getting back to the boat and in repairing the broken yawl. Meanwhile the crew kept on eating salt pork and navy bread.

On the 23d of June, when the *Nimrod* was a little below the site of the Aricara villages, near the mouth of Grand River, there arose one of those frightful tempests of wind, hail, and rain which were so frequent on the central prairies. For a little while the safety of the boat was despaired of. All the glass on the windward side was broken and the interior of the boat deluged with rain and hail. The hail accumulated in the cabin to the depth of a foot, and some of the hailstones were as large as turkey eggs. Captain La Barge made clay impressions of some of them and sent them to the St. Louis *Republican* as curiosities deserving public notice. Besides the damage to the cabins the wind carried away the pilot-house, which had to be replaced with a skin roof.

On another of Captain La Barge's voyages he encountered a storm which carried away the smokestacks. He extemporized some skin chimneys, which enabled him to complete the trip. The Captain was once summoned as an expert witness in a trial which grew out of a similar accident to another steamboat, whose owners had been sued for damages for not delivering freight. The defense was that a storm had so wrecked the boat that she could not proceed. The particular damage alleged was the blowing down of the smokestacks. La Barge explained how he had managed in a similar case, and the court instructed the jury against the defendant.

In another case La Barge's evidence, as an expert steamboat man, was decisive. It was a case of collision in which the pilot of the boat that was lost had not followed strictly the recognized signals and rules in passing the other boat. The owners had sued for damages. The defense was that the defendant's pilot had followed the strict rules of steamboating, and the other pilot had not. The main question was whether the defendant's pilot, when he saw the danger, should not have given way if possible, even if the other pilot was violating the rules, whether through willfulness or ignorance. La Barge was asked what course he would have pursued in the premises. He replied that, under any circumstances, it was a pilot's duty to avoid accident, if possible. The court agreed with this view.

The rest of the voyage of the *Nimrod* passed off without noteworthy incident. The boat reached Fort Union on June 22, started back June 24, and reached St. Louis July 9, after an absence of seventy-one days.

CHAPTER XIV.
CHANGED CONDITIONS.

Down to the date to which our narrative has now arrived, the steamboat business of the Missouri was mainly that of the fur trade. A small traffic was carried on with the settlements along the lower river and with the government establishment at Fort Leavenworth. In 1829 a regular packet was put on between St. Louis and Leavenworth, and this was kept up at intervals during the next fifteen years. But still the main business was the trade with the Indians or with Santa Fe and the parties of white hunters who roved all over the Western country. Its single noteworthy feature, as late as 1845, the annual voyage of the Fur Company's boat to the mouth of the Yellowstone.

At about the date last mentioned a profound change came over the business—a change inseparably connected with the foundation of civilization in the Far West. The emigration of the Mormons to Great Salt Lake was one feature of this new development. That singular sect, whose origin and doctrines have excited the contempt of the civilized world, as its marvelous growth and material achievement have commanded its admiration, was at this time about fifteen years old. Its founder was Joseph Smith, its birthplace Fayette, in New York State, and the year of its birth 1830. For causes which are differently stated by the friends and enemies of the church, Smith and his followers found it expedient to emigrate from New York. They went to Kirtland, O., where they laid the foundations of their New Jerusalem, and where they flourished with varying fortune for several years. In the meantime another location was also chosen, possibly as a refuge in case of expulsion from Kirtland— a situation on the very frontier of civilization, twelve miles west of Independence, Mo. Here the cornerstone of Zion was laid, under the sanction of divine revelation, and here the church began to erect its earthly temple. Hither in a few years came the faithful from Kirtland, having been expelled by the community, to whom their doctrine and practices had rendered them obnoxious.

In western Missouri their experience was even more discouraging than in Ohio. The neighboring communities would have none of them. The State authorities were appealed to by both sides, and finally entered the contest; the militia was ordered out, and things assumed the aspect of civil war. Blood was shed, and the Mormons were finally compelled to flee from the country, leaving Joseph Smith and Sidney Rigdon prisoners in the hands of their enemies. These worthies, however, soon escaped and joined the refugees near Commerce, Hancock Co., Ill.

Their first reception in Illinois was one of welcome, for the people of that State believed that they had been persecuted with uncalled-for severity by the citizens and State of Missouri. Under the impulse of this friendly feeling Smith secured a charter from the State, and forthwith began building the city of Nauvoo, on a site which has been universally admired for its great natural beauty. The powers conferred by this charter were very broad, and Smith became virtually emperor of an *imperium in imperio*. He was mayor of the city, *Lieutenant General* of the newly created Nauvoo legion, and President of the church. He acquired wide notoriety throughout the country, and became a political factor of no little importance in the State of Illinois. The colony flourished under the impulse of missionary effort, which sent proselytes hither from America and Europe alike. On the 6th of April, 1841, the corner-stone of still another temple was laid.

But the same causes which proved disastrous to the settlements in Ohio and Missouri soon began to operate in Illinois. The people were outraged at the immoral doctrines of the new sect, and alarmed at the arrogant defiance of civil authority by its spiritual and temporal head. Finally an act of violence under Smith's authority led to his arrest and that of his brother Hyrum, and their confinement in the Carthage jail, under guarantee of safety by the Governor of the State. But a mob was organized which overbore the civil authority, broke into the jail, and slew the brothers in cold blood.

For the future development of the sect, this was the most fortunate event in its history. It set the seal of martyrdom upon the founder of the church; it healed internal dissensions; it intensified the high purpose to succeed; and finally it opened up the career of the one man who above all others was qualified to carry the movement to success. This was that astute and gifted leader of men, prophet Brigham Young.

It was now apparent that there was no abiding place for the church upon the soil of the United States, and it was necessary to look beyond. From the narratives of those who had visited the regions west of the Rocky Mountains, Young determined to lead his people to the valley of the Great Salt Lake, at this time a possession of the Mexican Republic. In that remote and benighted wilderness his people could at least have freedom from persecution, for the civil authority of Mexico could scarcely reach so far. The movement was decided upon. Smith had been killed in June, 1844, and the general exodus began in the spring of 1846. In July, 1847, Young laid the foundation of the final home of his people on the shores of the Great Salt Lake.

In the course of this movement large bodies of Mormons remained encamped for long periods on both shores of the Missouri near Council Bluffs and Omaha. This situation became the great rendezvous for the expeditions before starting across the plains, and it was here that the Mormons came into relation with the steamboat traffic of the Missouri. Large quantities of freight and great numbers of passengers were brought up and disembarked here. The *Saluda*, whose tragic fate we have elsewhere described, was loaded with Mormons. In 1851 the steamer *St. Ange* carried up two hundred of these people, and the *Sacramento* four hundred. Many other boats, for fully a decade after 1846, brought up passengers and freight destined to the distant colony in the heart of the Rocky Mountains.

Another of the great movements of the time, which gave a marked impetus to Missouri River navigation, was the War with Mexico. This great event—great not so much in its battles as in its far-reaching results—had been gathering force for years. The influx of American settlers into the province of Texas caused the Mexican Government to adopt repressive measures toward them. This led to successful revolution on the part of Texas, and her independence was finally won by force of arms in 1836. For the next ten years Texas was practically an independent republic seeking annexation to the United States. The question of annexation was the determining issue in the national election of 1844, and the pro-annexationists prevailed. Texas was annexed in the spring of 1845, d in the following December was admitted as a State, against the protest of the Mexican Government. The administration ordered American troops to occupy certain disputed territory claimed by both Mexico and Texas. Collision with the Mexican troops followed: blood was shed, and the United States declared war.

Among the minor operations of the war from a military point of view, but of transcendent importance in their results, were the conquests of New Mexico and California under Harney, Doniphan, and Fremont. All the country so won became a part of the United States. It lay in the pathway of emigration to the West, and must sooner or later have given rise to grave complications. The inevitable issue was precipitated sooner than was expected, but the result must ultimately have been the same. The importance of this acquisition in the history of the nation cannot be overestimated.

The invasion of New Mexico naturally followed the line of the Santa Fe trail. The expeditions were organized on the frontier, mostly at Fort Leavenworth, but also at other points, such as Fort Kearney and St. Joseph. The transportation of troops and supplies to Westport, Leavenworth, and Kearney gave a great deal of work to the Missouri River boats, which thus became an important factor in one of our national wars.

Scarcely had the treaty of Guadaloupe Hidalgo, which closed the war, been signed, when an event took place in the newly acquired territory which completely revolutionized the situation of things in the West. This was the discovery of gold in California in 1848. Emigration had been moving to the coast, principally into Oregon, for the previous six years. The first large movement took place in 1843. I45 d 846 several parties crossed the Sierras into California, and there was a strong nucleus of American settlers there when the conquest came. The discovery of gold swelled this incipient stream into a mighty river. From every part of the world, by land and by sea, the rush to California began. The overland movement was one of the greatest and most wonderful migrations of a people which history records. It ran in full strength for several years, beginning in 1849, and by 1854 a vast but unknown number had crossed the plains.

There were various starting points from the Missouri River in this migration, although the different routes united before Fort Laramie was reached. Westport, Leavenworth, Fort Kearney, and Omaha became initial rendezvous, and a great deal of traffic for the emigrants was done by the river boats from St. Louis to these points.

Following the three great movements just described came the period of government exploration of the entire Western country, and the search for practical railroad routes across the mountains. Large exploring parties were sent into the field, and bodies of troops were dispatched to the Pacific Coast and to distant points in the interior.

The aggregate amount of business brought to the lower Missouri from these various causes was large. Viewed from the standpoint of transportation, the Western country in that day can be likened in shape to a fan. The handle was that portion which extended from St. Louis to the mouth of the Kansas River. Thence the various routes to all parts of the country diverged along the arms of the fan, which were outspread from Santa Fe on the south to Fort Union on the north. Most of the business below the point of divergence was done by steamboat. Vessels in large numbers plied the river over this first four hundred miles, and the amount of freight and passenger traffic carried by them was very great. Boats departed daily from St. Louis, carrying an almost inconceivable variety of articles for use of the emigrants, and nearly as large a variety of emigrants themselves. To one who witnessed this business in the noontide of its activity, it would have seemed scarcely possible that another generation should witness its total extinction.

Of the river business which grew out of the several movements just described, Captain La Barge had his full share. He knew the Mormons well. He had already seen much of them during their sojourn in western Missouri, and came into business relations with them on a considerable scale during their emigration of 1846 and subsequent years. He always liked them, and had several warm friends among them. He was introduced to Brigham Young by Peter A. Sarpy at Bellevue, where the American Fur Company post for that section was situated. The Mormons were encamped in this vicinity so long that they brought to Sarpy's post a large amount of business. La Barge himself became well acquainted with Young and with others of the principal men. Young impressed him from the first as a man of great ability. Apparently deficient in education and refinement, he was fair and honest in his dealings, and seemed extremely liberal in conversation upon religious subjects. He impressed La Barge as anything but a religious fanatic or even enthusiast; but he knew how to make use of the fanaticism of others and direct it to great ends. He was kind and considerate, but a firm and strict disciplinarian. In the Mormon movement he had found his niche. He saw in it his opportunity to achieve power and fame, to amass a fortune, and to become a great leader.

The freight business which came to the steamboats as a result of the gold rush was not of a desirable character. Many of the emigrants were so poor that it was difficult to collect from them, and once out of reach there was scarcely a chance of ever hearing from them again. This condition improved in later years, and the emigrant trade on the whole was one of great magnitude and importance.

Referring to the gold craze. Captain La Barge said:

"I was never seized with the craze. My wife wanted me to go, but I was too busy and was already making money. Had I been idle, or unsuccessful in business, I should undoubtedly have gone. I saw enough of the movement to show me how many chances of failure there were to one of success; and as I saw the thousands of disheartened adventurers who turned back without ever reaching the desired region, I never repented not going."

CHAPTER XV.

INCIDENTS ON THE RIVER (1845-50).

The annual voyages of 1845-46 were made on the steamer *General Brooks*. In the fall of the latter year Captain La Barge bought this boat for twelve thousand dollars, but sold her again at the close of the season. This was the first boat he had ever owned. He then went to Cincinnati, where he supervised the building of a new boat. She was named the *Martha,* and in her the voyage of 1847 made. Captain Sire, who for several years had gone up as master, now decided to leave the river, and Captain La Barge accordingly made the trip alone in full charge of the Company's business.

Besides the regular freight for the company trading posts, the boat carried up a large quantity of annuities for the several Indian tribes. A more extended reference to this annuity business and the abuses to which it led will be made further on. It is enough here to say that the agents were sent into the country without any protection; that the Company traders adroitly worked on their fears until they were fain to place themselves under the shelter of the trading posts; and that the Company was thus enabled to manage the government business to its own great profit. On this particular trip there was a new agent by the name of Matlock, and a good deal of time had to be spent at the various agencies to permit him to confer with the Indians.

At Crow Creek there was a band of Yankton Sioux near a trading establishment under charge of Colin Campbell. Here agent Matlock gave the Indians a feast and left part of their annuities, but not all, being induced by the Company's agent to deposit the balance at Fort Pierre. The Indians were sharp enough to see that they had not received all they were entitled to and naturally could not understand why. Campbell assured them that they would receive the balance at Fort Pierre. "Why not here?" asked the Indians. "Why make this long journey for what we can just as well get right here?" Campbell turned them off by saying that the Indian agent could attend to the matter there better.

The Indians sullenly acquiesced, evidently much dissatisfied. Campbell had cut ten or twelve cords of wood at this place for use of the boat, but it was not needed till the down trip. Captain La Barge feared, however, that, if it was left, the Indians, in their present temper, would bum it, and he therefore concluded to take it along. The Indians refused to let the wood be taken without pay, and seated themselves on the pile so that the men could not get at it. The captain was compelled to pay for the wood, although it had been cut by Company men. But the matter did not end here. Etienne Provost, who, as elsewhere stated, was employed on these trips to take charge of the rough and turbulent mountain men, was asked to attend to the loading of the wood, as it was feared there might be trouble. Provost came up on the boiler deck and sat down by La Barge, saying: "We are going to have some fun before that wood is on board." He then shouted "Woodpile! Woodpile!" and enough men rushed out to the bank, to take the whole woodpile at once. Provost ordered them to pick up all they could carry and then to move on to the boat one after another, so as to have no crowding or confusion on the gang plank. Meanwhile a dozen or more Indians were standing by, looking on. When the men were loaded up and were jammed close together in single file on their way to the boat, the Indians jumped upon them and began to belabor them with the rawhide horsewhips which they always had fastened to their waists. The men were frightened almost out of their wits, and dropping their wood, scrambled on board the best way they could. Provost lay back and roared with laughter, saying, "I told you we should see some fun."

He then went out himself onto the bank where the Indians were, and said, "Now, men, come out here and get this wood." They came and loaded up. "Now go on board," he said, and they went entirely unmolested. Provost went last, and before descending the bank, turned toward the Indians and asked them: "Why don't you stop them? Are you afraid of *me?*" The truth is they were afraid of him. They knew him well and respected him, and understood that he would stand no foolishness.

La Barge thought nothing further of the affair, for the Indians soon disappeared, as he supposed, for good. The wind was too high to proceed, and the boat remained at the bank nearly all the afternoon waiting for it to subside. "Everything quieted down," said the captain, in describing what followed, "and I was sitting in the cabin reading a paper, when all of a sudden there was a heavy volley of firearms and the sound of splintered wood and broken glass. This was instantly followed by an Indian yell and a rush for the boat, and in the uproar someone cried out that a man had been killed. The Indians got full possession of the forward part of the boat and flooded the boiler grates with water, putting out the fires. They had learned something of steam in the fifteen years that boats had been going up the river. My first act was to rush to my wife's stateroom, where I found Mrs.

La Barge unharmed. I told John B. Sarpy, who with his son was making the trip, to barricade her door with mattresses and to stay there until the trouble was over. I then hastened to the front of the cabin, but was met at the door by the Indians. Retreating, I met Colin Campbell, and asked him what the Indians wanted. Campbell replied that they wanted me to give up the boat; that if I would do so they would let the crew go, but if I resisted they would spare no one.

"After the first rush the Indians seemed timorous and uncertain, evidently fearing some unpleasant surprise in the unknown labyrinths of the boat. This gave me time for effective measures. I had on board a light cannon of about $2y$ inches caliber, mounted on four wheels. Unluckily it was at this time down in the engine room undergoing some repairs to the carriage. I had in my employ a man on whom I could absolutely rely—a brave and noble fellow, Nathan Grismore, the first engineer. Grismore had just finished the work on the cannon, and told me he thought he could get it up the back way, since the fore part of the boat was in possession of the Indians. He got some men and lines and soon hoisted the gun on deck and hauled it into the after part of the cabin. I always kept in the cabin some powder and shot for use in hunting. I got the powder, but the supply of shot was gone. Grismore promptly made up the loss with boiler rivets and the gun was heavily loaded and primed, ready for action. By this time the forward part of the cabin was crowded with Indians who were evidently afraid something was going to happen. I lost no time in verifying their fears. As soon as the gun was loaded I lighted a cigar, and holding the smoking stump in sight of the Indians, told Campbell to tell them to get off the boat or I would blow them all to the devil. At the same time I started for the gun with the lighted cigar in my hand. The effect was complete and instantaneous. The Indians turned and fled and fairly fell over each other in their panic to get off the boat. In less time than it takes to tell it, not an Indian was in sight. I had the cannon brought onto the roof, where it remained for an hour or more.

"As soon as the Indians were off the boat I began to look up the crew who had ingloriously fled at the first assault, leaving the boat practically defenseless. They had hidden, some here and some there, but most of them on the wheels (it was a sidewheel boat) where I found them packed thick as sardines all over the paddles. These were the brave mountaineers who were never slow in vaunting their courage and valorous performances! I was so disgusted that I was disposed to set the wheels in motion and give them all a ducking; but the fires had been put out by the Indians.

"The wind having subsided, we resumed our journey, and about a mile further on attempted to cross to the other shore. Failing in this we encamped for the night. On the following morning we buried the deckhand, Charles Smith, who had been killed when the attack began."

Captain La Barge said that this was the only time that he was ever caught napping by the Indians, and it taught him a lesson that he did not forget.

As already mentioned, Captain La Barge's wife was on board. It was always understood on the upper river that she was the first white woman to ascend the river from old Fort Lisa near the modern site of Omaha, Neb., to Fort Union, at the mouth of the Yellowstone. Her presence created great curiosity among the Indians. They would come on board and examine her with the liveliest interest, measuring her waist and the length of her hair, and wondering at the tastefulness and beauty of her dress. The leading squaws in great numbers visited her, and several adopted her as their sister. A good deal of time was

The original journal is silent about this affair, but the facts were suppressed, says Captain La Barge, by clerk Finch, of the American Fur Company, in order not to expose the questionable conduct of Campbell and Matlock in regard to the annuities. La Barge himself wrote the following marginal note opposite the entry for June 9: "The Indians fired on the boat while we were lying there and killed Charles Smith, deckhand." lost in satisfying their importunities to see her. Years afterward they would inquire of La Barge after their white sister, and would send her presents. She never failed to send them something in return. As late as 1885, when La Barge was in the government service on the survey of the Missouri River in the vicinity of the ancient Aricara villages, an aged half-breed squaw, old Garreau's daughter, told La Barge that she remembered seeing his wife on this early trip.

In the year 1848 Captain La Barge again went up the river with his boat *Martha,* on business for the Company. There were no noteworthy incidents on the trip except that the captain brought back quite a menagerie of the native animals from the upper country. There were buffalo, bear, beaver, antelope, elk, and deer. A large tank was made for the use of the beaver. All of the animals were for Kenneth McKenzie except the buffalo, which were for Pierre Chouteau, Jr.

On this trip La Barge had some difficulty with the Company, which induced him to sell his boat to them at the close of the season. He immediately contracted for a new boat which, when completed, he named the *St. Ange,* in memory of St. Ange de Bellerive, the first military governor of upper Louisiana. It was a fine boat, and probably the only one ever built entirely complete upon the ways, and launched with steam up ready to start the moment she struck the water.

As soon as the boat was done, La Barge, being no longer in the Company's service, went to work for the Quartermaster Department of the Army, hauling supplies up the river. He had made two trips to Fort Leavenworth, and on his way back on the second trip encountered a severe storm, which delayed him several hours. This delay, vexatious enough at the time, was a blessing in disguise. Instead of getting into port at St. Louis before dark, it was nearly an hour after midnight before he reached there. As he was nearing the mouth of the Missouri a broad gleam of light overspread the sky in the direction of the city. Its extent and brilliancy clearly enough indicated a great conflagration. When La Barge reached port it was to find the river front wrapped in flames. He steamed the whole length of the levee, seeking a safe place to land, but finding none, turned back, crossed the river, and tied up for the night at Bloody Island, on the east shore f

The Republican, March 19, 1849, in an editorial notice of the event, thus referred to Captain La Barge: "There is no Captain on the Western waters more highly esteemed than Captain La Barge. He is a St. Louisan born, and has been familiar with the river from early life." f This island took its name from the fact that it was a famous dueling ground. Its history in this connection dates from the

This conflagration, which is the historic "Great Fire" of St. Louis, commenced at about 10 P. M. on the night of May 17, 1849, d continued until 7 A. M. next day. Fire alarms had been heard several times early in the evening, but nothing had come of them, until about the hour above mentioned, when it was found that fire had broken out in earnest on the steamer *White Cloud*, which lay at the wharf between Wash and Cherry streets. The *Endors* lay just above her and the *Edward Bates* below. Both caught fire. At this time a well-intended, but ill-considered, effort to stop the progress of the fire was made by some parties, who cut the *Edward Bates'* moorings and turned her into the stream. The boat was soon caught by past century, but its fame rests upon a few celebrated contests, among which the following may be noted: Thomas H. Benton and Charles Lucas fought here twice, on August 12 and September 27, 1817. In the last encounter Benton killed his antagonist. Joshua Barton, brother of the first U. S. Senator from Missouri, and Thomas C. Rector fought here June 30, 1823, and Barton was killed. The most celebrated duel of all took place August 27, 1831, between Major Thomas Biddle, Paymaster U. S. A., and Congressman Spencer

Pettis of St. Louis. Both principals were killed. Another duel occurred in which one of the principals, B. Gratz Brown, editor of the Democrat, received a wound in the knee. When dueling fell into disuse the island became a noted resort for prize-fighters. Overlooking the island stood a large cottonwood tree, near which these duels were fought. It was certainly more than two hundred years old, and it fell from old age, July 18, 1897. the current and carried down the river; but a strong northeast wind bore it constantly in shore, and every time it touched it ignited another boat. An effort was now made to turn other boats loose before the *Bates* could reach them, but a fatality seemed to attend every effort. The burning boat outsped them all, and by frequent contacts set fire to many more. These in turn ignited the rest, until in a short time the river presented the spectacle of a vast fleet of burning vessels drifting slowly along the shore. The fire next spread to the buildings, and before it could be arrested had destroyed the main business portion of the city. It was the most appalling calamity that had ever visited St. Louis, and followed as it was by the great cholera scourge of 1849, it was a terrible disaster. At the levee there were destroyed twenty-three steamboats, three barges, and one small boat. The total valuation of boats and cargo was estimated at about $440,000, and the insurance thereon was $225,000; but this was not all paid, for the fire broke up several of the insurance companies.

Among the boats destroyed was the *Martha,* which La Barge had sold to the Company. She was loaded

The City of St. Louis passed an ordinance at this time that vessels should be moored with iron cables, and it placed permanent rings in the levee for that purpose, so that boats could not be cut loose in case of fire. with a full cargo for the mountains. The day after the fire La Barge received a note from Captain Sire, requesting him to call at the Company's office. He complied, and was met with an urgent appeal to go to the mountains with the Company's annual outfit. He was at that time engaged for a government trip to Leavenworth, but offered to go as far as Fort Pierre upon his return, if it were possible to do so. Sire replied that that was all they could expect. The trip to Leavenworth was completed in June, and La Barge immediately started for Pierre. He made a quick and successful voyage, and returned early in August.

The year 1849 of the terrible cholera years in the West. Thousands died in St. Louis, and there were many deaths on every boat that went up the Missouri.

In the following year, 1850, Captain La Barge went to the mouth of the Yellowstone for the American Fur Company. It was the quickest trip on record, being made in the extraordinarily short time of twenty-eight days up and back, doing all the Company's business at the various posts.

CHAPTER XVI.

INCIDENTS ON THE RIVER (1851-53).

The St. Ange left St. Louis on her voyage to Fort Union for the American Fur Company, June 7, 1851. She had on board about one hundred passengers, mostly employees of the Company. The cabin list included two distinguished Jesuit missionaries, Father Christian Hoecken and Father De Smet, bound for the Rocky Mountains.

The spring had been particularly backward and wet, and the Missouri was in one of its most dangerous floods. The whole bottom country was overflowed, and the river looked like a floating mass of debris of every description. Navigation, though relieved of the danger from snags, was much impeded by these floating obstructions, and the gathering of fuel was unusually difficult. The overflowed condition of the country made it malarial and unhealthy— as bad as possible for a year when the cholera was abroad in the land. Sickness in one form or another soon appeared among the passengers. In a little while the vessel, according to Father De Smet, resembled a floating hospital, and a feeling of gloom fell over the passengers. Father De Smet himself was seized with a bilious fever which completely prostrated him, and for a time his recovery was doubtful. When about five hundred miles up the river the cholera broke out. A clerk of the American Fur Company was the first victim, and from that time on for the next few days there were several deaths every day. The situation was a terrible one, and oppressed passengers and crew alike with the most dismal forebodings.

There was a physician on board of the name of Dr. Evans, a distinguished scientist who was making the voyage in the interests of the Smithsonian Institution. He did everything in his power to allay the plague. Father De Smet was too ill to do anything, but Father Hoecken worked incessantly, caring for the sick and watching over their spiritual needs. This heroic priest won the hearts of the passengers by his untiring labors in their behalf; but he so completely exhausted himself that he had no reserve strength to combat the disease if it should attack himself. He seemed everywhere at once, like a ministering angel, and Father De Smet earnestly besought him to spare himself somewhat or he would not hold out. Father De Smet's condition was so serious that he had asked Father Hoecken to receive his confession; but the latter did' not think his brother in immediate danger, and hastened to the bedsides of those who were in a more precarious condition. In the midst of his unselfish labors the zealous missionary was himself stricken. Father De Smet thus records the sad story of his death:

"Between one and two o'clock at night, when all on board was calm and silent, and the sick in their wakefulness heard naught but the sighs and moans of their fellow-sufferers, the voice of Father Hoecken was suddenly heard. He was calling me to his assistance. Awaking from a deep sleep, I recognized his voice, and dragged myself to his pillow. Ah, me! I found him ill and even in extremity. He asked me to hear his confession: I at once acquiesced in his desire. Dr. Evans, a physician of great experience and remarkable charity, endeavored to relieve him, and watched by him, but his care and remedies proved fruitless. I administered extreme unction; he responded to all the prayers with a recollection and piety which increased the esteem that all on board had conceived for him. I could see him sinking. As I was myself in so alarming a state, and fearing that I might be taken away at any moment, and thus share his last abode in this land of pilgrimage and exile, I besought him to hear my confession, if he were yet capable of listening to me. I knelt, bathed in tears, by the dying couch of my brother in Christ—of my faithful friend—of my sole companion in the lonely desert. To him in his agony, I, sick and almost dying, made my confession! Strength forsook him; soon, also, he lost the power of speech, although he remained sensible to what was passing around him. Resigning myself to God's holy will, I recited the prayers of the agonizing with the formula of the plenary indulgence, which Christ grants at the hour of death. Father Hoecken, ripe for heaven, surrendered his pure soul into the hands of his Divine Redeemer on the 19th of June, 1851, twelve days after our departure from St. Louis.

"The passengers were deeply moved at the sight of the lifeless body of him who had so lately been 'all to all,' according to the language of the apostle. Their kind father quitted them at the moment in which his services seemed to be the most necessary. I shall remember with deep gratitude the solicitude evinced by the passengers to the reverend father in his dying moments. My resolution not to leave the body of the pious missionary in the desert was unanimously approved. A decent coffin, very thick, and tarred within, was prepared to receive his mortal remains: a temporary grave was dug in a beautiful forest, in the vicinity of the mouth of-the Little Sioux, and the burial was performed with all the ceremonies of the Church, in the evening of the 19th of June, all on board assisting.'

On the return trip from Fort Union, Captain La Barge, despite the protests of the passengers, took Father Hoecken's remains on board and delivered them to the Jesuits at St. Louis, and they were buried in the Novitiate of the Society of Jesus at Florissant, whither Father De Smet was to follow twenty-two years later.

After the burial of Father Hoecken near the mouth of the Little Sioux River, Captain La Barge put everyone ashore, made the passengers roam around the neighborhood, unloaded and aired all the baggage, and completely renovated the boat. These measures, with the increasing healthfulness of the country as the boat entered the more arid sections, brought complete relief from the plague. Only one more death occurred, and in a short time everything assumed a normal aspect. The boat reached Fort Union on the 14th of July, and here Father De Smet left it to make a journey overland, southward to Fort John, on the Laramie River, where a great council of plains Indians was to assemble. Captain La Barge went on a hundred miles further, to the mouth of Poplar River, it being, as he then understood, the highest point reached by any steamboat; but it was not much, if any, farther than the *Assiniboin* went in 1834.

This may be a proper place to record some incidents in the career of Father De Smet which fell under Captain La Barge's observation. De Smet, as is well known, traveled a great deal in nearly all parts of the far northwest. Sometimes he went around by sea, and then came overland to the headwaters of the Missouri; sometimes he went by the Oregon trail; and at others by the Missouri River. La Barge, who saw much of him, found him always a pure and excellent man, very companionable, full of anecdotes, and fearless and brave in all situations. He was liked by everyone who knew him. The Mormons were well acquainted with him and thought much of him. The Indians had the very highest regard for his character, and he seemed always to be safe in their hands. The Government of the United States likewise held him in high esteem, and on several occasions called on him for responsible and delicate work among the Indians.

Father De Smet entertained the most affectionate regard for Captain La Barge. He presented him with autograph copies of all his works, and always referred to him in terms of deepest affection. The incidents which follow were witnessed by La Barge himself.

On one occasion near Poplar River a band of Blackfeet came down to the bank near where the boat was. In addition to the well-known traditional hostility of these Indians to the whites, there were other reasons for believing that they were at this time in an ugly temper and meditated trouble. Father De Smet, grasping the situation, said, "It looks as if those Indians mean mischief. I will go out and meet them." La Barge remonstrated, saying that De Smet was not acquainted with these particular Indians, and that they might kill him, when, if they knew who he was, they might spare him. But De Smet knew that his reputation had traveled where he himself had not been, and he believed that they would recognize and protect the Black Robe, as they called him. He accordingly donned his cassock, and with the crucifix before him, went ashore and walked boldly to where the Indians were. As he had expected, they received him well, made him sit down on a buffalo robe, and then lifted him up and carried him on the boat. La Barge gave them a feast and presented the chief with a suit of clothes, which greatly pleased his vanity. After a time the Indians withdrew without attempting any harm.

Although the spring of 1851 had been very backward and wet in the lower country, it was not so higher up, and when the *St. Ange* arrived at the Aricara villages the com crop of those Indians was found to be actually suffering from drouth. The Aricara chief, White Shield, came on board and said to La Barge, who understood his language well:

"I am glad to see you, and I hear the Black Robe is on board."

La Barge replied that that was so. The chief then continued:

"I want to ask him a favor. It is very late in the season and no rain. Com ought to be up now. We want the Black Robe to send us rain."

La Barge took the Indian back to De Smet's room and said to the priest. "Father, here is the White Shield, who wants you to make it rain, for the com is not up yet."

De Smet, who knew the White Shield well, laughed heartily, and said he would do all he could. He then asked La Barge if the boat was going to remain there all day, and being informed that it was, he said to the White Shield: "Go to your village and put your lodge in order, and call in some of the chiefs.

The Aricara language is related to that of the Pawnees, which La Barge, as we have seen, had learned in his first years in the Indian country.

I will come and offer prayer to the Almighty and ask him to be merciful and grant your requests; and I am satisfied that, if you deserve it, the Great Spirit will look down and favor you."

Captain La Barge and several of the passengers went along with the father, and the interpreter translated the prayer to the Indians. They left the Indians satisfied, and at noon had them on the boat for a feast, after which they returned to their village. As good fortune would have it, along about three or four o'clock in the afternoon, there came up a heavy thunder shower which fairly deluged the place. Father De Smet laughed and said:

"They will think I did it. They will give me all the credit for it."

Some time after the shower Pierre Garreau, a French Canadian, who had spent all his life among the Indians, and had become almost an Indian himself, came to the boat and said to La Barge:

"I want you to help me. I want to find out how Father De Smet did that."

"Did what?" asked La Barge.

"Made it rain. I will pay a good price if he will tell me. I will give him ten horses."

La Barge took him back to De Smet, where he presented his request himself. De Smet told him to be a good Christian, and pray when he wanted it to

. rain, and if he deserved it, it would come. Garreau went away disappointed, for he fully believed that the father had some secret art by which he produced so signal a result. After he had gone, De Smet laughed and said: "Did I not tell you they would say I did it?"

After La Barge returned from this trip he laid the boat up for repairs, and soon after sold her. He had now about made up his mind to quit the river and retire from active business. He had already accumulated a snug fortune for those days, and concluded to enjoy it. He made the best financial move of his life in the purchase of a large tract of land in what is now Cabanne Place in St. Louis. Had he held on to this purchase, the mere growth of the city would have made him immensely wealthy. But retirement from business is one of the hardest things for a man to do, even in old age. For a man in the prime of life, as La Barge was at this time, being only thirty-six, it was not to be expected; and fate soon threw in his way a temptation that brought him back to the river.

La Barge Avenue, St. Louis, extending from Union Avenue west to the city limits, was in part given by Captain La Barge and recorded in his name. A later generation, with an amazing indifference to the work of one of the most noted characters in the history of the city, has changed the name to "Maple Avenue."

In the spring of 1852 he met in town one day Captain Edward Salt-Marsh, who had just arrived from Ohio with a handsome new boat. She was called the *Sonora*, as almost everything in those days was given a California name. "Nothing would do but that I should go and inspect his boat," said La Barge. "I found her an excellent craft, and soon learned that Salt-Marsh was disposed to sell her. A desire to purchase at once took possession of me and led to a lengthy negotiation, which ended in my buying the boat for thirty thousand dollars. Next day I went into town and raised the entire amount."

The Captain this year made a contract with the Company to take their annual outfit up the river. He went to Union and back, but there were no especial incidents on the trip. After the return of the *Sonora* he ran in the New Orleans trade for the rest of the season. This was a yellow-fever year in that section, and so many boats had left the river that Captain La Barge found plenty of business.

There were some untoward incidents on the Fort Union trip this season which decided La Barge not to go up for the Company the following year. He sold the *Sonora* in the fall of 1852, purchased a small boat, the *Highland Mary,* with which he ran in the lower river the entire season of 1853. He sold his boat in the fall of that year.

CHAPTER XVII.

ICE BREAK-UP OF 1856.

DURING the season of 1854 Captain La Barge was in the employ of the government most of the time. In the previous winter Colonel Crossman, of the army, Quartermaster at St. Louis, contracted with a company of boat-builders on the Osage River for a steamboat for government use. When the hull was nearly completed Captain La Barge went up and brought the boat down by the use of sweeps. He supervised her completion and remained on her as pilot during the entire season. This boat was called the *Mink,* from the color selected in painting her.

The American Fur Company chartered a boat to take up the outfit of 1854, but the crew mutinied, and the voyage proved a failure. Mr. Chouteau then asked La Barge to recommend him a boat for the next year's trade and join with him in purchasing her. It so happened that two St. Louisans, Sam Gaty and a man named Baldwin, had recently won a prize of forty thousand dollars in the Havana lottery, and were using it in building a boat. They sold the boat

200 in her unfinished state, the Company purchasing a half interest and La Barge and John J. Roe each one fourth. La Barge supervised her completion and named her the *St. Mary,* after a new town which P. A. Sarpy had just laid out a few miles below the modern Council Bluffs, Ia., and which has been long since entirely washed into the river.

Captain La Barge made the annual voyage of 1855 in this new boat. Mr. Charles P. Chouteau, son of Pierre Chouteau, Jr., accompanied the trip. The only incident of particular moment on this voyage was the transfer of Fort Pierre to the United States Government in accordance with the terms of a sale which had been consummated the previous spring. This important event, which will again be referred to more at length, marked the beginning of the conquest of the upper Missouri country by the army of the United States. The *St. Mary* was used in making the transfer of the post to the War Department and in moving the Fur Company's property to a new situation some distance above the old site, near the mouth of Chantier Creek.

General Harney was in command of the troops sent to the upper Missouri in 1855, and La Barge saw him at Fort Pierre. The Captain always liked him, and considered him one of the best friends of the Indians that the army ever produced—a terrible fighter when fight was unavoidable, but always desirous of accomplishing his purposes by peaceful means. The Captain recalled an incident of Harney's intercourse with the Sioux which created a great deal of mirth on the frontier at the time.

While holding a council at Pierre with about three thousand Sioux, the General told them of the great power of the American people and the uselessness of their trying to resist them. He was anxious to exhibit some proof that would appeal to the native imagination. Finally a thought struck him. Chloroform was just coming into use in surgery, and the hospital equipment with the expedition had some of it along. "I will show you the great power of the white man," said the General with impressive gravity. "I will show you how he can even kill and bring to life again." He called the surgeon, explained what he wanted, and then, through the interpreter, commanded that a dog be killed and afterward restored to life. He cautioned the surgeon to be extremely careful not to overdo the matter. The surgeon proceeded to chloroform the dog, while the Indians looked on in mute astonishment, if not with superstitious awe. After the dog was insensible the General called the chiefs and told them to satisfy themselves that he was actually dead. The surgeon was then ordered to resurrect the dog. He applied the usual restoratives, but the dog slept on. He nipped his tail with a pair of pincers, but still no sign of life. The surgeon finally gave it up, and the white man's marvelous power did not materialize. The Indians looked on, and putting their hands to their mouths said: "Medicine too strong, too strong."

After the return of the *St. Mary* to St. Louis, Captain La Barge, as was his wont, ran in the lower

One of the medical officers accompanying the troops, and possibly the surgeon in this case, was Dr. George L. Miller of Omaha, Neb., who had early established himself in the West to seek his fortune there, and afterward became one of Nebraska's most eminent citizens and well known throughout the country. He had gone up with the troops for temporary service because they had no regular surgeon. Dr. Miller returned to Omaha on the St. Mary, and many years later prepared an account of his personal experiences on the trip. His reference to Captain La Barge is interesting in this connection. He described him as "a short, stout, alert, and energetic man, with the eye of an eagle, which had been trained by twenty years' service as a student of the mysterious and muddy waters of the Missouri." A few years before these reminiscences were written by Dr. Miller, Captain La Barge's brother John died, and Dr. Miller had mistakenly understood it to be his old river friend of 1855. The event called forth this further reference to the Captain: "The death of Joe La Barge, the brown-faced and black-eyed pilot, two or three years ago, caused a pang of regret in the hearts of tens of thousands who dwell along the valley of the great river, and who knew and admired him both in character and calling." river trade the rest of the season. In the following winter, February 27, occurred the famous ice "breakup" of 1856 on the Mississippi River at St. Louis. The winter had been very cold and the ice was three or four feet thick and the water low. The break-up was not caused in the usual way by the thawing of the ice, but by a rise in the river from above, which caused the ice to move before it had become much disintegrated. It was an appalling and terrible example of the power of a great river when restrained in its course. The following account is from the pen of an eyewitness:

"The ice at first moved very slowly and without any perceptible shock. The boats lying above Chestnut Street were merely shoved ashore. Messrs. Eads & Nelson's Submarine No. 4, which had just finished work at the wreck of the *Parthenia,* was almost immediately capsized and became herself a hopeless wreck. Here the destruction commenced. The *Federal Arch* parted her fastenings and became at once a total wreck. Lying below were the steamers *Australia, Adriatic, Brunette, Paul Jones, Falls City, Altona, A. B. Chambers,* and *Challenge,* all of which were torn away from the shore as easily as if they were mere skiffs, and floated down with the immense fields of ice. The shock and the crashing of these boats can better be imagined than described. All their ample fastenings were as nothing against the enormous flood of ice, and they were carried down apparently fastened and wedged together. The first obstacles with which they came in contact were a large fleet of wood-boats, flats, and canal-boats. These small fry were either broken to pieces or were forced out on the levee in a very damaged condition. There must have been at least fifty of these smaller water craft which were destroyed, pierced by the ice or crushed by the pressure of each against the other.

"In the meantime some of the boats lying above Chestnut Street fared badly. The *F. X. Aubrey* was forced into the bank and was considerably damaged, the noble *Nebraska,* which was thought to be in a most perilous position, escaped with the loss of her larboard wheel and some other small injuries. A number of the upper-river boats, lying above Chestnut Street, were more or less damaged. Both the Alton wharf-boats were sunk and broken in pieces. The old *Shenandoah* and the *Sam Cloon* were forced away from the shore and floated down together, lodging against the steamer *Clara,* where they were soon torn to pieces and sunk by a collision with one of the ferryboats floating down. The Keokuk wharf-boat maintained its position against the flood and saved three boats below, viz., the *Polar Star, Pringle,* and *Forest Rose,* none of which was injured.

"After running about an hour the character of the ice changed, and it came down in a frothy, crumbled condition, with an occasional heavy piece. At the end of two hours it ran very slowly, and finally stopped about 5 1-2 o'clock P. M. Just before the ice stopped and commenced to gorge, huge piles, twenty and thirty feet in height, were forced up by the current on every hand, both on the shore and at the lower dike, where so many boats had come to a halt. In fact these boats seemed to be literally buried in ice.

"The levee on the morning after the day of the disaster presented a dreary and desolate spectacle, looking more like a scene in the polar regions than in the fertile and beautiful Mississippi Valley. The Mississippi, awakened from her long sleep, was pitching along at a wild and rapid rate of speed, as if to make up for lost time. The ice coat of mail was torn into shreds, which lay strewn along the levee, and was in some places heaped up to a height of twenty feet above the level of the water. Where the boats had lain in dense crowds only a few hours before, nothing was to be seen save this high bulwark of ice, which seemed as if it had been left there purposely to complete the picture of bleak desolation. The whole business portion of the levee was clear of boats, except the two wrecked Alton wharf-boats, which were almost shattered to pieces, and cast like toys upon the shore in the midst of the ridge of ice. There was not a single boat at the levee which entirely escaped injury by the memorable breaking up of the ice on February 27, 1856."

Captain La Barge retained a vivid recollection of this great catastrophe, for he was the only steamboat man who succeeded in extricating his boat from the wreck. The sight was something terrible to him, and a marvelous exhibition of power. The ice piled up in enormous masses as easily as a child would heap up sand, and then it collapsed and gave way. There were three of these pilings-up, or gorges. The noise of the crushing ice was terrific. Some of the boats were smashed to splinters; some were sunk, and others were pushed far up onto the bank.

The *St. Mary* was lying at the wharf when the movement began. La Barge at once got up steam and prepared to do what he could to save her. Sarpy came down to see him, and said to him, "Do just what you think best with the boat. If anyone can save her you can. Draw on me for anything you want." It was a very risky thing to trust one's life in a chaos of wreckage like that. Hooper, the mate, came and said that he should go too if the Captain was going to risk the river. He thought he could get five or six men to venture. The final giveway came about dark, and La Barge backed the boat away from the shore, let her drift in the ice, and thus escaped the crush which came along the shore. He drifted some twenty miles downstream before he could extricate himself from the ice.

La Barge went to Fort Union for the Company again in 1856. On this trip Lieutenant Gouveneur K. Warren, afterward general and corps commander in the Civil War, took passage on the boat nearly all the way from St. Louis. He had with him a corps of scientific assistants, among them the eminent geologist Dr. F. V. Hayden, who was then just beginning his explorations of the West. Lieutenant Warren sketched the course of the river from the pilot-house as the boat proceeded, taking compass bearings and estimating the distances. He speaks in his report of the uniform courtesy extended him by Captain La Barge in facilitating his operations. The Captain remembered him well, as he was in the pilothouse nearly all the time. He was very active, and kept his men vigorously employed gathering information. At night he went on shore and took observations. La Barge became very much interested in his work, and assisted him in every possible way, often stopping the boat to allow him to do some particular work. He seemed so interested and pleased with everything, and so intelligent and well posted, that he quite won the Captain's admiration. He was, as Captain La Barge remembered him, a handsome man, with a fine head and clear eye, at that time rather slender, but well built and erect. He was always pleasant, and was liked by his men, but was nevertheless a strict disciplinarian. We can easily discover in the Captain's recollections the youthful portrait of the future hero of Little Round Top at Gettysburg, and the accomplished leader of the Fifth Corps.

The Captain also distinctly remembered Dr. Hayden, and related a certain incident which came very near proving disastrous to that enthusiastic explorer. Hayden was a man of rather small stature, talkative and companionable, well informed, and very energetic and eager in his work. On one occasion his devotion to his scientific pursuits came very near getting him into danger. The incident in question occurred at the site of old Fort Clark, which stood upon a high cut bank. "We laid up here for an entire day," said the Captain in narrating this event. "The bank was full of fossils, some of them very rare. I had told Hayden of this on a former trip, and he was anxious to investigate the place. He went down under the bank, pick in hand and his rifle over his shoulder. An Aricara village was on the top, and while he was absorbed in his investigations some young bucks took it into their heads to have a little fun at his expense. They commenced pelting him with small pebbles, corncobs, etc., from the top of the bank, at the same time keeping themselves concealed from his view. For some time Hayden could not see where the missiles came from, but at length caught sight of the Indians, and instantly leveled his rifle at them. I had been a quiet spectator from the boiler deck of the boat, and quick as thought called to him to desist or he was a dead man. He lowered his gun and came on board and hunted no more fossils under that bank. If he had fired he would certainly have been killed, and as it was, the Indians were greatly incensed that he should have leveled his gun at them.

Upon this trip a disagreeable incident happened which led Captain La Barge to leave the Company's service for good. He had as clerk of the boat a son of one of the partners. The young man's wife was also on board, going up for the pleasure of the voyage. La Barge had been particularly requested by the clerk's father to use his best offices for her protection, comfort, and pleasure in the wild and lawless country to which she was going, and he promised to do so. Everything passed off pleasantly until Fort Clark was reached, when one of the partners of the Upper Missouri Outfit, the bourgeois of the post at Fort Clark, came on board to accompany the boat to Fort Union. He was naturally a rough, arrogant, blustering character, disposed to override everyone, and on two previous occasions La Barge had been compelled to deal pretty severely with him. He was, nevertheless, a man of great energy, well versed in the business of the fur trade, and a good man for the Company. He was therefore tolerated where a less capable man with his faults would have been gotten rid of.

"When he came on board," said Captain La Barge, "he went to the office and told the clerk to assign him a stateroom so that he could have his baggage sent to it. The clerk promised to attend to it and the bourgeois withdrew. The clerk and myself then looked over the register to see what we could do for him. There was only one room that could be made available except by causing passengers who had secured and paid for their rooms to vacate them. This room was occupied by two clerks, who' were compelled to give it up and sleep on cots outside. It was a forward stateroom, and hence not so desirable as those further aft, but still a good room, and the only one that was available. I directed the clerk to have the bourgeois' baggage put in, and to show him the room when he should request it. About 9 P. M., when the boat was tied up for the night, and I was in the office writing up the journal, the bourgeois came in and asked the clerk for his room. The clerk took him out and showed him his room and told him that two of the clerks had given it up for him. The bourgeois turned up his nose and exclaimed, 'What! that room for, a member of the firm? Can't I have a room in the after cabin, where the bourgeois are usually assigned?' He was told that it was impossible without ousting others who could not reasonably be disturbed. He did not ask me, for he knew I would not grant it. Then drawing himself up in a pompous fashion, he said to the clerk, calling him by name: I will occupy your room to-night and you may occupy this,' and added other suggestions not calculated to mollify the feelings of the young husband.

"The clerk came into the room deathly pale, but made no response to the bourgeois' insulting insinuations. I overheard the whole conversation, and determined to remain up and see the affair out. After a while the bourgeois came to the door of the office and said to the clerk: 'Good-night, Mr.—.'

'Good night, Mr.—,' replied the clerk, and the bourgeois withdrew and started for the ladies' cabin. I immediately stepped out and followed him. He walked directly back to the clerk's stateroom and was about to take hold of the door knob, when I seized him by the collar, jerked him around, gave him a smart kick in the direction of the forward cabin, followed it up by two or three others, and in short order landed him in front of the boat yelling 'M u r d e r !' and calling for help. Culbertson and others came out, but I told them not to interfere, as I was simply protecting a lady from insult. The bourgeois would not be quiet, and I ordered my mate Hooper to put him on the bank. This was promptly done, the boat was held off shore by a spar, the gang plank drawn in, and the bourgeois could not get back on board. The weather was so warm that he would not suffer from the cold, and the pestering mosquitoes, which swarmed in the willows, kept him active all night.

"When I returned to St. Louis I made no report of this affair, leaving it to the clerk, whose wife's honor had been protected, to lay the matter before his father. Instead of reporting the facts he represented that I had treated the bourgeois with uncalled-for severity, and that such things ought not to be allowed to go on. He said nothing of the real cause of the trouble, although his wife, a refined, cultured, and beautiful woman, drove to my house as soon as she returned, and told my wife how thankful she was for what I had done.

"A few days after my return from Union I was summoned to the office, and was there informed that the men in the upper country thought me altogether too hard on them, and that, to avoid future difficulty, it was best to terminate our relations. I replied that I felt so fully justified in my action that I should retire from their service with the utmost willingness if such was their view of the affair. This was in the fall of 1856, and was the last time that I worked for the Company.

"Three years later I was again called to the office and thus addressed by the father of my ungrateful clerk:

"'I have called you in to scold you for your conduct.'

"'Why so, Mr.—?'

"'You remember the cause of the trouble in 1856 that led to our separation?'

"'Very distinctly.'

"'Why did you not defend yourself? Why did you not make me a full report?'

"'I thought, sir, it was your son's place to lay the matter before you, as the whole trouble had been on his and his wife's account. I had promised you that I would protect her, and all I did was in fulfillment of that promise. I am glad that you now know the truth of the matter.'

"'Perhaps you are right; it was my son's place to tell me; but he was influenced by others and never mentioned it.'

"The old gentleman was very indignant over the affair, and ever after treated me with the greatest consideration."

As has been stated already, this was the last service of Captain La Barge for the American Fur Company. Many years of the most active part of his life had been spent in their interest. They never had a pilot on whom they could more confidently rely, and his careful management of their expeditions was worth hundreds of thousands of dollars to them. But their hard and exacting ways, often sullied with open injustice, gave rise to misunderstandings, which on several occasions virtually compelled him to quit their service and finally led to permanent separation.

CHAPTER XVIII.
THE HEAD OF NAVIGATION REACHED.

The decade from 1850 to 1860 saw a very rapid growth in the steamboat business of the Missouri River. The stream of emigration across the plains continued practically unchecked. Settlement was rapidly filling up the lower valley of the river, and by 1856 had reached as far as Sioux City, and all the modern towns below that point had commenced their existence. Government exploration was being pushed with vigor in all directions into the country beyond. The Indians were becoming restive under the pressure of settlement; their annuities were increasing, and the presence of troops in all parts of their country was becoming more imperative. The long Indian wars of the Missouri Valley were beginning.

All these developments had their effect upon the steamboat traffic of the Missouri River, for that stream was the one great transportation route into the heart of the West. Some idea of the magnitude of the business may be gleaned from the records of the times as published in the newspapers along the river.

In the year 1858 there were 59 steamboats on the lower river and 306 steamboat arrivals at the port of Leavenworth, Kan. The freight charges paid at that point during the season amounted to $166,941.35. In 1859 the steamboat advertisements in the St. Louis papers showed that more vessels left that port for the Missouri River than for both the upper and lower Mississippi. In 1857 there were 28 steamboat arrivals at the new village of Sioux City before July 1. There were 23 regular boats on that part of the river, and their freight tonnage for the season was valued at $1,250,000. The period from 1855 to 1860 was the golden era of steamboating on the Missouri River. It was the period just before the advent of the railroads. No other period before or after approached it in the splendor of the boats. All the boats were sidewheelers, had full-length cabins, and were fitted up more for passengers than for freight. It was an era of fast boats and of racing. It was the heyday of that most important personage, the Missouri River pilot.

While this rapid development of traffic on the lower river was going on, the American Fur Company was laying its plans to carry steamboat navigation to Fort

Benton. We have elsewhere told how the *Assiniboine* in 1834 reached a point near the mouth of Poplar River, a hundred miles above the Yellowstone, and being caught by low water, was compelled to stay there all winter. For the next nineteen years this remained the farthest point reached by steamboats. In 1853 the *El Pa* went about 125 miles further, to a point five miles above the mouth of Milk River. El Paso point, as this place came to be called, marked the limit of steamboat progress up the river for the next six years.

In 1859 final step, or very nearly so, was taken in reaching the real head of navigation. The record of this event is quite as definite as are those of the entrance of steamboats into the mouth of the Missouri in 1819 and the voyage of the *Yellowstone* to Fort Union in 1832. In the spring of 1859 the American Fur Company sent up two boats with its annual outfit, its own boat, the *Spread Eagle,* and a chartered boat, the *Chippewa*. The *Chippewa* was a light boat, and her owner, Captain Crabtree, contracted to take her to Fort Benton, or as far as it was possible to go. At Fort Union he defaulted in his contract and sold the boat to the Company for just about the charter price for the voyage. Such freight as the *Spread Eagle* carried for Fort Benton was then transferred to the *Chippewa,* making a total cargo of 160 tons. Captain John La Barge, brother of Joseph La Barge, and pilot of the *Spread Eagle,* was assigned to charge of the *Chippewa* on her adventurous undertaking. Mr. Charles P. Chouteau went along as the Company's representative.

The boat made her way successfully, and without any notable incident, to within fifteen miles of Fort Benton, and discharged her freight at Brule bottom, where Fort McKenzie stood in former years. Her arrival at this point was on July 17, 1859, forty years and two months after the *Independence* entered the mouth of the river f

This noteworthy event must be classed as one of the celebrated feats in steamboat navigation. The *Chippewa* had reached a point further from the sea by a continuous water course than any other boat had ever been. She was now 3560 miles from, and 2565 feet above, the ocean, and the whole distance had been made by steam on a river unimproved by artificial works.

In 1860 the *Chippewa* and the *Key West* completed the short remaining distance to Fort Benton, and made

"Captain John La Barge, one of the oldest and best steam boat men on the river, takes command of the Chippewa, and if the trip to Fort Benton can be made, he will make it!"—Sioux City Eagle, July 23, 1859. f For a complete record of this event, see letter from Alfred Vaughn, Indian Agent for the Blackfeet—Report Commissioner of Indian Affairs for 1859, fast to the bank in front of the old post July 2 of that year. On June 16, 1866, the steamer *Peter Balen* ascended the river to the mouth of Belt Creek, six miles from the Great Falls, and thirty-one miles above Fort Benton. This is believed to be the farthest point reached by steam on the Missouri River. The feat was accomplished during the June flood and would have been impossible at ordinary stages. Fort Benton has always been considered the head of navigation on the Missouri River.

In 1861 the heroic *Chippewa* made her last trip up the river. Again bound for Fort Benton, she reached the end of her voyage and of her career at a point a little below the mouth of Poplar River, Mont., since known, from this connection, as Disaster Bend. She was loaded with American Fur Company goods and Blackfeet annuities, and had a goodly quantity of alcohol on board. One Sunday evening in the month of May, while supper was being served, the boat was discovered to be on fire. She was immediately run ashore, the passengers were put off, and she was set adrift to avoid the danger from an expected explosion of gunpowder that was in the hold. The boat floated across the river and about a mile downstream, when she blew up, just as the upper works were fairly consumed to the water's edge. The explosion was terrific, and packages of merchandise were found at a great distance from the place. No lives were lost, and the personal effects of the passengers were saved. The fire was caused by some deckhands, who went into the hold with a lighted candle to steal some liquor.

CHAPTER XIX.

FORT BENTON.

Few, if any, towns in the Far West country possess so unique and varied a history as Fort Benton. With the exception of some of the old Spanish villages in the southwest it is the oldest settlement in the mountain country, for the traders made their first establishment there in 1831. The true historic career of Fort Benton did not embrace more than half a century, yet in that brief space it saw more of romance, tragedy, and vigorous life than many a city of a hundred times its size and ten times its age.

The commercial importance of Fort Benton arose, of course, from its situation at the head of navigation on the Missouri River; but this was not the cause of its first location there. The surrounding country was the home of the Blackfeet Indians—great fur producers, but in early times inveterate enemies of the whites. From the time when the traders began to penetrate those distant regions it was their ambition to open up trade relations with this fierce and refractory tribe. Attempts were made in the years 1807-10 and again in 1822-23, but wholly without success. The Indians always evinced a deadly hostility, attacked the trappers, killed a great many, drove them out of the country, and gave them no opportunity to explain their pacific purposes.

In 1831 Kenneth McKenzie, ablest of the American Fur Company traders on the upper Missouri, resolved to make another attempt. He had already securely established himself at Fort Union, near the mouth of the Yellowstone. Fortune threw into his hands at this time the very instrument required for his purposes —an old trapper who had long served under the Hudson Bay Company in the Blackfoot country north of the boundary. His name was Jacob Berger. He understood perfectly the language of these Indians and knew many of them personally. McKenzie prevailed upon him to go to their country with overtures of peace and the promise of a trading post. The real origin of the enmity of the Blackfeet had been the apparent favoritism of the whites, in years gone by, toward their hereditary enemies, the Crows; and McKenzie felt confident that, if he could once get their ear and explain the true purpose of the traders toward them, he would secure their friendship and custom.

Berger set out with a small party in the fall of 1830, carrying unfurled an American flag, and traveled upward of four weeks before he saw an Indian. Finally he came upon a large village in the valley of the Marias River. The sight so terrified the little band that they were for instant flight before they should be discovered. Berger, however, persisted in his mission, and the party moved forward, scarcely expecting to be alive another hour. They were quickly discovered, whereupon a number of mounted warriors started at full gallop to meet them. The whites halted and Berger advanced with his flag. The Indians paused and Berger made signs of peace, and called out his own name. As he was well known to the tribe, they recognized him at once. There was a rush to shake hands and Berger and his party were taken to the village, where, to their infinite relief, they were received with every demonstration of good will.

Berger remained at the village for some time, and made the Indians fully acquainted with the purpose of his mission. He finally induced about forty of the leading men to return with him to Fort Union, where they could confer with McKenzie direct. The journey was long, and the fickle nature of the Indians showed signs of weakening before it was nearly completed. They began to fear treachery, and it took all of Berger's ingenuity to keep them from turning back. Finally, as a last resort, when almost at their journey's end, he pledged them his scalp and his horses if they did not reach the fort in one day more. They agreed to this eminently fair proposition, and before the day had passed they saw, from the top of a hill, in the plain below them, the imposing palisades and bastions of Fort Union. This was about the beginning of the year 1831.

McKenzie did all in his power to impress the delegation favorably. He made them liberal presents, and sent a trader with an outfit of goods to remain in their village during the winter. Finally he promised them a permanent trading post the following year. Before the year had passed he induced the Blackfeet and Assiniboines to make a treaty with each other, and he thus established peace all along the northern border. In the fall of 1831 he sent a complete outfit under James Kipp to the Blackfoot country for the purpose of establishing the promised post. After a long and tedious voyage Kipp reached the mouth of the Marias River and selected the point of land between the two streams for the proposed establishment. It was begun about the middle of October. The Indians appeared soon after his arrival, but Kipp requested them to withdraw for seventy-five days, until he could finish the work. They went away and returned punctually on the day fixed. To their astonishment they found the fort entirely finished and everything ready for the trade. This post was very properly named, from the sub-tribe of the Blackfeet in whose country it was located, Fort Piegan.

Thus was the white man's first foothold established in the land of the Blackfeet, near where the great post of Fort Benton stood in later years. Kipp drove a thriving trade during the winter, and in the spring went down to Union with the returns and with all his men, for they refused to remain if he went. It is said that the Indians burned the post after Kipp withdrew. Whether from this cause or from some other, it was not rebuilt upon the original site. D. D. Mitchell, one of the Company's most capable servants, was sent up in 1832 to reopen trade with the Blackfeet. On his way up he lost his boat in a storm, with all the property, worth some thirty thousand dollars, and two men, one of them a Piegan Indian. The Indians who were with him suspected foul play and Mitchell had all he could do to maintain himself while sending back to Union for another outfit. He succeeded, however, and in due time reached the mouth of the Marias.

Not liking the situation selected by Kipp, he went up the river some seven miles farther, and chose a spot on the left bank in a fine bottom with abundant growths of timber near by. The erection of the new post was one of the dramatic incidents of the early fur trade. There were several thousand Indians present, suspicious of the whites and ready for trouble upon any pretext. The men worked like beavers in getting up the pickets, and during this time slept on the keelboat. It required the utmost tact and firmness on the part of Mitchell to prevent an outbreak, and several times it seemed as if all were lost. The work was finally completed, and once within the fort the little party felt safe. The new post was named Fort McKenzie, a merited tribute to the man who had accomplished a feat which the traders had hitherto considered impossible.

In the summer of 1833 Alexander Culbertson, next to McKenzie the greatest of the American Fur Company traders, went up with Mitchell from Fort Union, and began his long and eventful career on the upper river. Prince Maximilian was a guest of the party, and remained at Fort McKenzie nearly all summer. While there he was treated to a genuine Indian battle. The Assiniboines, becoming weary of peace, broke the treaty of two years before, and fell upon a band of Piegans who were encamped around the fort. They killed several Indians in the first onset, but were quickly repulsed by aid of the inmates of the post, and were finally driven back beyond the Marias. Mitchell and Culbertson took part in the fight, and the venerable Prince became its historian.

The history of Fort McKenzie had more of excitement and incident about it than any of the other early trading posts. The Blackfeet and the Crows were deadly enemies of each other, and many were the bloody encounters between them. The Crows often came to seek their enemy in his own country, and the Blackfeet went to the Crow country on the Yellowstone, where the inmates of Fort Cass witnessed the counterpart of scenes which fell under the eyes of the traders at Fort McKenzie. It is said, but upon uncertain authority, that the Crows once actually laid siege to Fort McKenzie, but as they were a friendly tribe to the whites, this may be taken with some allowance. It is certain, however, that for many years the warfare between these two tribes raged with great fury, though not with much loss to the traders, for the booty captured from one party found its way directly to the trading post in the country of the other.

The thrilling incidents with which the annals of Fort McKenzie abounded in these early years would fill a volume; but we can note only the more important. The year 1837 was the year of the terrible smallpox scourge among the tribes of the Missouri Valley. Great care was taken at Fort Union to dispatch the annual outfit for Fort McKenzie without carrying the smallpox along with it. The expedition was in charge of Alexander Harvey, one of the most noted and desperate characters which the fur trade produced. Harvey took every possible precaution, but in spite of his efforts the disease broke out in his party. He therefore thought it prudent to stop before he reached Fort McKenzie and send word to Culbertson, who had been in charge of the fort since 1834, when Mitchell left. Culbertson wisely decided to leave the cargo at the mouth of the Judith until the disease had run its course. There were large numbers of Indians encamped near the fort awaiting the arrival of the boat, and when they learned of the proposed delay they became suspicious and insisted that the boat should be brought up. Culbertson expostulated with them, but all in vain, and to avoid the capture and destruction of the boat and its crew, he yielded to their demands.

The result was exactly what had been foreseen. The disease was communicated to the inmates of the post and to the Indians as well. The latter completed their trade and left the fort before the pest actually broke out among them, and the garrison remained for some time in ignorance of what their fate had been. For upwards of two months not an Indian was seen, and Culbertson, fearing the dreadful truth, resolved to go in search of them. With a single companion he set out for the Three Forks of the Missouri, where the Piegans usually spent their autumns hunting beaver. They finally came upon a village of about sixty lodges, only to find it absolutely deserted, with dead bodies strewn in every direction, and carrion birds of prey the only sign of life anywhere around. The smallpox had done its work well, and the few survivors of the village had fled in scattered groups among the surrounding mountains. The mortality among the Bloods and Blackfeet had been as great as among the Piegans, and Culbertson estimated the total loss among the three bands at six thousand souls. The Grosventres, for some cause, escaped with small loss.

The annals of Fort McKenzie during the next six years find their chief sensational interest in the exploits of Alexander Harvey. Many were the desperate deeds committed by him, and it required all the steadying authority of Culbertson to offset his sinister influence among the Indians. Harvey was, however, an excellent trader, and rendered the company good service. He was left in charge of the post during the occasional temporary absences of Culbertson at Fort Union, and in spite of his many outrages upon the Indians, and even upon the whites, was considered too valuable a man to lose.

Under Culbertson's prudent management Fort McKenzie had become, next to Union, the most paying establishment on the river. The Company were so pleased with his record that they decided to send him to Fort John, on the Laramie River, to build up the trade of that post, which was doing a losing business on account of bad management. Culbertson protested that it would be a mistake to take him away from McKenzie, but the Company overruled him, and Francis A. Chardon, one of their most experienced clerks, was sent to relieve him.

Chardon was the same manner of man as was Alexander Harvey, and it goes without saying that such a pair traveled rapidly the highway to commercial ruin. Chardon, being new to his duties and new to the post, relied a great deal upon Harvey, who became the real head of the establishment. The natural consequences of this arrangement quickly followed. Some little offenses committed by the Indians, which a prudent trader would have passed by without trouble, were made the excuse for one of the most atrocious crimes ever committed by either white man or Indian upon the other. The plan was to fall upon the unsuspecting Indians the next time they should come in to trade, and to kill all they could and confiscate their property. It only partly succeeded, owing to the failure of the actors to co-operate exactly; but it went far enough to arouse the hatred of the Indians to the highest pitch. They began a war of vengeance, and soon rendered the situation at Fort McKenzie untenable. Chardon accordingly moved down to the Judith River, and erected a new post on the left bank of the Missouri, opposite the mouth of the smaller stream. He named the post Fort Chardon. Fort McKenzie was burned, some say by Chardon himself and some by the Indians. The fort lost its old name and became known as Fort Brule, or burned fort, a name which still survives in Brule bottom, where Fort McKenzie stood. The massacre took place early in the winter of 1842-43.

There has been a good deal of confusion about this date, and it cannot yet be considered as definitely settled. The weight of authority is as given above. Chardon had other difficulties with the Indians which may have been confused with this affair. Thus the journal of one of the inmates of the Blackfoot post (whether Fort McKenzie or Fort Chardon is uncertain) says: "February 19, 1844. Fight with the north Blackfeet, in which we killed six and wounded several others; took two children prisoners. The fruits of our victory were four scalps, twenty-two horses, 350 robes, and guns, bows, and arrows, etc." This answers very closely to the description of the "Blackfoot

As a result of their reckless management, Chardon and Harvey had by this time ruined the trade with the Blackfeet tribes. In this emergency the Company turned to Culbertson, acknowledged their error in removing him from Fort McKenzie, and besought him to return and restore things to their old-time condition. Culbertson went back in the summer of 1844, abandoned and burned Fort Chardon, and established a new post twelve miles above the modern Fort Benton. The fort was built on the right bank of the Missouri, and was named Fort Lewis, in honor of the great explorer, Captain Meriwether Lewis.

On his way up from Fort Union this season Culbertson was accompanied by Jacob Berger, James Lee, and Malcolm Clark. Clark had served at Fort McKenzie five years before. He was a noted frontier character of good family connections, an unsuccessful student at the West Point Military Academy, a man of fine physical presence, and possessed of a bold and desperate character, which brought to his name the stigma of more than one crime. Clark and his companions seem to have plotted the murder or severe punishment of Alexander Harvey; for when Harvey came down from Fort Char don to meet the boat, he was attacked by Clark and Lee and barely escaped with his life. He fled to the post, barricaded himself, induced the inmates to stand by him, and would not admit even Culbertson without a guarantee of personal safety. He then closed up his affairs at the post, left the Company's service, went down the river, and soon after became senior member in the opposition firm of Harvey, Primeau & Co. He returned to the upper river, built a small post near the mouth of Shonkin Creek, and did a fair business for several years, when he sold out to his old employers.

With Chardon and Harvey away, Culbertson soon won back the trade of the Blackfeet. The site of Fort Lewis, however, proved unsatisfactory. The valley of the Teton River, a tributary of the Marias, which flowed parallel with the Missouri for many miles, was a favorite camping ground of the Indians. Fort Lewis was a long way off, and across the Missouri from this valley. Accordingly, in the spring of 1846 the post was dismantled, moved down the river, and set up in the fine open bottom where the village of Fort Benton now stands.

The post was thus finally settled in its future permanent location, although the name, Fort Lewis, was still retained for several years. Business flourished under Culbertson's management, and he at one time had three outlying posts in the country round about. In 1850 he determined to rebuild the post of adobe, after the manner of Fort John, on the Laramie. The soil was well adapted to the purpose, and although the work was begun late in the season, it was completed, thanks to an open fall, before winter set in. On Christmas night, 1850, it was dedicated with a grand ball, and was rechristened Fort Benton, in honor of Senator Thomas H. Benton, who had so often rescued the Company from the peril of its own malefactions. The name Fort Benton, as applied to the post of the Blackfeet, and to the head of navigation on the Missouri River, thus dates from the year 1850, nineteen years after the first trading post was established in that vicinity.

No events of other than a routine nature transpired at Fort Benton until the year 1853, when the extensive exploring expedition of Governor I. I. Stevens took the field to find a northern railroad route to the Pacific Ocean. These explorations brought a great deal of business to Fort Benton, and added a new feature to the life of that hitherto almost unknown post. Growing out of this work came the effort to negotiate treaties with the Blackfeet similar to those which had been formed at Fort Laramie three years before with most of the plains tribes. Congress made a large appropriation to cover the expense of the negotiations, and Governor Stevens and Alfred Cummings were appointed treaty commissioners. The necessary gifts for the Indians were purchased, the American Fur Company was awarded the contract for their transportation, and in due time Commissioner Cummings and party left St. Louis on the Company's steamboat *SV. Mary*.

There were on board, besides Commissioner Cummings, Major Culbertson, Indian agents Vaughn and Hatch, and a friend of Captain La Barge, an army officer, who later became paymaster in the army. At Fort Union the goods were transshipped in keelboats for Fort Benton, while the passengers took wagons for the same destination. Arrived at Milk River crossing, the party met Governor Stevens just returning from the Pacific Coast, and here the details of organization of the Commission were decided upon. There was much dispute over the question of precedence, and although Governor Stevens finally yielded to his colleague, the relations of the two men were so embittered that their subsequent work lacked harmony and effectiveness.

From Milk River the party went on to Fort Benton, but the boats were not able to get up that far except with very great delay, and it was decided to hold the expected council at the mouth of the Judith River. The goods were stopped at that point and hither repaired the Commissioners and the various Blackfeet bands to the number of about two thousand. The work was completed and in about ten days the Indians departed with their lavish presents. The era of the fur trader had ended and that of the Indian agent had come. In this case, as in all that had preceded it, the change, so far as the Indians were concerned, was a change for the worse.

These events bring our sketch of the history of Fort Benton down to the point already reached in our regular narrative. The arrival of the first steamboat in 1859 epoch in her history. Followed, as it was, almost immediately by the discovery of gold in Montana, and the consequent rush of emigration, it changed the whole order of things at the post. Stores and other buildings began to appear, and in 1865 a town site was laid off. The young city grew with astonishing rapidity and became a place of very great importance. Strange indeed must it have seemed to the Indians and to the old trappers to behold upon this spot, where for so many years there had been only a single palisade—sole habitation of white men within five hundred miles—buildings of metropolitan style and quality, trains of wagons coming and going, and lines of noble steamboats lying at the bank along the entire front of the town. It was a wonderful metamorphosis, scarcely paralleled in any other city of the country. Mushroom towns have sprung up all over the West, but no permanent city from causes like those which built up Fort Benton. Her rise and greatness were due solely to her position as a strategic point in the commerce of the far Northwest, not from any great mineral discovery in her neighborhood. Her supremacy she maintained until other commercial routes had rendered useless the great natural highway which found its terminus at her door f

June 11, 1866, there were seven steamboats at one time at the levee of Fort Benton. f In this sketch of Fort Benton I have drawn somewhat, for the period after 1843, from the notes of Lieutenant James H. Bradley, as published in vol. iii. Proceedings Mont. Hist. Soc. The notes were taken by dictation from Alexander Culbertson. Unfortunately, as in most cases of personal narrative, this one abounds in errors, and is controlled throughout by the desire of the narrator to magnify his own importance in the events he describes. The notes possess, however, great intrinsic value, and are an important contribution to the history of the West. The American Fur Company, founders of Fort Benton, continued to do business on the upper river until 1864, when they sold out to the firm of Hawley, Hubbell & Co., under the style of the Northwestern Fur Company. The negotiations were concluded in the winter of 1864-65, and the actual transfer accomplished in the following season. In 1869 the Northwestern Fur Company sold out all its interests below Fort Union to Durfee & Peck, and in 1870 abandoned all the trade above Fort Union.

Their preservation is due to the zealous forethought of an army officer who recognized the importance of collecting original data on the history of the West before its principal actors should have passed away. He did not live to prepare these notes for publication himself. They found their way to the Montana Historical Society, which, with the intelligent zeal that has always characterized that body, has given them to the public in a well-gotten up volume of the society's proceedings.

Lieutenant James H. Bradley was born in Sandusky, O., May 25, 1844; enlisted as a private in the 14th Ohio Volunteers, April, 1861; re-enlisted in the 45th Ohio Volunteers, June, 1862; mustered out as Sergeant, July, 1865; appointed Second Lieutenant 18th U. S. Infantry, February 23, 1866; promoted to First Lieutenant, July 9, 1866, transferred to 7th Infantry, November 28, 1871; killed in the Battle of the Big Hole by the Nez Perce Indians, August 9, 1877.

CHAPTER XX.

LINCOLN ON THE MISSOURI.

HAVING permanently left the service of the American Fur Company, Captain La Barge spent the three years, 1857-59, mainly on the lower river, not generally going above Council Bluffs. In the summer of 1859 he built a fine new boat, one of the best that ever went up the river. Pierre Chouteau, Jr., having heard of his undertaking, sent to him and offered any assistance that might be needed. The Company still cherished a high appreciation of Captain La Barge's services and would gladly have taken him back into their employ. The captain thanked Mr. Chouteau, but never took advantage of his offer. When he had finished his boat he named her the *Emilie,* for one of his daughters. Soon after this he received a polite note from Mr. Chouteau, telling him to order a complete stand of colors for the boat and he would pay the bill. The captain was much embarrassed, for he knew that Mr. Chouteau had made the offer under the impression that the boat had been named in honor of his wife. When La Barge declined his generous offer and explained why, Mr. Chouteau said: "That's all right. I am glad you have told me so frankly. You did well to name the boat for your daughter."

The *Emilie* was one of the famous boats of the Missouri River. She was 225 feet long, 32 feet beam, with a hold 6 feet deep, and could easily carry 500 tons. She was a sidewheel boat, built on the most approved lines, and an exceedingly beautiful craft. Captain La Barge was designer, builder, owner, and master, and set out on his first voyage with her October 1, 1859, his forty-fourth birthday.

Before the boat was completed he entered into a contract with the Hannibal and St. Joseph Railroad, which had just reached the Missouri River at St. Joseph, to run from that point up and down the river in connection with the road. The *Emilie* was accordingly taken at once up the river, and remained all the fall in that section, going up as far as Fort Randall once or twice.

It was during the boating season of 1859 that Captain La Barge first saw Abraham Lincoln. Among the more obscure incidents in that great man's career were his visits to the Missouri River in the summer and fall of this year. In August he visited Council Bluffs, and in December several towns in Kansas. The purpose of his first visit was not political, although during his stay at the Bluffs he was induced to make a political speech. He had evidently come out to take a look at the great West, and possibly also to make some investments in real estate. At any rate, in November following he purchased from N. B. Judd lot 3, block 1, of Riddle's Subdivision of Council

Bluffs. In 1867 this property was conveyed back to Mr. Judd by the Lincoln heirs. It is a very singular fact that the adjoining lot 4 of this subdivision was owned by Clement L. Vallandigham, Mr. Lincoln's greatest political enemy.

General Grenville M. Dodge, who later became a distinguished officer in the Civil War, was at this time handsomely for appearing before an Iowa audience during a campaign in which he was not interested. He then, with many excuses and a lengthy explanation, as if conscious of the nauseous nature of the black Republican nostrum, announced his intention to speak about the 'eternal negro/ to use his own language, and entered into a lengthy and ingenious analysis of the nigger question, impressing upon his hearers that it was the only question to be agitated until finally settled. He carefully avoided going directly to the extreme ground occupied by him in his canvass against Douglas, yet the doctrines which he preached, carried out to their legitimate results, amount to precisely the same thing. He was decidedly opposed to any fusion or coalition of the Republican party with the opposition of the South, and clearly proved the correctness of his ground, in point of policy. They must retain their sectional organization and sectional character, and continue to wage their sectional warfare by slavery agitation; but if the opposition South would accede to their view and adopt their doctrines, he was willing to run for President in 1860, a Southern man with Northern principles, or in other words, with abolition proclivities. His speech was of the character of an exhortation to the Republican party, but was in reality as good a speech as could have been made for the interest of the Democracy. He was listened to with much attention, for his Waterloo defeat by Douglas has magnified him into quite a lion here." engaged in surveys for the proposed Union Pacific railroad. He had just come in from the plains, and Lincoln, hearing of the fact, sought him out and had a long talk with him in regard to his surveys. His great interest in the matter and his skill in drawing out information soon gave him all that the young surveyor knew. The latter thought no more of this at the time than that possibly he had been giving away secrets that belonged to his employers only. In 1863, while in command of the district of Corinth, Miss., he received a dispatch from General Grant directing him to proceed to Washington and report to the President. He was a good deal perturbed over the matter, for he feared it might be something pertaining to his military work that had not given satisfaction. When he appeared before Mr. Lincoln he found that the President wanted to consult with him in regard to the eastern terminus of the proposed Pacific railroad, which would soon have to be determined. Mr. Lincoln had remembered the conversation in Council Bluffs, and now sought assistance from the same source from which he drew so freely on the former occasion. The result was that Council Bluffs instead of Omaha was fixed as the terminus, and that is why the Union Pacific railroad begins just across the river in Iowa, and not, as would have seemed natural, on the west shore of the river.

Late in the fall of 1859 Mr. Lincoln visited Kansas. He arrived at St. Joseph December 1, *via* the new Hannibal and St. Joseph railroad. He was met at the station by D. D. Wilder, and M. W. Delahay, who escorted him at once to the ferry. Mr. Wilder was a member of the reception committee, and had spent several days in the office of Lincoln & Herndon the previous summer. While waiting for the boat they sat down on the bank, and Lincoln talked freely of the recent exciting political events in Illinois. The party then crossed to Kansas, the first stop being at El wood, where Lincoln spoke on the night of December 1. The next day he went to Troy, Kan., where he gave an address, and in the evening he made a speech at Doniphan. The following day he went to Atchison and spoke in the Methodist church. Lincoln's speeches on these occasions were essentially the same as that delivered at a later date at Cooper

Union, New York. Lincoln seems to have gone to Leavenworth on the 4th of December. He remained there two or three days, delivering two speeches at Stockton's Hall and holding a public reception. His long stay at this place was probably due to his having to wait for the steamboat to take him back to St. Joseph. He left Leavenworth on the 7th of December, accompanied by Mr. Parrott, the Kansas delegate to Congress.

It was on the occasion of one of these visits to the Missouri River that Captain La Barge met Mr. Lincoln. It is understood that Mr. Lincoln made his journey to Council Bluffs by boat, either from St. Louis or St. Joseph, and returned home across the State; and that on his Kansas visit he went back by boat from Leavenworth to St. Joseph in December. On one of these trips he traveled on Captain La Barge's boat. The Captain retained with great distinctness his impressions of the appearance and personal peculiarities of the distinguished passenger. The tall and relatively slender build of Mr. Lincoln, his high hat, sallow complexion, and not very elegant costume, gave him a somewhat comical appearance at first sight. He seemed to La Barge rather quick in his movements, and apparently a good walker. The captain noticed that he was scarcely ever alone, there being always someone listening to him. Although he made no speeches on his way up, he had an audience all the time, and his agreeable address, and interesting way of putting things, made him a constant center of attraction.

La Barge remembered that he frequently came into the pilot-house, and asked many questions, particularly about the fur trade and the Indians. He expressed his desire to make a visit to the upper country. Before he left the boat he asked La Barge if he would not procure for him a fine buffalo robe and send it to him, giving him to understand that he should of course expect to pay him well for all expense he might be put to. La Barge promised to do so. Lincoln was not at this time much talked of for the Presidency, and in Missouri was unpopular on account of his attitude toward slavery.

Captain La Barge did not take his boat down the river in the fall of 1859, because the ice cut him off. She was laid up a little below Atchison. He himself went to St. Louis, and in February returned

155

with his family. In the spring of 1860, when the ice was about to break up, the citizens of Atchison offered to furnish fuel for the boat if La Barge would attempt to cut through the ice to St. Joseph. He undertook it, running his boat up on the ice until her weight broke it in, and in that way succeeded in getting through. The captain remained in the service of the railroad all summer, running to Kansas City and Omaha and intermediate points. In the fall he started for St. Louis, but was caught by the ice at Liberty, Mo., and compelled to lay up his boat there. It was at this point that he first heard of Lincoln's election. When John Baxter, keeper of Liberty Landing, came on board with the news, La Barge said to him: "Up go all your niggers." "Oh, you don't think that'll make any difference, do you?" "Up go all your niggers," replied La Barge; "they will all be set free." "And they were all set free," remarked the captain in narrating this dialogue, "and mine with the rest, for I had some."

CHAPTER XXL

THE CIVIL WAR.

In a great many ways the War of the Rebellion affected the commerce of the Missouri River. Missouri was a slave State, and most of her citizens along the river were Southern sympathizers. It is stated that all the Missouri River pilots except two were in sympathy with the South, and that General Lyon had to go to the Illinois River for pilots when he wanted to move his troops up the river in June, 1861.

The steamboat business on the river felt the weight of the war almost immediately upon its breaking out. Most of the business was with the loyal people and was, of course, considered by the Confederates as a legitimate subject of confiscation. Guerrilla bands infested the country along the river, fired into the boats, and did all they could to break up the business. They succeeded in driving most of the traffic off the lower river; but at the same time the demands of the war stimulated the trade higher up. There was an increased movement of government troops and stores, and in the later years of the war many refugees from both armies passed up the river to the mountains. The discovery of gold in Montana added greatly to the river commerce during these years. The injurious effects of the war, therefore, were mainly confined to the river below Kansas City.

The peril to navigation due to the operations of the guerrillas was a formidable one. Wherever the channel ran close to the high wooded banks or other sheltered localities, ambush and attack could always be expected. The danger was mainly from the south bank. It became necessary to tie up at night away from this bank, and Captain La Barge followed the practice of anchoring in mid-stream. The pilot-houses were regularly equipped with shields of boiler iron, semi-cylindrical in form, inclosing the wheel, and capable of being moved so as to be adjusted to the changing course of the vessel. These shields were of great service on the upper river also, for the Indians at this time were as dangerous in that section as were the guerrillas farther down. Occasionally, when there was much government freight aboard, troops were sent up on the boat until

Kansas City was passed. The passions aroused by this internecine strife deadened human kindness, and made men as ferocious and brutal as wild beasts. This was particularly true of the lawless bands of guerrillas whose desultory operations have been in all wars the most cruel and most difficult to suppress or control. Brigadier General Loan, of the Missouri State Militia, in reporting the tragedy which we shall next relate, said: "The guerrillas and Rebel sympathizers are waging a relentless, cruel, and bloody war upon our unarmed and defenseless citizens, and are determined to continue it until the last loyal citizen is murdered, or driven from the State for fear of being murdered." Such was the true situation along the south bank of the Missouri River, and it was only by the most vigilant precaution on the part of the steamboat men that they did not suffer more than they did. We shall relate one instance in which these precautions did not avail.

In the latter part of March, 1863, the steamboat *Sam Gaty* was on her way up the Missouri with a heavy load of freight and passengers, bound for the far upper river. There were on board several persons of wealth on their way to the newly discovered gold fields of Montana. There were besides quite a number of paroled Union soldiers and some forty contrabands, as the negroes freed by the war were called. While passing under a high wooded bank near Sib-ley, Mo., the boat was attacked by a band of guerrillas under the leadership of one Hicks, who had for some time been the terror of the surrounding country. The boat was ordered to come to the bank and promptly obeyed, whereupon the guerrillas immediately boarded her. The attack was unexpected, and the passengers were seated around the cabin engaged in games and conversation when the appalling fact of their situation dawned upon them. A rush was made to conceal valuable property, and the paroled soldiers made haste to get into citizens' clothes. The poor negroes could do nothing. The guerrillas made quick and heartless work. They robbed the passengers of all the valuables to be found on their persons, and one man narrowly escaped summary death for attempting to slip his gold watch into his boot. All the property on board that seemed to be of any use to the government was thrown into the river. The safes were broken open and robbed. Some of the paroled soldiers were taken off the boat and shot. All of the contrabands were driven ashore, where they were shot down in cold blood. Their shrieks and cries were plainly heard on the boat. After this attack the boat was allowed to proceed.

Vengeance followed quickly in the wake of this atrocious crime. A body of Kansas troops under a Major Ransom pursued and overtook the guerrillas, attacked and destroyed their camp, took twenty-one horses, killed seventeen men in combat and hanged two, and completely dispersed the organization.

Captain La Barge had his full share of troublesome experiences that followed the outbreak of the war. As a slave-owner in a small way, and as a man born and bred in the old ante-bellum atmosphere that surrounded the institution of slavery, his natural sympathies were with the South. But when it came to a decision he did not hesitate a moment. As between union and disunion he was for union. It required a degree of self-denial and patriotism which many Northerners have never fully appreciated to stand by the country when one's training and natural sympathies would have led him to the other side. Captain La Barge remained a Union man, took the oath of allegiance, and throughout the war rendered constant service to the government. He soon came to see the wisdom of his decision, and before the war was over his sympathies had swung into full line with his action.

In 1861 Captain La Barge was coming down the river on the *Emilie* from Omaha, and, as usual, stopped at St. Joseph for freight and passengers. A good many people got on board, most of them Southern sympathizers going south. When the boat rounded out into the stream the passengers went up on deck and cheered for Jefferson Davis. The news of this event was telegraphed to Colonel R. D. Anthony of Leavenworth. This distinguished agitator and ardent Union man called a meeting of the citizens, and it was decided to hang La Barge the moment the boat arrived. The Captain had a stanch friend in Leavenworth of the name of Alexander Majors, of the firm of Russell, Majors & Waddell, overland freighters. He was waiting to take passage to his home in Lexington, Mo. When the boat approached there was a great crowd on the levee. The instant the prow touched the bank Majors leaped on board and told the Captain not to make fast, as the crowd proposed to hang him. The Captain asked the clerk what business they had for Leavenworth. He replied that there were only a few bills to collect. "Let them go for now," said the Captain, and tapping the bell to depart, drew back into the stream. When the crowd saw that they were outwitted, they swung their rope into the air and yelled that they would get him at Wyandotte. "All right," replied the Captain, "I expect to stop there," but when he reached that place he kept right on.

On one of the down trips in the season of 1861 the *Emilie* arrived at Boonville just as the Confederates were evacuating that place upon the approach of the Federals under General Lyon. La Barge knew nothing of what was transpiring there, and his first intimation of any unusual state of things was a volley of cannon shot whistling over the boat. The Captain signaled that he would halt, and rounded to above the town. The Confederate General Marmaduke came on board and with him Captain Kelly and a company of troops. "I knew Marmaduke well," said La Barge, "and asked him as soon as he got on board what the matter was. He replied, 'I want you to turn around and take General Price up to Lexington. He is sick and cannot stand the overland ride.' I replied that I could not think of such a thing; that I was in the service of the government. He then took possession of the boat, placed me in arrest, and forced me to take the boat back to Lexington. I protested again, saying that the crew would look to me for pay for this extra work, and the government would hold me responsible for failure to fulfill my contract. Marmaduke replied, 'I will pay you every cent you have to disburse on account of this trip.' After Price came on board Marmaduke left, and wethen steamed up to Lexington, where the boat was turned over to me and I was told to shift for myself. I suppose they thought I ought to consider myself fortunate to get off at all. They never paid me anything, although they might easily have done so, for the first thing done upon landing at Lexington, as I was told, was to sack all the banks of that town. As to my getting away, that was far from being a matter of much satisfaction. It was, of course, known in the Federal lines that I had carried Price up the river. How should I answer for myself upon my return? I went to Price, told him the dilemma I was placed in, and asked him to help me. He gave me a very strong letter, stating that I had acted under duress, and had been forced to go back against my repeated protest.

"It was with no slight misgivings that I turned the *Emilie* downstream and started in the direction of Boonville. I knew that there was trouble in store for me. When I approached the Federal lines a volley was fired at the boat, apparently with the definite purpose of hitting her. I promptly rounded to and the firing ceased. A young Lieutenant by the name of White came on board with a guard of a dozen men to arrest me. I had known White in St. Louis as a commission clerk, a young man of no account, but who, having now some authority, felt disposed, like all inferior men, to exercise it with a severity in inverse proportion to his ability. He doubtless thought it a great feather in his cap to have as prisoner a man who would scarcely have deigned to notice him in any other situation. He was insolent and arbitrary, and lunging his sword toward me, would order me to walk faster. I was taken to General Lyon's quarters, and when in that officer's presence, he said to me: You are in a very bad scrape here, sir.' I took Price's letter from my pocket and handed it to him, saying, General, please read that; it may help to straighten matters out.' He read the letter, but pretended not to think much of it. After hemming and hawing over the matter for a while he said: Do you know anyone here who can tell me who you are?' He knew very well who I was, for he had been with Harney in the Sioux War of 185455 and we had met then. I asked him to name the members of his staff, and I could tell. He finally mentioned Frank Blair. I said with some irony, 'I know Frank Blair very well, and I think *he* knows me.' We then walked up *to* Blair's quarters. He shook hands cordially and said, I understand that you are in a bad fix here.' 'It looks like it,' I replied. 'Rather be at home than here, I presume,' he continued jokingly. 'Much rather,' I replied. Lyon showed Blair Price's letter. They consulted together for a little while and Lyon then said to me,

' You can take possession of your steamboat and go home.' I found the boat in Lyon's fleet where it had been taken, and all of her provisions confiscated. I was not long in getting up steam, and left the inhospitable region with the utmost expedition.

"I did not like Lyon. He was a Yankee, and his disposition seemed to be to crush everyone who did not think as he did. His language and bearing toward me were so insolent and exasperating that they left a lasting rancor in my mind.

"This affair cost me about five thousand dollars, although I was partially reimbursed for the stores taken. I did not go up the river again that season, being too much vexed and disgusted with my late experience. I sent the boat up under charge of a man of the name of Nick Wall, who ran her until my government contracts were completed."

In the year 1862 Captain La Barge was again impressed temporarily into the service of guerrillas. On October 16 of that year a body of Confederates was at Portland, Mo., when the steamboat *Emilie*

This was the opinion naturally held by Southern sympathizers in Missouri. The unbending will of this stern and ardent patriot would overbear and crush without compunction anyone who had even a taint of disloyalty about him. Though La Barge had taken a stand which was quite as honorable, and more self-sacrificing than that of Lyon, still the latter could not come along. The *Emilie* stopped to put two men ashore, when a gang of Rebels concealed behind a woodpile took possession of the boat and compelled Captain La Barge to set them across the river. He was forced to unload his deck freight and take on 175 horses and as many men. Scarcely had they started across when a force of Union cavalry of the Missouri State Militia arrived, but not in time to arrest the operation.

These were the only occasions on which Captain La Barge had trouble on the river on account of the War. Like all other boatmen, he welcomed the close of this conflict and the tranquillity which it brought to the river business.

There was an organization in the military establishment of the United States, growing out of the progress of the war, of which very little is known. It was called the United States Volunteers, and consisted of six regiments and one independent company. It was composed chiefly of deserters from the Confederate army and prisoners of war who had taken the oath of allegiance to the United States. forget that the Captain's environment and training had made him more sympathetic with the Southern cause than a Northerner could possibly be. Lyon's temperament, moreover, aggravated the severity of his patriotism. He was not popular with his associates in the old army on account of his overbearing disposition. These troops served continuously on the Western plains and in the Northwest, except the 1st and 4th regiments, which served mainly at Norfolk, Va. On the Missouri River, and perhaps elsewhere, they were commonly spoken of as "Galvanized Yankees." In 1864, when Fort Rice was established near the mouth of the Cannon Ball River, it was garrisoned by the 1st Regiment of U. S. Volunteers under Colonel Charles A. R. Dimon. This officer was one of the remarkable characters of Missouri River history, and made a great impression along the valley, considering his brief service there. He was the particular bugbear of the traders, and the character which they have given him can be best expressed by spelling his name with an "e" in the first syllable. It was said that he ordered his men shot down on the least provocation, and that many of the regiment were slain in this way. Numbers of his men are said to have deserted through fear of his tyrannical and ungovernable temper. One of the traders has left a record of his own special grievance.

In the winter of 1864-65, as already stated, the American Fur Company sold out to the Northwestern Fur Company, more commonly known as the firm of Hawley & Hubbell. In the following spring these two gentlemen went up the river with Mr. C. P. Chouteau on the American Fur Company boat, the *Yellowstone,* to make the transfer of the posts and property. There were many passengers of different political creeds on board, including a number of ex-Confederates. At a point about one hundred miles above Fort Sully news of Lincoln's assassination was received, and the passengers of all shades of opinion expressed their horror of the event. When the boat arrived at Fort Rice, Colonel Dimon, according to this authority, came down to the boat with a large guard of soldiers and placed the whole party under arrest on the charge of jubilating over the assassination of the President. The traders thought the whole proceeding was a scheme of Colonel Dimon to advertise his intense loyalty. He told Chouteau, whose Southern proclivities were well understood along the river, that he would take him out on the bank and shoot him like a dog. Chouteau was thoroughly frightened and trembled like a leaf, for there was no knowing what the impetuous officer might take a notion to do.

Hubbell and Hawley determined to go down to Sioux City and report to General Sully the detention of their boat and the conduct of Colonel Dimon toward themselves and others. Chouteau gave them a yawl and wrote a letter to the General. Dimon ordered them not to go without first reporting to him. Although his authority to give such an order is doubtful, the men did not dare to disobey for fear of being shot. When they appeared they were required to submit all their letters to his inspection. The particular letter he was after was one he believed Chouteau had written, but Hubbell and Hawley had slipped it into the breech of a Henry rifle and left it in the boat. Finally they were permitted to go. They made a rapid trip, partly by river and partly by land, and immediately reported their grievances to General Sully. The General promptly gave them a written order to Colonel Dimon to release their boat. Armed with this they returned to Fort Rice by the steamer *G. W. Graham,* and in an incredibly short time, considering the distance and mode of travel, appeared before Colonel Dimon. General Sully's order eased matters up somewhat, but still the traders had a good deal of trouble with the irate post commander.

How much there was in the stories about Colonel Dimon is doubtful, but probably about an equal mixture of fact and fiction. Certainly the view of the traders concerning him was not shared by General Sully, if we judge from the following extracts from his own correspondence with General Pope. Writing from Sioux City under date of June 10, 1865, he says:

"I admire his energy and pluck, the determination with which he carries out orders; but he is too young —too rash—for his position, and it would be well if he could be removed. He is making a good deal of trouble for me, and eventually for you, in his overzealous desire to do his duty... His regiment was raised and organized by Ben. Butler, and he is too much like him in his actions for an Indian country, but he is just the sort of a man I would like to have under me in the field." Upon his arrival at Fort Rice a month later he thus commented upon Colonel Dimon:

"I am much pleased with the appearance of this post and the way military duty is performed. Colonel Dimon is certainly an excellent officer. A few more years of experience to curb his impetuosity would make him one of the best officers in our volunteer service."

Pope in the meanwhile authorized Sully to take such action in regard to Colonel Dimon as he saw fit. A board of officers was convened to investigate complaints against him, and on the strength of their report he was relieved July 21, 1865. He resumed command of the post, however, October 10, 1865, but was mustered out of the service on the 27th of the following month. He was subsequently brevetted Brigadier General of Volunteers for gallant and meritorious service during the war. Colonel Dimon probably showed an excess of severity toward the traders where the average officer showed far too little. That explains their chief ground of dislike of him. Add to this the "impetuosity" of temperament referred to by General Sully, and we have a pretty close analysis of a situation which caused a great flurry on the Missouri River in its day. As a matter of fact a great many of the men in the 1st Volunteers died at Fort Rice, but from disease, and not by execution under Dimon's order. A number of men did desert, and seventeen of them walked all the way to Fort Union. One of these men made a pen drawing of that post which is probably the most accurate now in existence.

CHAPTER XXII.

GOLD IN MONTANA.

IF the Civil War operated to drive commerce from the lower Missouri River, other forces were at work at the head waters of that stream to multiply it many fold. At the time when the attention of the nation and of the world was centered on the tempest that had burst over the eastern portion of the Republic, a few hardy miners were prospecting the country around the upper tributaries of the Missouri in their ever-restless search for gold. It is a singular fact that the gold-bearing regions of western Montana, the very first in the mountain country to be extensively frequented by white men, should have been the last to give up the secret of their hidden wealth. For nearly twenty years emigration had been pouring into the West. The Mormons had settled a few hundred miles to the south. Settlement had gained a permanent foothold on the Pacific Coast from Mexico to the British line. The Pike's Peak gold discoveries were rapidly filling up Colorado. The reflex wave of emigration was rolling back from the Pacific Coast across the Sierras and the Cascades into Nevada, eastern Oregon, and Idaho. But as yet there were no settlers to speak of in the mountains of Montana, and that country was still practically unknown to the general public. It is a remarkable fact that a section of country in that neighborhood, which is now considered the most wonderful in the world, was the very last of all the national domain to be discovered and explored.

The wave of gold discovery in the Northwest moved from the west toward the east. In 1860-61 it made known the rich deposits in Idaho on the Salmon and Clearwater rivers. Next came the findings just west of the Continental Divide, and then the rich discoveries on the head waters of the Missouri. The existence of placer deposits within the limits of the present State of Montana had been asserted as early as 1852. A Canadian half-breed of the name of Beneetse is said to have found pay dirt in that year on a small tributary of Deer Lodge River, one of the sources of the Columbia. The stream has since been known as Gold Creek, and the place of discovery is about fifty miles northwest of the modem city of Butte. Four years later,

1856, the discovery was confirmed by a party who were traveling from Great Salt Lake to the Bitter Root Valley. In the same year a man turned up at Fort Benton with what he asserted was gold dust. He came from the mountains in the Southwest, most likely from the Deer Lodge Valley. None of the people at the post were gold experts, and they hesitated about receiving the dust; but Culbertson finally took it on his own responsibility, giving for it a thousand dollars' worth of merchandise. Next year he sent it down the river, and it was found to be pure gold, worth fifteen hundred dollars. This was the first exchange of gold dust in Montana.

The next step in the progress of discovery must be credited to James and Granville Stuart, two of Montana's most distinguished pioneers. They had been spending the winter of 1857-58, with a number of other people, in the valley of the Bighole River, a tributary of the Missouri, and in the spring of 1858 went over to the Deer Lodge Valley to investigate the reported findings on Gold Creek. They remained there for a time and found paying prospects, but were so harassed by the Blackfeet Indians that they were compelled to leave. They moved to a safer locality, but here James Stuart met with an accident which came near proving fatal, and the two brothers left the country and went to Fort Bridger. Although they had made no great discovery, their report was considered as confirming those already made of the existence of gold in the Deer Lodge Valley.

Before these prospects were any further developed attention was wholly diverted to the important discoveries in Idaho already referred to. A great stampede to the Salmon and Clearwater rivers began. Emigrants poured in both by way of Salt Lake and the Missouri River, and an even larger inflow came from the Pacific Coast. But before the rush from the East had gathered full force discoveries in Montana arrested its course and held it permanently in a new and greater Eldorado.

In the winter of 1861-62 a considerable floating population, among them the Stuart brothers, remained in the Deer Lodge Valley. The Stuarts commenced sluicing in a systematic way on Gold Creek, and their work was the beginning of the gold mining industry in

Montana. Although nothing particularly remarkable was found, it was enough to attract attention, and reports soon got abroad that the findings were very rich. The greater part of the emigration from the East in the year 1862 was bound for the Idaho mines, but did not get beyond the Deer Lodge Valley, or other points in western Montana. Among these parties was one from Colorado, including J. M. Bozeman, for whom the town of Bozeman, in the beautiful Gallatin Valley, is named. The new-comers made a rich discovery on a branch of Gold Creek, which was named, from the place whence the party came, Pike's Peak Gulch.

Another party from Colorado, bound for the Idaho mines, were deflected north by the difficulty of getting through the Lemhi Mountains and by favorable reports from the Deer Lodge Valley. Two of their number discovered gold on Grasshopper Creek, in the southwestern corner of the present State of Montana. They carried the news to the main party, who had gone on to the Deer Lodge, and all returned to investigate the discovery. The report of the two men was found to be true, and prospecting in that part of the country was carried on extensively. This work resulted in the finding of a very rich deposit by a party under one White, for whom the spot was named White's Bar. Here the town of Bannock sprang up, and before the end of the year boasted a population of five hundred souls. Other rich discoveries were made in that vicinity, while far to the north the deposits on the Big Prickly Pear Creek were found. It was now apparent that the whole country on the head waters of the Missouri abounded in gold, and the work of prospecting assumed enormous proportions.

Two other important expeditions came from the East this season, bound for the Idaho mines, but were stopped in their course, like that from Colorado, by the new discoveries in Montana. One of these was the firm of La Barge, Harkness & Co of St. Louis, and the other was a body of emigrants who accompanied what was known in its day as the Northern Overland Expedition from St. Paul. This expedition was of a semi-official character, under a Federal appropriation of five thousand dollars, and its ostensible object was to open a wagon road from St. Paul to Fort Benton. It was under the command of Captain James L. Fisk, who, a private soldier in the 3d Minnesota Volunteers, was appointed Captain and Quartermaster and placed in charge. About 125 emigrants accompanied the expedition. The journey was made in safety, and was full of interesting happenings. It contributed one of the most important additions ever made to population of the rising State.

The spring of 1863 was marked by one of the most noted gold discoveries ever made. During the previous winter a considerable party, under the leadership of James Stuart, was organized at Bannock City, to explore and prospect the country on the sources of the Yellowstone. A portion of this party, including William Fairweather and Henry Edgar, went by the way of Deer Lodge Valley to secure horses, having fixed on the mouth of the Beaverhead River as the place of joining the main party. Through some unavoidable delay the smaller party did not arrive on time and Stuart went on without them. The Fairweather party discovered Stuart's trail and made forced marches to overtake him. The route lay up the Gallatin Valley and across the divide to the Yellowstone, and thence down the valley of that stream. Soon after reaching the Yellowstone the smaller party were plundered by a band of Crows of everything except their guns and mining tools. The Indians had the generosity to give them in exchange for their mounts old broken-down horses of their own.

The party gave up their pursuit of Stuart and started back for Bannock City. On the 26th of May they stopped for noon on Alder Creek, a little branch of one of the main tributaries of Jefferson Fork of the Missouri. Here, as a result of a chance examination of a bar by two men, Fairweather and Edgar, the famous Alder Gulch discovery was made, and the richest placer deposit in the history of gold mining came to the knowledge of the world. The news of this wonderful discovery drew to the spot a large part of the population of the Territory, and the town of Virginia City sprang up as if in a night. For several years it was the principal town in the Territory and became its first capital. In less than two years it had grown to a city of ten thousand souls.

The next important discovery was made in the fall of 1864, in what was named at the time Last Chance Gulch. The deposits were very rich, and the history of Alder Gulch was re-enacted here. The town which arose on the spot was named Helena, and soon outgrew its sister to the south. It became, and for many years remained, the principal town of the Territory. In 1874 it was made the Territorial capital, and after Montana was admitted to the Union, it was made the permanent capital of the State.

Other discoveries followed those here mentioned, many of them rich and of permanent value, but none equaling those of Alder and Last Chance gulches. The Territory at once took rank with California and Colorado as a gold-producing territory, and has held its high place ever since.

The mighty metamorphosis which, in the space of five years, came over the country at the headwaters of the Missouri, produced an equally marvelous change in the commercial business of that stream. The river gave a sure highway for travel to within one hundred to two hundred miles of the mines. There was no other route that could compete with it, for this could carry freight from St. Louis to Fort Benton, in cargoes of one to five hundred tons, without breaking bulk. The emigrants themselves went in large numbers by overland routes, but a great number also by the boats; while nearly all merchandise, including every necessary of life, and all mining machinery and heavy freight, came by the river.

The steamboat trade jumped suddenly to enormous proportions.. Prior to 1864 there had been only six steamboat arrivals at the levee of Fort Benton. In 1866 and 1867 there were seventy arrivals. The trade touched high-water mark in 1867, and at this time presented one of the most extraordinary developments known to the history of commerce. There were times when thirty or forty steamboats were on the river between Fort Benton and the mouth of the Yellowstone, where all the way the river flowed amid scenes of wildness that were in the strictest sense primeval. To one who could have been set down in the unbroken wilderness along the banks of the river, where nothing dwelt except wild animals and wilder men, where the fierce Indian made life a constant peril, where no civilized habitation greeted the eye, it would have seemed marvelous and wholly inexplicable to find this river filled with noble craft, as beautiful as any that ever rode the ocean, stored with all the necessaries of civilization, and crowded with passengers as cultured, refined, and well dressed as the cabin list of an ocean steamer. What could it all mean? Whence came this handful of civilization and what brought it here? Certainly a most extraordinary scene, flashed for a moment before the world and then withdrawn forever.

It was not the steamboat alone, however, that made up the romantic history of Missouri navigation in these exciting times. There were every year many men from the mines who wanted to return to the States because they were weary of the country or wished to carry down the crude wealth which they had secured. The steamboats came up only in the spring, and if passengers were not ready to go down it was necessary to seek other conveyance. The usual resource in such cases was the mackinaw boat. It was a perfectly comfortable and very cheap mode of traveling, with only one drawback—danger from the Indians, who, at this time, were intensely hostile all along the river. It was regarded as a sort of forlorn hope to go down in an open boat, and yet many tried it every year. Generally they got through all right, with their precious freight, but there were some terrible tragedies as the penalty of such reckless daring.

Some statistics have survived showing the magnitude of the steamboat business on the Missouri River during these years. In the year 1865, 1000 passengers, 6000 tons of merchandise, and 20 quartz mills went to Fort Benton. In the year 1867 forty steamboats had passed Sioux City before June I on their way up the river. They carried over 12,000 tons of freight, most of it for Fort Benton. There was not much downstream traffic, although all the boats carried gold dust. In 1866 one boat, the *Luella,* had on board $1,250,000 worth of dust.

The profits of a successful voyage were enormous. The reported profits for some of the trips of 1866 were as follows: The *St. John,* $17,000; the *Tacony,* $16,000; the *W. J. Lezuis,* $40,000; the *Peter*

Balen, $65,000. In 1867 Captain La Barge cleared over $40,000 on the trip of the *Octavia.*

Freight rates from St. Louis to Fort Benton in 1866 were 12 cents per pound. Insurance rates were 6 1-2 per cent, in the case of sidewheel boats and 8 per cent, with sternwheel boats. The fare for cabin passengers was $300. It was not everyone, however, who had a share in the high prices of those times. The master of the boat received $200 per month; the clerk $150; the mate and engineer each $125. The pilot was the only member of the crew who could command what salary he pleased. So indispensable were his services that as high as $1200 per month was paid for the best talent.

CHAPTER XXIII.

INCIDENTS ON THE RIVER (1862-67).

IN the summer of 1863 Pty of twenty-one men and three women went down the Missouri in a mackinaw boat from Fort Benton. They reached the vicinity of the mouth of Apple Creek, near where Bismarck, N. D., now stands, just as the Sioux Indians, whom General Sibley was driving out of Minnesota and across the country to the Missouri, arrived on the banks of that stream. They had just been defeated in three engagements, with General Sibley and were in a very angry temper. They attacked the boat and fought the little party an entire day, and finally killed them all and sunk the boat. It was reported that the whites killed ninety-one Indians in the fight, and that the captain of the boat, whose name is supposed to have been Baker, "made such a brave defense that the Indians were struck with admiration for him and wanted to save him." The boat had a large amount of gold dust on board, and some of it was recovered by the Mandan and Aricara Indians. An air of mystery has always hung over this affair, and the details will probably never be known. For some unexplained reason, certain individuals who were believed to have had some knowledge of it refused to disclose anything.

In 1864, while Captain La Barge was at Fort Benton, a number of miners applied to him to purchase a mackinaw boat. He refused to sell because he felt sure that it meant death to them to try to run the gantlet of the Indians in that way. They replied that they were afraid to go overland on account of road agents. The Captain told them they had less to fear from road agents than from Indians. The road agents might take their gold, but the Indians would spare neither treasure nor life. They were unconvinced, however, and as the Captain would not sell the boat, they stole it and set out. While passing a high cut bank, about thirty miles below Fort Berthold, where the channel ran close to the shore, they were attacked by a war party of Sioux and all killed. Pierre Garreau, the well-known interpreter, went down from Berthold and recovered a part of the gold dust. La Barge saw some of it among the Indians the following year.

In 1865 the steamer *St. Johns,* on her way down the river, was attacked by the Indians and the mate instantly killed. The boat was under full headway and out of reach before it was possible to return fire. In the same year the *General Grant* lost three men. They had been sent ashore at a wooding place to make fast a line, when they were pounced upon by the Indians and killed.

On April 23, 1865, a band of Blood Indians near Fort Benton stole about forty horses belonging to a party of beaver-trappers, of whom Charley Carson, a nephew of "Kit" Carson, was one. On the night of May 22 these men, having gotten on a drunken spree, attacked a small party of Blood Indians who happened to be near Fort Benton, but were not known to be the thieves, killed three, and threw their bodies into the Missouri. The survivors fled toward the south and met a large band of warriors near Sun River, on their way north. Exasperated at the outrage upon their brethren, they were ready for any measure of revenge, and accident soon threw the desired opportunity in their way.

At the mouth of the Marias River lay the steamboat *Cutter*. A town site had been laid off at this point and named Ophir, and some timber had been cut in the valley of the Marias for use in the erection of buildings. The principal proprietor of the nascent village was a passenger on the *Cutter,* and the business of that boat seems to have been connected with the building of the town. On the afternoon of May 25, about half-past two o'clock, eight men left the boat with a wagon and three yoke of oxen to bring down some of the timber, and an hour later two men went on horseback to join them, for it was felt that there might be trouble from the Indians, and that the party should be as strong as possible. These men were all well armed. Their route lay up the valley of the Marias along its right bank, which they ascended about three miles. At this point the valley, which was quite broad below, narrowed to a width of four hundred yards. There was a growth of timber quite dense close to the river, but open farther back. Just above this point the bluffs crowded close upon the river, seamed with ravines and gullies, like all the river bluffs along the Missouri. The roadway at the foot of these bluffs was very narrow.

Beyond this defile the valley opened out again, and there was another belt of timber. In the upper opening the Indians seem to have been in camp and to have been discovered by the wood-choppers just as the latter were passing the defile. It was probably the same band which we have noted as being near Sun River two days before. The wagons were instantly turned about, although in a most disadvantageous situation. The Indians saw the whites at about the same time. They were lying in wait for another party with a mule train, and were intending, after attacking it, to try to take the steamboat. As soon as they saw the wood-choppers they at once attacked them and killed every man and captured all the property. The bodies of the slain were found scattered along the river, fifty to one hundred yards apart, except one, that of N. W. Burroughs, which was found half a mile further downstream, where he was overtaken on his flight to the boat. Of the Indians the head chief and one other were killed and a third dangerously wounded. The Indians, to the number of about two hundred, immediately moved toward the British line.

The attack occurred about four o'clock and the firing was distinctly heard on the boat. A party prepared to go out and investigate when a hunter came riding in from the bluffs, saying that the whites were being assailed by a large party of Indians. Three scouts set out immediately, and after proceeding about two miles and a half found the body of Mr. Burroughs. It being certain that all the rest had been killed, and not knowing where the Indians were, it was not thought best to go farther at the time. Next morning a party went out with wagons and brought in the bodies, all of which were found. They were buried in one grave, side by side, with a head board giving the names and date.

The names were N. W. Burroughs, George Friend. Franklin Friend, Abraham Low, James H. Lyons, Harry Martin, FrankCaptain La Barge arrived at the mouth of the Marias on the *Eilie Deans* soon after this affair and saw the fresh graves. He remembered the circumstance particularly, because, among the guard, which had been stationed there after the massacre, was the identical "Yankee Jack" who had whipped the two Irishmen on the *Robert Campbell* in 1863.

About September, 1865, eight men left Fort Benton in a skiff for the States. They were attacked by some forty Indians near the mouth of Milk River and five of their number were killed. The fight lasted over five hours. One of the men who was killed, T. A. Kent by name, is said to have actually killed thirteen Indians before he himself fell.

In the year 1866 there were several noted open boat voyages down the river. One of these was made by a party of ten miners, who purchased a mackinaw at Fort Benton in which to transport themselves and their gold dust. When in camp on an island about sixty miles above Fort Randall, one of the men, of the name of Thompson, got up in the night, took an ax, killed one companion and wounded another. He was apparently bent on the destruction of the entire party. The rest of the men, suddenly awakened by the cries of their comrades, and believing that they, Angevine, George Allen, James Andrews, and James Perie (colored) were attacked by Indians, rushed to the boat with the wounded man and made off, leaving the murderer and his victim alone on the island. Whether robbery was the motive of the deed, or whether it was caused by insanity, was never known.

More fortunate was another mackinaw party that went down the same season. It consisted of seventeen men, and made the trip from Fort Benton to Sioux City in twenty-two days. They brought down over two hundred thousand dollars in gold dust.

The third party of this season consisted of one man in a yawl and about twenty others in a mackinaw. They made the entire trip without loss, although they were attacked, some 225 miles below Benton, by about five hundred Blackfeet. The river was in flood stage, and thanks to its great width and swift current the boats were able to keep out of range of the Indians and to pass quickly beyond their reach.

The most important mackinaw trip ever made down the river was in 1866 under the leadership of J. B. Hubbell of the firm of Hawley & Hubbell. Hubbell had advertised that his steamboat would leave

Fort Benton on her second trip about September 15, promising, if she did not get to Fort Benton, to take the passengers down in a mackinaw until they met her. As late as October 20 she had not appeared, and accordingly about thirty passengers started down in a mackinaw. The boat was a very elaborate one, built for this particular trip. It was eighty feet long, twelve feet beam, housed in on both sides by bulletproof walls for a distance of fifty feet, with sleeping bunks along the sides, and open spaces at bow and stern for managing the boat. Two masts rigged with square sails were provided.

The boat was run until after dark every night and was started before daylight in the morning. Wherever possible she was tied to a snag out in the stream for the night so as to make it impossible for the Indians to attack by surprise. When the party arrived at Fort Union they learned that the steamer had been up, but had gone back. After some deliberation it was decided to undertake the rest of the journey and trust to luck not to be caught by the ice. Everyone took a hand at the oars and rapid progress was made. Game was plentiful and the boat was full of gold dust, and in spite of the fear of ice and Indians the party were in the best of spirits. They arrived at Sioux City November 22, with the river running full of ice. Two days later and they would have been frozen in. Mr. Hubbell received $175 per passenger.

A singular incident happened in the summer of 1867, growing out of the wreck of one of the river boats. In July of that year the steamer *Trover* was wrecked at a point 240 miles below Fort Benton. The *Ida Stockdale* happened along about the time, took her freight and passengers to Benton, and on the way back took off her machinery and carried it to St. Louis. When she left the wreck there were two colored boys asleep in the hold, and the boat went off without knowing they were there. On waking up and finding themselves alone, without a thing to eat or any means of defense, and surrounded by a wilderness wholly unknown to them, they were completely paralyzed with fright; but recovering their presence of mind they saw that they must find some relief immediately or they would die of starvation. They left the wreck and started down the river. In crossing a small tributary of the Missouri one of the boys was drowned. The other kept on night and day, most of the time back from the river, to avoid the bends and the swamps and underbrush. He had nothing to eat except a little bark and some flower blossoms and did not stop a moment for sleep. His keeping back from the river caused him to miss the boats and trading posts. Finally, almost famished and exhausted, he beat his way through a dense willow growth to the bank of the river in the hope that some boat would come along before he should die. Shortly afterward a steamer hove in sight—the *Sunset*—on her way up the river. She was a veritable sun *rise* to the poor boy, who began waving an old white hat, almost the only article of clothing he had left. The people on the boat saw the signal and sent the yawl out and brought the boy in. His face was almost raw from mosquito bites, and he was so weak that he could scarcely stand. He was found at a point twenty-five miles below Fort Rice, or 642 miles, by river channel, below where the *Trover* was wrecked. He traveled this distance in nine days. With all the cut-offs duly allowed for, he must have averaged seventy miles a day during this time, and all the while without food. Were it not that the facts seem well established, such an example of physical endurance would be incredible. The name of this little hero was Frederick Good and his home was in St. Louis.

CHAPTER XXIV.

LA BARGE AGAIN IN OPPOSITION.

With a view to entering, upon a large scale, into the newly developing business at the head waters of the Missouri, the firm of La Barge, Harkness & Co. was formed in St. Louis in the winter of 1861-62. The members were Joseph La Barge, Eugene Jaccard, James Harkness, John B. La Barge, and Charles E. Galpin. Each partner put in ten thousand dollars. Two steamboats were purchased— Captain La Barge's boat, the *Emilie,* and a light draft boat, the *Shreveport*. In the division of duties and responsibilities among the partners Jaccard was to attend to the affairs of the firm in St. Louis, the La Barges were to manage the steamboat business, Galpin was to look after the trade along the river, and Harkness was to go to the mines with an outfit of merchandise, and was to remain there and develop a business with those rapidly growing communities.

When it was known that Captain La Barge was to make a spring trip to Benton, he was overwhelmed with applications, not merely from those who wanted to go to the mines, but from business men and capitalists who wished to join the enterprise. He could easily have organized a capital of a million dollars, but he adhered to his first plan and pushed his preparations with vigor. The *Shreveport* was first gotten ready to sail and left port April 30, 1862. Captain John La Barge was master. The *Emilie* followed on the 14th of May.

As a performance in steamboating the voyage of the *Emilie* was a great success. She was loaded to the guards with some 350 tons of freight and 160 passengers. Captain La Barge himself had never been more than a hundred miles above Fort Union; yet he made the whole trip, 2300 miles, in a little less than thirty-two days, and would have finished it sooner but for the fact that he had to help the *Shreveport* the last hundred miles of the distance. The boats arrived at Fort Benton at noon June 17, and at 6 A. M., June 19, the *Emilie* started down the river, reaching St. Louis on the 3d of July. Her speed up averaged 71 miles per day; down, 152 miles.

An exciting incident of the trip was the passing of the American Fur Company's boat, the *Spread Eagle*. The new opposition of La Barge, Harkness & Co. was a formidable one, and the Company bestirred itself with unusual vigor to be first on the ground with its annual outfit. The *Spread Eagle*left St. Louis with three days the start, but was overtaken by the *Emilie* near Fort Berthold. For the next two days the boats were near each other most of the time. The day after leaving Berthold the *Emilie* passed her rival for good. When the officers of the *Spread Eagle* saw that they were beaten they played a desperate game, which showed to what lengths the Company's servants would go when it was a matter of rivalry in trade.

At the point where the race took place there was a towhead (a newly formed island) which at the stage of the river then prevailing was covered with water. The main channel, and at ordinary stages the only channel, passed on the right-hand side going up, and this channel the *Spread Eagle* took. But the water was now high enough to give a good channel on the other side of the towhead. As the distance by this channel was somewhat shorter, and as the *Emilie* was the faster boat anyway, it was a good chance to get well ahead and out of the way. La Barge promptly seized the opportunity. The pilot of the *Spread Eagle* with quick eye realized that he had been outmaneuvered, and seeing no other way to prevent the *Emilie's* passage, determined upon wrecking her. He accordingly left the main channel and made for the chute that the *Emilie* was entering. He steamed alongside of her for a moment, but found that he waslosing ground. The boats were scarcely fifty feet apart, when the pilot of the *Spread Eagle,* seeing that he could not make it, deliberately put his rudder to port, and plunged the bow of the boat into the *Emilie* immediately opposite her boilers. Several of the guards were broken and the danger of wreck was imminent. La Barge was in the pilot-house at the time and was not looking for such a move, for he did not believe that even the American Fur Company would play so desperate a game when human life was at stake. He instantly called out to Bailey, the pilot of the *Spread Eagle*, to stop his engines and drop his boat back or he would put a bullet through him. The passengers likewise became thoroughly aroused, and some of them got their arms and threatened to use them if the *Spread Eagle* did not withdraw. These threats were effective; the *Spread Eagle* fell to the rear and was seen no more on the voyage. She was four days behind at Benton, and a week on the whole trip. She lost four men on one of the rapids by the grossest carelessness. A crew had gone to the head of the rapids to plant a deadman, and having finished this work dropped down to the boat in their yawl. Instead of passing alongside of the steamer they made directly for the bow, and on reaching the boat the swift current instantly rolled the yawl under and the crew were drowned.

When the *Spread Eagle* returned to St. Louis charges were preferred against Bailey for having attempted to wreck the *Emilie*. He was brought to trial before the steamboat inspector and his license was canceled. It was a hard blow to him, for steamboating was his trade, and he had a large family to support. About a month afterward he went to La Barge saying that he had been trying to get the inspector to reinstate him, but that he would not do it except upon La Barge's recommendation. Bailey admitted his guilt, but said that he had acted at the instigation of the Company's agents, and he begged La Barge to reinstate him for the sake of his wife and children. The Captain was never good at resisting appeals of this sort, and he accordingly went to the inspector and got Bailey reinstated.

When the *Emilie* was reported as back from her trip, the old gentleman Chouteau sent his carriage to bring La Barge to the office.

"At what point did you turn back?" he asked when La Barge arrived, for the phenomenally quick trip indicated that the *Emilie* did not reach Fort Benton.

"Fort Benton, sir," replied La Barge.

"Tut, tut! I know you could not have done that. Tell me candidly where you left your trip."

"Fort Benton, sir."

"We'll see about it. I don't believe it, don't believe it."

"Sorry you doubt my word, but it is nevertheless true."

"Where did you leave the *Spread Eagle?*"

"'Way below Benton; found her cordelling."

"Well, if you got to Fort Benton you made a good trip; but I don't believe it."

As soon as Captain La Barge reached St. Louis he loaded his boat with merchandise for the new posts along the river, intending to go back until he should meet the *Shreveport,* a much lighter-draft vessel, and transfer the cargo to her for the rest of the trip. The *Shreveport* left Fort Benton July 6, and met the *Emilie* at Sioux City. The transfer of cargo and passengers was made, and the *Emilie* returned to St. Louis. The *Shreveport* went as high as the mouth of Milk River, the farthest of the new posts except that near Fort Benton. After the *Emilie's* return from her second voyage she went to work for the government, carrying stores from St. Louis to Memphis, and remained in this service all winter.

The river portion of the season's operations of the new firm had been a complete success. Three large cargoes had been sent up the river, two to Fort Benton and one to the lower posts. Of these posts there were four—La Framboise, near old Fort Pierre; another near Fort Berthold; Fort Stuart, near the mouth of Poplar River, and Fort Galpin, near the mouth of Milk River. It remains to notice what was done at Fort Benton and in the projected expedition to the mines.

The operations at Fort Benton and beyond were placed in the hands of Mr. Harkness. The first step was to build a post at Fort Benton, where it was intended to locate the principal establishment of the firm. The site chosen was near the spot where the Grand Union Hotel later stood. The work was begun June 28, Mrs. La Barge driving the first stake. The inclosure was made three hundred feet long by two hundred feet wide, and the post was named Fort La Barge.

Before the *Shreveport* set out to return to St. Louis, a considerable party made an excursion to the Great Falls of the Missouri. Among them were Father De Smet, Eugene Jaccard, member of the firm; Giles Filley of St. Louis, and his son, Frank; Mrs. John LaBarge, Miss Harkness, W. G. Harkness, Tom La Barge, and Mrs.

Culbertson, the Indian wife of the noted trader. Mrs. La Barge and Miss Harkness are supposed to be the first white women to have seen the Great Falls of the Missouri. Four days after their Teturn the *Shreveport* left for St. Louis, taking with them all who had come up only for the trip.

The *Shreveport* having gone, and affairs at Fort La Barge being well under way, Harkness set out July 9 with an ox train laden with assorted merchandise for the mines in the Deer Lodge Valley. When the boat left St. Louis it was expected to go to the Salmon River mines, but the recent discoveries in Montana gave a better prospect nearer home. In fact the demand for goods, even at Fort Benton, was brisk, and the firm had carried on a thriving trade ever since the arrival of the boats. Harkness followed the usual trail up the Missouri River and Little Prickly Pear Creek, through the broad valley on the border of which the city of Helena now stands, and thence to the valley of the Deer Lodge. Nothing of unusual note transpired on the trip. Harkness did not like the experience, except the trout fishing. His journal is full of complaints at the hardship he was compelled to undergo, and he plaintively asks if he "will ever live to reap the benefit." He generally "nooned at 11 A. M." in order to "catch trout for dinner." Hereached the Deer Lodge Valley July 23, near the point where the town of that name now stands. Here he found a fellow passenger on the *Emilie,* Nicholas Wall of St. Louis, who had reached the mines some days before, and who was destined to figure prominently in the future affairs of La Barge, Harkness & Co.

After remaining in this section and prospecting around for eleven days, Harkness grew disgusted at the prospect, placed such of his goods as he did not sell in the hands of Nick Wall to be sold on commission, and set out for the Missouri "glad to be on the road home." On the Sun River he met the Northern Overland Expedition from St. Paul. He visited the Great Falls on his way down, and arrived at Fort La Barge August 18. Harkness was now "tired and out of spirits," and "adjusted his expense accounts

What is now the town of Deer Lodge, Mont., was first named La Barge City, and was so known for about two years. The name was given by two friends of Captain La Barge, John S. Pemberton of St. Louis and Leon Quesnelle, a descendant of the Quesnelle who seems to have been the first permanent settler at Bellevue, Neb. Quesnelle had been in the Deer Lodge Valley for some time, and had a ranch near where the town was afterward built. Two years later the town site was organized by James Stuart and others, surveyed and laid out by W. W. De Lacy, and rechristened Deer Lodge. The original town site plot of La Barge City is in possession of the Montana Historical Society and turned over everything to the store." He had evidently had enough of this kind of life, and forthwith ordered "a boat built to go down the river." The boat was launched August 26 and was christened the *Maggie*. Harkness lost no time in getting away, and left Fort La Barge at 4 A. M. on the 28th. No incidents occurred on this trip which are of much interest. The party reached Omaha September 30, where Harkness "sold the *Maggie* for five dollars," and took passage on the *Robert Campbell* to St. Joseph. From that point he went by rail and the Mississippi River to St. Louis where he arrived October 6.

The foregoing details, taken entirely from the diary of Harkness, show in what unfit hands the important business of the company in the upper country had been intrusted. From his arrival at Fort Benton until his departure was only two months and a half, including a trip of several hundred miles to the Montana mining regions. Only eleven days did he spend in establishing his trade in that section, the most important point of all, and then practically gave his goods away to Nick Wall, for the company never received a cent for anything left with that gentleman. Yet Harkness was the partner who was to remain in the upper country two years. "He was back in St. Louis almost as soon as I was," said La Barge, with just indignation, in commenting on the affair. Such were the first season's operations of the firm of La Barge, Harkness & Co. In most respects the firm had made a brilliant beginning. The prospects in the river portion of the business were all that could be asked. Only Harkness' weak management of his part of the enterprise can be criticised. He was not the man for the place, and lacked the courage and hardihood for that kind of work, and he threw away an opportunity from which a more enterprising man would have made a fortune.

CHAPTER XXV.

'VOYAGE OF 1863THE TOBACCO GARDEN MASSACRE.

Deferring for the present our narrative of the fortunes of La Barge, Harkness & Co., we shall recount one of those mournful tragedies and one of those instances of official corruption which marked the later history of the Indian tribes along the Missouri River. When Captain La Barge, in the spring of 1863, undertook to leave the government service on the Mississippi, to get ready for his trip to Fort Benton, he was told by the Quartermaster in St. Louis that he could not have the boat, for the government had further use for it. Not having time to go to Washington to see about it, he sold the boat for twenty thousand dollars to the Hannibal and St. Joseph Railroad, and left to that company the task of securing its release. He then chartered the *Robert Campbell,* and, with the *Shreveport,* prepared for a voyage to Fort Benton. It proved to be a notable trip. The cargo and passenger lists of the *Shreveport* were made up almost exclusively for the mines and for the posts of La Barge, Harkness Co. The *Campbell* was loaded with annuities for the Sioux, Crows, Blackfeet, and Assiniboines, together with some other freight, making a cargo of nearly five hundred tons. The *Shreveport* got away from port in the latter part of April, but the *Campbell* was subjected to annoying and even disastrous delay by the failure of the annuities to arrive on time. Captain La Barge, who had the contract to transport the annuities, had been ordered to have his boat in readiness on the 1st of April. The goods did not arrive, and he was held in St. Louis for forty-two days before he could start on the long journey. It was considered of the highest importance to start as soon as the ice disappeared in order that the trip, both coming and going, could be made during high water. As the year 1863 happened to be a low-water year, the delay which Captain La Barge suffered made it impossible to complete the voyage. Even on the 12th of May, the day of starting, only a portion of the goods had arrived, and the rest were taken on at St. Joseph, whither they were sent by rail.

The boat proceeded on her way, determined to accomplish the trip if it were possible to do so. The water was unusually low for that time of year, and it took nearly a month to get to Sioux City, which ought to have been reached easily in a third of the time. Owing to the great danger from guerrillas below Kansas City, a force of thirty soldiers accompanied the boat as far as St. Joseph, Mo. This precaution was very timely. Every boat that was met in the lower river reported attacks with occasional loss of life. Owing to the presence of soldiers on the *Robert Campbell*, and Captain La Barge's precaution to anchor midstream at night instead of lying at the bank, he got through all right. At Miami and at Cogswell's Landing parties tried to board the boat, but without success.

Among the passengers on the *Campbell* were two Indian agents, Henry W. Reed and Samuel M. Latta, the former for the Blackfeet tribes and the latter for the Sioux, Crows, Mandans, and other tribes in that region. Henry A. Boiler, whose work, "Among the Indians," achieved some notoriety in its time, was likewise on board, as were also Alexander Culbertson and his Blackfoot wife. In all there were some thirty passengers, and this number was considerably increased at the various landings as far up as Sioux City. The value of the annuity goods on board was upwards of seventy thousand dollars.

The Indians all along the Missouri above the Niobrara were at this time intensely hostile, but knowing that their annuity goods were about to arrive, they held aloof from any desperate measures until these were received. It would have been a wise thing to have sent a company of troops all the way on this important trip, but not a soldier was to be had. The boat reached Fort Pierre June 20, and here several of the Sioux bands were assembled to receive their annuities. It appears that the Two Kettles band were in a great state of exasperation over the recent killing of eight of their number by the soldiers near Fort Randall. After a considerable amount of parleying the distribution of the annuities commenced, but for some reason, which Captain La Barge never heard explained, only a portion (about two-thirds, as he estimated it) of the goods to which the Indians were entitled were put off. The Indians could not be deceived in the matter and were very angry. They went to the Captain and appealed to him to see justice done them. They had the fullest confidence in him, for they had known him for years, and he had always treated them honestly. He was now helpless, however, and could only tell them that he was under the orders of the agent and had no control whatever over the goods. They then assured him that they should follow the boat and cause it all the trouble they could, but they would not harm him if they could avoid it.

They were as good as their word. All the way from Pierre to Union, six hundred miles, these Indians followed the boat. It is a remarkable fact, when we stop to think of it—this pursuit of a steamboat on its laborious voyage through the Western prairies, seeking at every turn to destroy it and kill its passengers and crew. There was some deep and far-reaching cause that could create and support so bitter and vindictive a spirit as this. The warning of the Indians to Captain La Barge was taken by him at its full value. The boat was thoroughly barricaded with the cargo by piling it so as to protect the vulnerable points, and all the firearms on board were made ready for use. These precautions proved to be of the highest importance. At every woodpile Indians appeared and attacked the crew. At every favorable point shots were fired into the boat. On one occasion a bullet passed through the pilot-house, barely missing the pilot, Atkins, who was at the wheel. We shall relate some incidents that occurred on the way to Union, one more comical than serious, but one tragic and deplorable as any in frontier history.

The *Shreveport* had gone up the river in advance of the *Robert Campbell,* but being unable, on account of low water, to get beyond Snake Point, or Cow Island, 130 miles below Fort Benton, had discharged her cargo on the bank and had returned down the river. She met the *Robert Campbell* at Apple Creek, thirteen miles below Bismarck, and was there stopped by Captain La Barge. A part of the cargo of the larger boat was transferred to the *Shreveport,* and the two then proceeded up the river, the *Shreveport* being sometimes ahead and sometimes in rear. The hunter on the *Shreveport* was Louis Dauphin, already referred to as one of the bravest men and most noted characters of the upper country. He now acted as hunter for both boats. It was his custom to go along ahead of the boat, beating up the country and securing whatever game was worth stopping the boat for. Whatever he killed, as an elk or deer, he would hang on a pole or tree near the bank where it could be seen from the boat, and would then continue his hunt. One day about noon Captain La Barge's eye, which was constantly studying the river ahead, fell upon a curious object floating downstream. It looked like a hat, but, strange to say, was standing upright on the water, with no tendency to sink at all. It caused the Captain no little perplexity. In the windy country of the Missouri it was no uncommon thing for hats to be blown into the river, but he had never before seen one ride like that. He followed it with his glass until it was near the boat, when up it rose, securely perched on the head of a swimmer who proved to be no other than the hunter Dauphin. "I had to take to the water this time," he said as he climbed on board. "They were too many for me. You are going to have trouble at the Tobacco Garden. The Indians are gathered there to the number of at least fifteen hundred and intend to capture the boat." The general amusement which Dauphin's subaqueous adventure had caused on the boat was quickly dispelled by the sad fulfillment of the predictions which he brought back.

Just above the mouth of Rising Water Creek the boats stopped to wood, and were hailed by some Grosventres (of the Missouri, Minnetarees) who offered some meat if a boat were sent out for it. These Indians, a friendly tribe, had been out hunting for two weeks and were just returning well laden with meat. The women had made some bullboats and were about to ferry it over the river. The men had meanwhile turned most of their horses out to graze, keeping only one each fastened by lariats. Some meat was exchanged for coffee and other articles and the *Robert Campbell* resumed her voyage. Just as she was starting one of the squaws uttered a piercing scream, and the people on the boat saw a Sioux Indian riding at full speed for the Grosventre herd, brandishing a red cloth, and followed by a large body of his tribe. The Grosventre squaws took to their boats and the men to the tied horses. The *Campbell* drew in to the bank and took men and horses on board and set them across the river. The poor Grosventres lost nearly their entire herd and all the fruits of their hunt.

The name "Tobacco Garden" on the Missouri River designated the bottoms at the outlet of Tobacco Creek, on the left or north bank of the river, eighty-eight miles below the mouth of the Yellowstone. The origin of the name is uncertain, but the place has long been well known to river men. Near this point, but on the opposite shore, was a bottom, covered with large trees, but open and free of underbrush. The south bank of the river was a "caving bank," or one that was being undermined by the river. At this time there was a very narrow beach at the water's edge, above which the bank rose perpendicularly to a height of six or eight feet. The channel was close to the shore and a boat in passing had to come within thirty or forty yards of the bank. Even if anchored to the sandbar immediately opposite, it could not get more than sixty yards away. It was an ideal place to "hold up" a boat, and the Indians were shrewd enough to understand this perfectly.

It was toward noon of the 7th of July that the two boats hove in sight of the Tobacco Garden, and there, true to Dauphin's prediction, they beheld on the south shore a large body of Indians assembled with the evident purpose of stopping them. There was no use in trying to run a gantlet like that, and accordingly the boats made fast to the opposite sandbar, the *'Shreveport* about one hundred yards below the *Robert Campbell*. A parley ensued with the Indians, who were so near that it was perfectly practicable to talk back and forth. La Barge asked them what they wanted. They said they wanted the balance of their annuities; they wanted no trouble, but simply their just dues. The agent refused them the goods, but "requested the Captain to send his yawl and bring aboard some of the chiefs and head men that we could have a talk and... make them a present of sugar, coffee, tobacco, etc., and by this means quiet them." The Indians likewise wanted the yawl to be sent out, but wanted the agent to go with it. They would then send their principal chiefs back with him to the boat, where everything could be talked over. They were very shrewd, and the agent almost fell into the trap. The Captain told him that he could not possibly think of ordering the yawl out, considering the disposition of the Indians and their evident purpose of mischief. Latta replied: "Why, I'll go; I'm not afraid." "All right," answered the Captain, "if you can get volunteers; I will not order a crew out." They then went to the mate, Miller by name, and a crew was made up to take Latta to the shore. When the yawl was ready the Captain sent word to the agent, who had disappeared upstairs. The latter sent back a reply that he

Letter from S. N. Latta, agent, to W. P. Dole, Commissioner Indian Affairs, dated Yankton, Dak., August 27, 1863. See report Com. Ind. Affs., 1863, p. 170. was suddenly taken ill and could not possibly go, but to send the men and bring the chiefs on board.

The crew of the *Robert Campbell* were not lacking in physical courage, and the necessary force to man the yawl was easily made up. It was a little after noon when the yawl left the boat. There is no truth in the statements of Boiler and Larpenteur that the men were forced to go and clung to the side of the steamer until the mate threatened to cut off their fingers if they did not let go. It was easy enough for them to get out of going if they chose to. The crew of the yawl consisted of seven men. The steersman,, a gallant fellow of the name of Andy Stinger, sat in the stern. Two men of the names of O'Mally and Chris Sharky sat in the bow. There were four oarsmen, one of them a young man of the name of Martin, and the other, one of the Irishmen who had been

The two Indian agents profess in their reports not to have anticipated any trouble. Latta would hardly have ordered the yawl out if he had suspected what actually occurred. Reed, the Blackfoot agent, says that they "continued to hollow to us for some time, and showed great signs of friendship, and wanted us to come ashore." The sum of it all is that the two men who were officially in charge of the trip entirely failed to understand the gravity of the situation, which was thoroughly appreciated by those, like Culbertson and La Barge, who had had long experience with the Indians. The sending of the yawl and the consequences which followed must ever remain charged to the account of Samuel N. Latta, Indian Agent. whipped by "Yankee Jack," as related elsewhere. The yawl put off, and as the distance was very short, it quickly reached the opposite shore. It struck the beach head on and then swung around under the force of the current, so that it lay alongside of the bank.

A chief and three Indians were under the cut bank on the beach when the yawl arrived. One of the Indians stood exactly opposite Stinger, with a gun in his hand covered with a leather case. The other two Indians were armed with spears. The chief was a fierce-looking man, and it seemed as if his eye would pierce one through and through. Stinger motioned him to get into the yawl. The men meanwhile were sitting quietly with their oars across their laps. The chief gave some quick directions and in an instant the two Indians with spears jumped into the boat and the one with the gun stripped the leather case off. Stinger knew what this meant, and with great presence of mind instantly threw himself into the water on the river side of the boat, where it was fortunately four or five feet deep. Slipping up along the boat he seized it by the gunwale amidships and dragged it from the bank. The movement, however, quick as it was, was not quick enough. The two young bucks who had leaped into the boat thrust their spears into the bodies of two of the oarsmen, killing them instantly. A third was killed by the Indian with the gun, who had missed his chance at Stinger, and a fourth was severely wounded by an arrow from the bank. The two men in the bow instantly threw themselves into the bottom of the yawl.

The Indians had no time to carry the attack further. The crews of both the steamboats were watching with breathless anxiety the progress of events. When they saw Stinger jump into the water they thought him killed. Someone exclaimed, "There goes Andy," and instantly both boats responded with their entire armament. This included two howitzers on the hurricane deck of the *Robert Campbell* and one on the *Shreveport,* together with weapons of various sorts belonging to the passengers and crew. One rattle-brained Irishman was so upset that he brandished his revolver in the air, firing off into space without the slightest regard as to the whereabouts of the enemy. The fire, on the whole, was very effective. Numbers of the Indians were seen to fall, and Captain La Barge afterward learned through Pierre Garreau, the interpreter at Fort Berthold, that there were eighteen men and twenty horses killed and many wounded. The Indians soon withdrew, and in about an hour some were seen trying to get water for their wounded near a pile of driftwood half a mile below. It was an intensely sultry day. The howitzers were turned on them and they disappeared.

Returning to the yawl, we find that Andy Stinger, protected behind the gunwale, was steadily pulling the boat into the stream and swimming toward the sandbar as the current drifted him down. When about halfway across he called to the men to get up, while he himself climbed into the yawl, which was then rowed to the bank. The people on the two boats were so absorbed with the battle that no one thought of going to the assistance of the yawl crew. The wounded man and the two who were unharmed got out and walked up the beach. Stinger was thus left alone to drag the yawl and its mournful cargo up alongside the boat. This apparent neglect fired him to a desperate pitch, and he let go some powerful language to the mate and others of the crew. Captain La Barge presently came aft and looked into the yawl. He said not a word, but turned away shaking his head in a manner that showed plainly enough what was passing in his mind.

Such was the celebrated "affair at the Tobacco Garden." After the return to St. Louis Captain La Barge was talking to a friend about it when Andy Stinger happened to pass by. He said, loud enough for Andy to hear: "There goes the hero of the Tobacco Garden." The brave steersman treasured up these words as his proudest title during the rest of his life. Long years passed away before Captain La Barge heard from him again. He did not even know whether his old boatman was. still alive when, in the fall of 1896, thirty-three years after the massacre, he received a most cordial and affectionate letter from him, and two years later had the pleasure of meeting him again.

"KNOB VIEW, CRAWFORD, CO., MO.

Sept. 2, 1896.

"MY DEAR OLD CAPTAIN

"JOSEPH LA BARGE,

"*My Dear Friend:* I should like to hear from you whether you are still in the land of the living. Thank God for his mercies. Dear Captain I should be happy to be with you a few hours and have a good talk over the hardships of our past life steamboating, especially on the *Robert Campbell* in 1863 going to the mountains. It would give me great pleasure to see you and all your family once more. It is a great many years since I have heard anything from you. Please let me hear from you soon. My love and friendship to you and all your family. I remain your true friend until death. From the Hero of the Tobacco Garden on *Bob Campbell* in 1863.

"WM. ANDY STINGER.

"P. S. Address

" Wm. A. Stinger,

"Knob View, Crawford Co. Mo.

"Farewell Dear Captain. May God bless you all with health and strength."

Commenting upon the affair at the Tobacco Garden, Captain La Barge said:

"This event was one which could not have happened under ordinary circumstances. Master of both boat and cargo, I should never have permitted the yawl to go ashore. I was under orders of the agent in everything except the mere handling of the boat, and was bound to give him such opportunities to meet the Indians as he desired. I had gone to the extreme of my freedom of action when I refused to order a crew to go ashore for him, but could not well decline to let men volunteer. It was a lamentable affair, and one of the many crimes which must ever lie at the door of the Department of Indian Affairs in Washington. Here was an agent who gave every evidence of being corrupt and in collusion with the Fur Company, for he retained about a third of the annuities due the Indians and stored them in the Company's warehouse, from which they never reached the Indians except in exchange for robes, as in the case of private merchandise. Moreover, the agent was utterly ignorant of Indian character, full of the self-assurance which goes with ignorance, and not knowing himself what to do became the passive tool of the crafty and trained agents of the company."

There are numerous authorities upon the affair of the Tobacco Garden. The reports of both the agents Latta and Reed

About 3 P. M. the boats resumed their voyage, as the Indians had entirely disappeared. On the following morning the burial of the victims took place at a point about forty-seven miles above the Tobacco Garden. They were buried on an eminence on the south side of the river nearly opposite the mouth of Little Muddy Creek, and a cedar cross was planted at the head of their grave. The boat then pursued her way up the river and arrived at the mouth of the Yellowstone on the 8th of July. Here the Indians were seen again, and a few shots were fired by them at the boats, but no injury was done. describe it. Henry A. Boiler, in his "Among the Indians," describes it at length, as does Larpenteur in his "Forty Years a Fur Trader." The testimony of Captain La Barge and Andy Stinger, who in each other's presence related the matter to the author, is here produced for the first time.

In his edition of "Larpenteur's Journal," referred to above, p. 352, Dr. Elliott Coues makes the following statement: "I have offered in writing to Captain Joseph La Barge to print in this connection any statement concerning the affair that he might wish to make and would be willing to sign; but up to date of going to press have not heard from him."

The inference from this is that Captain La Barge could not controvert Larpenteur's statements, or he would have done so when the opportunity was given. This offer was sent to Captain La Barge through the author of the present work. The old gentleman retained in his old age the same spirit of haughty disdain for willful attempts to injure the reputation of others that characterized his whole life, and he indignantly refused to notice the matter. Time will set this right," he said. The truth

The herculean labors of Captain La Barge on this memorable voyage won the plaudits of all who observed them. He seemed to be everywhere present, and the only man on whom reliance could be placed. "We got to the mouth of the Yellowstone," says agent Reed, "after the most untiring efforts, especially on the part of Captain La Barge, who seemed to know the only channel to be found in the Missouri." The Captain was constantly exposed to danger, and personally conducted all soundings of the river, going far from the

195

boat with a few men in the yawl. The responsibility resting upon him was very great. The lives of the passengers, the safety of his valuable cargo, the danger from the Indians if their expected goods should be lost, and his own large pecuniary stake in the voyage, all rested upon his own shoulders. is that Charles Larpenteur, although very long in the Indian country, was never a man of high standing there, and proved a failure in whatever he undertook. Like all such men, he nursed the delusion that the world was in league against him, and he took advantage of the opportunity offered by the preparation of his memoirs to even matters up. Nearly everyone with whom he deals comes in for a round measure of abuse, until one is led to believe that Larpenteur was a saint, solitary and forlorn, wandering disconsolate among the children of Beelzebub. Larpenteur was probably an honest man in his business relations, but never an able man, and his attempts to account for the consequences of his own deficiencies by attributing them to the rascality of others, does not add to the value of his memoirs as historical material. Bad as the early population of that country was, it was not entirely composed of scoundrels.

CHAPTER XXVI.

THE BLACKFOOT ANNUITIES.

At the mouth of the Yellowstone the voyage of the *Robert Campbell* came abruptly to an end. There was only a depth of two feet over the Yellowstone bar, and it was a physical impossibility to proceed. The annuities had now been delivered to the lower tribes so far as Captain La Barge was concerned, but there still remained undelivered those going to the Crows, Assiniboines, and Blackfeet. The annuities for the first of these tribes were to be delivered wherever these Indians could be found, but those of the Blackfeet were to be delivered at Fort Benton. Fortunately, the Assiniboines came in while the boats were at the Yellowstone, and their annuities were delivered. Dr. Reed, the agent for the Blackfeet, then advised La Barge to abandon the idea of going further, and to store the goods at Fort Union until the following spring. This the Captain was very loath to do. He knew only too well the complications that might arise, particularly as such a course compelled him to place himself in any degree within the power of the American Fur Company. It seemed, however, the only thing to do. The *Robert Campbell* simply could not get any further. The *Shreveport* had not been able to get above Snake Point, and since that time the water had fallen materially. It was now the 8th of July, and no further rise could be expected; in fact no boats reached Benton that year. The only alternative to storing the goods was to haul them by wagon to their destination, and for this purpose the transportation could not be had. The Captain very reluctantly concluded to follow the agent's advice, particularly as the bulk of annuities were for the Indians belonging to his own agency. An arrangement was made with William Hodgkiss, agent of the American Fur Company, and five days were consumed in transferring the cargo to the warehouse. Full receipts were given by Agent Hodgkiss, and these were witnessed by Captain W. B. Greer, U. S. Army. In addition to the receipts the Captain secured from Agent Reed a written statement of the circumstances in order that his action might have the fullest explanation possible. In those days, when the government felt that it was being

This was the same man who served as clerk to Captain Bonneville in the latter's celebrated expeditions. He died March 15, 1864. robbed right and left by dishonest contractors, and every claim was looked upon with suspicion, the adjustment of any matter of that sort was extremely difficult, and the innocent were made to suffer with the guilty.

As soon as the business at Fort Union was cleared up the two boats turned their prows down the river and made the best of their way toward the lower country. When they arrived at Crow Creek, eighty-two miles below Pierre, they met General Sully, who was engaged in his expedition against the hostile Sioux. The General invited La Barge to his tent and told him he should have to impress one of the boats into his service for a time. As the *Shreveport* was much the lighter boat it was considered best to take her. Captain La Barge's brother, however, absolutely refused to remain, and accordingly Captain La Barge had to. It was also necessary to use military authority to secure a crew. The *Robert Campbell* then went on her way to St. Louis, and Captain La Barge commenced hauling supplies for General Sully. He went up as far as the mouth of the Little Cheyenne, and there awaited the result of General Sully's expedition, which was a victorious battle with the Indians. He then dropped down below old Fort Pierre, when he was ordered to proceed to Fort Leavenworth and report to General Easton. By that officer he was directed to take a cargo to Sioux City. Though late in the season, the trip was successfully accomplished. Captain La Barge then returned to St. Louis, where he arrived late in November, and reported to the commanding officer at that point. He had now been continuously at work for over six months, during one of the most trying seasons ever experienced upon the river. His nightly sleep scarcely averaged five hours, and he was constantly under the weight of a terrible responsibility. Nothing but an iron constitution could have withstood the incessant strain.

As soon as Captain La Barge could straighten matters up at home he set out for Washington to see the Indian Commissioner in regard to his past season's contract. He received full payment for everything delivered, but nothing for the annuities still undelivered and nothing for his great loss caused by the delay of the Indian Department in delivering the goods to him on time. He was, however, given a new contract to transport the goods to their destination the following year.

In order to pursue this particular subject to its final outcome we shall step ahead of our narrative to the year 1864. Captain La Barge went up the river that year with the steamer *Effie Deans,* leaving space on the boat for the undelivered annuities. Arrived at Fort Union he first fell in with Captain Greer, who had witnessed the receipt of Agent Hodgkiss for the goods the previous summer. Captain La Barge told him that he had come to take the annuities to their destination. "I don't believe that you will find much," said Captain Greer. "The Company has traded it nearly all for robes."

Agent Hodgkiss had died during the winter, and Captain La Barge presented the receipts to the new agent, Rolette. The latter refused to deliver the goods except upon payment of the extortionate storage charge of two thousand dollars. He expected that this charge would cause Captain La Barge to refuse to take the goods. The sum, however, was tendered, whereupon the agent refused to deliver them except upon the prior surrender of Agent Hodgkiss' receipts. Suspecting that a large part of the goods were missing, the Captain declined this condition, but offered to give a receipt for all goods he should take from the warehouse. Driven from every position, the agent openly avowed that he could not deliver all the goods, for he did not have them all. He stated that, under instructions from Commissioner Dole, transmitted through the Company, he had delivered a large portion of the goods to the Grosventres and many packages to other Indians. The delivery of the balance could, therefore, not be made except upon surrender of the receipts of the previous year. Captain La Barge asked to see the receipts of the Indians to whom the goods had been delivered. The agent had none, although it was an invariable rule to secure such receipts for all annuities delivered. The alleged order from Commissioner Dole was then called for, but that could not be produced, the agent stating that it came by messenger, who delivered it verbally.

"You acknowledge, then, that a large portion of these goods you have not got," asked Captain La Barge.

"Yes," replied the agent; "they have been delivered during the winter and have reached their proper destination."

All these proceedings were witnessed by the officer, Captain Greer, whom Captain La Barge had taken the precaution to have present. From what Captain Greer had told him, and from the trader's inability to account satisfactorily for the disposition of the goods, Captain La Barge became thoroughly convinced that they had been used in trade, and he very wisely declined to surrender his receipts. As the trader would not give up the rest of the goods except upon a surrender of the receipts for all, the Captain went on his way without them.

In the meanwhile Dr. Reed, who had been relieved as Agent of the Blackfoot tribes, went up on the American Fur Company boat *Yellowstone* to turn over his charge to the new agent, Mr. Gad E. Upson. Mr. Chouteau had received the contract for taking up the annuities for the year 1864. He took them only to Cow Island, where, for some reason, possibly low water, they were put on the shore and the boat turned back. Mr. Upson, who had gone down from Benton to Union early in the spring, went back on the *Yellowstone* with Mr. Reed. The boat, after unloading, turned back, and a day later met the *Effie Deans*. La Barge reported to Dr. Reed the facts as to the goods at Fort Union. Mr. Chouteau, who was on the *Yellowstone,* was called in and professed to disapprove of Rolette's course, but did nothing to rectify it. So far as Captain La Barge knew at the time or ever learned afterward, this large quantity of Indian goods was traded out to the Indians by the so-called American Fur Company and constituted an unqualified theft from the government. The final outcome of the affair, so far as Captain La Barge was concerned, was a loss of nearly twenty thousand dollars. He died a poor man, with the government in his debt by a sum that would have given ample comfort to his declining years.

Blackfoot annuities, 142,862 lbs., freight St. Louis to Fort Benton, at 11 cents per pound, $15,714.82' Crow annuities, 12,572 lbs., freight St. Louis to the mouth of Milk River, at 8 cents 1,005.76

Demurrage, 33 days at $300 per day,...9,900.00 Only payment ever received on this claim, Balance unpaid, $19,414.03.

CHAPTER XXVII.

COLLAPSE OF THE LA BARGE-HARKNESS OPPOSITION.

The steamboat *Shreveport*, with the annual outfit of the new firm for the year 1863, did not get above Cow Island on account of the extremely low stage of the river. No other boat went as far as that within two hundred miles. Harkness and John La Barge put the cargo out upon the bank and hastened back to the assistance of the *Robert Campbell*. This event further illustrated the incapacity of Harkness. No arrangement was made for the transportation of the goods to Benton, although he knew that a considerable portion of the freight belonged to outside parties, and that the firm had contracted to take it through to that post. This precipitate action was due in part to danger from the Indians. In the year 1863 the tribes along the river were all in a state of unrest, and some of them actually on the warpath against the whites. Fort Union was practically in a state of siege all summer, and the danger to steamboats was a very formidable one. It was held by some parties that the sudden termination of the voyage was due to news received of the famous discovery of the Alder Gulch placers and the desire to go back and notify the firm; but of this there is not the slightest probability. Whatever the explanation, the act itself was disastrous upon the fortunes of the firm.

Among the number of outside parties who had freight on the *Shreveport* was the firm of John J. Roe and Nicholas Wall, both of St. Louis. Wall represented the firm in Montana and Roe remained in St. Louis. Some little account of Wall's career and his previous relations with Captain La Barge will be of interest, to show how far a man may forfeit the sentiment of gratitude when his business interests are in any way involved. La Barge had previously been connected with Wall in a business way. In 1861 Wall joined the Confederate sympathizers, in St. Louis, and was captured by General Lyon in the affair of Camp Jackson, St. Louis, May 10, 1861. The prisoners taken there were all paroled, but were confined to the limits of the city. At Wall's urgent appeal La Barge became bondsman for his good conduct and secured his freedom of action. He worked for La Barge during the rest of the season of 1861.

In the winter of 1862 Wall asked La Barge to assist him in getting to Montana. La Barge gave free transportation on the *Emilie* to Fort Benton for himself and his goods, and advanced him seven hundred dollars to get to the mines. Wall did a successful business in the Deer Lodge Valley in 1862, and in the fall of that year returned to St. Louis, where he entered into a partnership with John J. Roe. The outfit which this firm were to send to the mines was taken up on the *Shreveport*. It was through La Barge's patronage that Nick Wall was extricated from a perilous situation and placed in a position to do a good business. His method of repaying his benefactor will presently appear.

When Wall heard that the *Shreveport* could not reach Benton and had discharged her cargo on the bank at Cow Island, he organized a wagon train and went down after his own freight and that of several others. In the spring of 1864 he returned to St. Louis, where he and Roe presented a claim to La Barge, Harkness & Co. for forty thousand dollars' damages, on goods that were not worth at the outside ten thousand dollars in St. Louis. Captain La Barge agreed to pay the full price of the goods and charge no freight, but his offer was refused. He then told Roe and Wall that they could bring suit at once. Roe replied that he was too sharp to think of bringing suit in St. Louis; he would bring it in Montana, where he knew that the chances were much more in his favor. Robert Campbell and John S. McCune, two of St. Louis' leading citizens, protested against this proceeding, and agreed to give bonds for the full payment of all damages. Roe refused all compromise and Wall returned to Montana and brought suit.

In the meanwhile, affairs at Fort La Barge were showing the effect of absence from that post of any responsible member of the firm. Joseph Picotte, brother of Honore Picotte, a distinguished trader of the American Fur Company, had been left in charge in 1862; but word having been received that he was not properly attending to his work, he was relieved by Robert H. Lemon, who had been highly recommended by Robert Campbell. Lemon proved to be of less account even than Picotte, and actually took the wholly unauthorized step of turning the firm's property over for safekeeping to the American Fur Company. The receipt for this transfer, signed by Andrew Dawson, agent American Fur Company, is still among the La Barge papers. The transaction took place August 31, 1863, and included not only the storage of all the firm's property at Fort La Barge, but the payment of their employees' wages, and the removal of the *Shreveport* freight from Cow Island to Fort Benton. The sum of one thousand dollars was to be paid for storage, and the goods were to be held as security for the payment of this sum and all other liabilities of the firm on account of wages, transportation, or other cause. Thus the entire business of the firm at Fort Benton was practically surrendered to their great rival, and the new "opposition" was crushed almost at its beginning.

As soon as Wall began legal proceedings the goods were seized and held, pending the outcome of the trial. This did not come off until 1865, when a verdict was rendered against La Barge, Harkness & Co. of twenty-four thousand dollars, which was paid in due course. All the firm's property in Montana was absolutely lost, including a large quantity of furs ruined by the long detention. The total loss amounted to fully one hundred thousand dollars.

The lawsuit itself was an important one at the time. It involved the rights and obligations of carriers on the Missouri River. It was the first important legal case in the history of the Territory. It brought into distinguished notice one of the picturesque and leading characters in the pioneer history of Montana, Colonel Wilbur F. Sanders, who became one of Montana's first representatives in the Senate of the United States. On the part of the defense the case was badly managed. None of the principals was present at the trial, which was held at a point nearly three thousand miles from their home. With a skillful defense it would probably not have resulted so disastrously as it did.

The immediate result of the trial was the dissolution of the firm of La Barge, Harkness & Co. It went out of business upon an honorable footing. Every liability was paid in full, but so much of it fell upon Captain La Barge that it seriously impaired his fortune. He cherished, not without reason, a very bitter feeling toward some of the parties who were instrumental in the downfall of his business, and particularly toward the American Fur Company. There is no doubt that that concern furthered the result in every possible way. It was a principle of their business to crush all opposition, and they made no exception in this case. But it is evident that the real cause lay in the reckless management of affairs at Fort Benton and at the mines, and for this Harkness was alone responsible.

The collapse of the La Barge, Harkness & Co. business marked the inception of a system of land transportation in Montana which grew to enormous proportions. It was known as the Diamond R <R> Company. Among the ill-gotten gains of John J. Roe, in his successful effort to break up a rival company, were a large number of oxen which La Barge, Harkness & Co. had brought up the river to transport freight between Fort Benton and the mines. Roe organized a transportation company, using these oxen as a nucleus for commencing the business. By various changes of ownership it passed into the hands of Montana men. It soon became a great company, with a complete organization of agents, issuing its bills of lading to all points, both in and out of the Territory. At one time it employed no less than twelve hundred oxen and four hundred mules, besides a large number of horses, and the sustenance of these animals was a source of no slight income to the small farmers of that section. It went out of business in 1883.

CHAPTER XXVIII.

CAPTAIN LA BARGE IN MONTANA.

Captain La Barge sold the *Emilie* late in the winter of 1862-63. the following winter he made an unexpected sale of the *Shreveport*. Henry Ames & Co., pork packers, sent their clerk one day to see if the Captain would sell the boat. He replied that he did not care to, but would if the price were satisfactory. Being invited to come to the office of the firm, he was told that the boat suited them and was asked to name a price.

"Twenty-five thousand dollars," he said.

"Give the Captain a check for twenty-five thousand dollars," said Ames, turning to his clerk.

"Don't you want a bill of sale and the customary evidence that she is clear of debt?" asked the Captain, in some surprise.

"No," was the reply; "you say she is so, and I will take your word."

La Barge went down to the levee, transferred the boat, and then went to the bank and cashed the check. He recalled this last circumstance by the fact that the teller handed him the amount in twenty-five notes, each of one thousand dollars.

This sale took place in the winter, and it behooved the Captain to cast about at once for a boat for the next annual voyage. A new boat was being built on the Ohio River by the Keokuk Packet Company, John S. McCune, President. Not proving satisfactory for their purposes, she was brought to St. Louis and offered for sale. La Barge found her well fitted for his work, and negotiated a purchase at forty thousand dollars. McCune retained a one-fourth interest. She was called the *Effie Deans*.

The boat was loaded with the usual assortment of freight, and left St. Louis March 22, 1864, with forty-nine passengers and a cargo of 160 tons. She succeeded in getting only to the Marias River, where the cargo was discharged. The boat was sent back in charge of John La Barge, and the Captain himself remained in the upper country. He hired wagons and took his property up the river, selling part of it in Benton and the rest in Virginia City. He remained in the mining regions upward of two months, although he finished his business in much less time. On account of the danger from outlaws, or road agents, it was necessary to await an exceptionally good opportunity for getting away. The Captain had decided to return *via* Salt Lake City, because to go by way of the Missouri in an open boat would have meant little less than suicide. The feeling of the Indians was so bitter at this time that no one could pass their country in safety unless well protected.

The Captain had almost a hundred thousand dollars in gold dust to take with him, and he knew that this was not a secret with himself. He caused it to be given out that he expected to depart on a certain day, but actually stole away several days before, and was safely in Salt Lake City before the announced date of his departure. The coach he was to have taken was held up by the road agents and a passenger of the name of Hughes was killed.

In Salt Lake City Captain La Barge remained for some time arranging for the rest of his journey home. He could not hire a coach from Ben Holiday, proprietor of the overland line, for less than eighteen hundred dollars. The Wells-Fargo Express Company wanted twenty-five hundred dollars to send the dust by way of San Francisco, and would assume no responsibility. These conditions were not satisfactory, and the Captain purchased a team and wagon, with which he and three or four others undertook the journey alone. Their gold dust was carried in bags of thick buckskin.

While in Salt Lake City the Captain renewed his acquaintance with Brigham Young and other Mormons whom he had known on the Missouri. An old friend of his of the name of Hooper, who had turned Mormon, and later became a delegate from the Territory to Congress, called as soon as he heard that La Barge was in town. He also found there another friend, Hopkins by name, whom he had known from boyhood. Hopkins tried his best to induce La Barge to join the Mormons. He assured the Captain that if he would sell out in St. Louis and come to Utah it would be his fortune. As proof of this, he referred to himself and others, who, he said, had gone into Mormonism, not for any love of the doctrine, but as a simple business proposition. Hooper and Hopkins had both been unsuccessful in St. Louis. La Barge had taken them up on his boat to Fort Kearney, about 1852, and had always esteemed them good men. He asked the wife of one of them one day why her husband had never married again, since the doctrine of the Church and the sentiment of the community sanctioned it. "He doesn't dare to; he knows *I* would leave him if he did," she replied.

The Captain called on Young several times. That dignitary received him very hospitably, took him to the Tabernacle and other places of interest, and presented him to several of his families. They went to the theater together, where they sat in a box with Young's favorite wife, the other wives being ranged in seats below. Young never said anything intended to convert La Barge to his religion. Other members of the Church did, and particularly Orson Hyde, who was a man of education and a very persuasive talker. La Barge heard a sermon by Heber Kimball—a rough old fellow who took off his coat, rolled up his sleeves, and waded in. His language was coarse and vulgar, and would not bear repetition in refined ears.

The route of the Captain's party, on leaving Salt Lake City, was through Weber Canon to Fort Bridger. They stopped there a short time with Captain' Carter, who, for many years, did business at that frontier post. From there they made their way east, and left the mountain country *via* the valley of the Cache a la Poudre River. In the valley of the South Platte they met an old man of the name of Geary, who told them that a band of hostile Indians was scouring the country between them and Denver, and that they had better conceal themselves for a few days on an island in the Platte River. They acted upon this advice, and when they judged the danger to be past they resumed their journey. They had gone but a little way when they came to a spot where a party of emigrants had been massacred only a day or two before. Their timely measure of precaution was therefore well taken.

The rest of the journey was made without noteworthy incident. The party reached the Missouri at Nebraska City just in time to catch the last boat to St. Louis. They arrived home about December i. Captain La Barge found that the *Effie Deans* had returned and had been chartered by McCune's company to go to Montgomery, Ala. She made this trip in safety, returning to St. Louis before ice closed in. Probably no other boat ever made so long a trip on inland waters in a single season, including also a sea voyage, as did the *Effie Deans* in 1864. The distance on the Missouri up and back was 4570 miles; that on the Mississippi to the Gulf and back was 2522 miles; that from Mobile to Montgomery and back was 676 miles; and that across the Gulf from the mouth of the Mississippi to Mobile and back not less than 600 miles. The whole distance traveled was about 8400 miles.

In April, 1865, Captain La Barge started up the river again on the *Effie Deans*. At Nebraska City came the news of Lee's surrender, and at Decatur that of the assassination of Lincoln. There was great commotion among the passengers at the news of this terrible deed. There were many ex-Confederates on board, some of whom expressed their satisfaction at the event, and there might very easily have been trouble between them and the Union passengers; but Captain La Barge skillfully avoided all difficulty.

The voyage, though a tedious one, was completed without serious delay or accident. Captain La Barge sent the boat back in charge of the pilot, Captain Ray, and himself started with another outfit of goods for the mines. This time he went to Helena, which had sprung into existence since his last trip to Montana. He bought a small house in which to store his goods and he and his son acted as salesmen.

In the meanwhile Captain La Barge's brother had again involved St. Louis parties in serious difficulty on account of the non-delivery of freight. John S. McCune had shipped to Fort Benton a fine cargo of goods on the *Kate Kearney,* Captain John La Barge, master. The very hostile attitude of the Indians caused the Captain to abandon the trip a little above Fort Union. When the news reached the mines suits were brought against McCune aggregating some three hundred thousand dollars. As soon as word reached St. Louis, McCune saw the gravity of the situation, and instantly dispatched a message to La Barge in Montana *via* the overland route. It fortunately reached the Captain before he had finished his business in Helena, and he set out forthwith for Fort Benton, leaving his son in charge of the store. He felt certain that Captain Ray, the pilot of the *Effie Deans*, would not abandon the cargo, and he was not mistaken. When Ray met the *Kate Kearney*, on his return trip, he transferred the cargo to the *Effie Deans*, and brought it back to Fort Galpin, a little above the mouth of Milk River, but could get no further on account of low water. He then sent an express to Fort Benton for teams. Captain La Barge was there at the time, and at once procured thirty ox teams of five yoke each, with the necessary wagons, and started for Fort Galpin. There he took all the freight and delivered it safely at its destination. It was a prodigious task, but its timely completion saved McCune from a disastrous loss. The suits were all withdrawn, and the cost of transportation by wagon was the sum of the extra expense.

La Barge left the Territory late in the season with fifty thousand dollars in gold dust. He went by way of Salt Lake City, where he and two others chartered a coach to take them through to Nebraska City. When within about fifty miles of Denver the stage driver refused to go farther on account of the Indians, and the party were compelled to hire a wagon and go the rest of the way alone. At Nebraska City they found the steamboat *Denver*, on which they went to St. Joseph, and thence by the railroad to St. Louis.

Captain La Barge had not been heard from in two months. He at once went to McCune's office to relieve the fears under which that gentleman had so long been laboring. McCune came up to him, looked the travel-worn Captain in the face, and said: "I don't dare to ask you any questions. I am afraid to know the worst."

"Don't be alarmed," said La Barge; "I think I have straightened everything out all right."

"Are there no suits pending?" asked McCune.

"No; they are all settled, and here are the receipts."

"How much has the misadventure cost me?"

"Not to exceed ten thousand dollars all told." McCune was overjoyed at the news, for he feared that he was ruined. As it was, in spite of the extra expense, he would reap a handsome profit. He threw his arms around La Barge and embraced him for joy at the unexpected deliverance, and could never thereafter do enough for him.

IN connection with his work for the government it became necessary for Captain La Barge to make several visits to Washington. Considering the interesting period through which the national Capital was then passing, it was to be expected that these visits should present some features of note. The Captain went to Washington in all three times, once in each of the winters of 1862-65.

On the occasion of his first visit he was a member of a party who called upon the President to present him with a fine robe of fur. Three years before this Captain La Barge had promised Lincoln to procure for him a good buffalo robe; but the rapid march of events and the great matters that weighed upon the public mind had so far kept him from fulfilling his promise. On the present occasion it was proposed to give the President an elegant robe composed of ten beaver skins, the whole richly lined and embroidered.

The members of the party were Dr. Walter A. Burleigh of Yankton, Dak.; Captain La Barge, Charles E. Galpin, and several others. Dr. Burleigh acted as spokesman. The delegation were shown to a room apart from the general reception room, and Lincoln, after a little while, came in, saying that he had sent them in there so that he might have some uninterrupted talk with them about the West. He remembered at once the old steamboat Captain with whom he had ridden on the Missouri, and he greeted La Barge with great cordiality. After some general conversation Dr. Burleigh arose, took the robe, asked the President to stand up, and then threw it over his shoulders. Lincoln folded it around him like a blanket and danced about for an instant in Indian fashion. He seemed greatly delighted with the gift. He then asked the party many questions about the West, for the Indian troubles were at that time causing the administration a great deal of annoyance.

Galpin's mission to Washington was to secure reimbursement of a ransom which he had paid for the liberation of a white female prisoner, who had been captured the year before at the time of the Minnesota massacres. Galpin had been sent by La Barge from Fort La Framboise to rescue the prisoner, and had been compelled to pay fifteen hundred dollars. Captain La Barge took her down in his boat to Sioux City, whence she was sent home. He had Galpin go with him to Washington to assist in presenting the matter to the Bureau of Indian Affairs. The ransom money was reimbursed in full.

In the winter of 1863-64 La Barge saw the President again. The only subject of importance which was touched upon on that occasion was the Indian, in whose welfare he always displayed the deepest interest. As it was a subject which had often aroused the Captain's indignation and pity, he made the most of his opportunity to acquaint the President with the facts. He told him of the gross frauds practiced on the Indians, and how their annuities, under present conditions, had to pass through the hands of some of the worst rascals on the face of the earth, who deliberately cheated the Indians right and left. Lincoln replied that he knew it; that, under the stress of war, he was not able to send just the men he would like to into that country as Indian agents, and that too many of them were importunate place-seekers of worthless character whom members of Congress were anxious to get rid of somewhere. "But wait," said he, "until I get this Rebellion off my hands, and I will take up this question and see that justice is done the Indian."

The Captain made his third visit to Washington in the winter of 1864-65. His particular business was to secure payment on his government contracts, which had been approved by the Department of War and the Bureau of Indian Affairs, but disallowed by the Treasury. He went to Secretary Chase, but was told by that gentleman that all Missourians were *prima facie* Rebels, and that that was why his account was being held up. La Barge did not relish this very much, as he had been doing business for the government all through the war, and had even gone so far as to take the oath of allegiance. He went to Lincoln and laid the matter before him. The President smiled at Chase's remark, gave La Barge a card with his autograph on it to hand to Chase, and. said he presumed that would fix matters all right. La Barge went back, and the account was paid without further delay. La Barge, with his usual distrust of the American Fur Company, suspected that some of its members had been giving him a bad character in Washington in order further to cripple his opposition.

On the occasion of his interview with the President he brought up the matter of the Blackfoot annuities, explicitly charging that these goods had been wrongfully disposed of and had not reached their proper destination. Lincoln sent for the proper officer of the Indian Department to hear La Barge's accusation. This officer stated that he had receipts signed by the Indian chiefs saying that they had received their annuities. The signatures of the Indians were witnessed by agents of the American Fur Company. La Barge declared that the receipts were false; that he had himself carried these goods and knew that the Indians had not received them, but that they had been appropriated by the American Fur Company and sold. "Well," said the official, "there are the receipts; we cannot go back of them; they have been considered final evidence in such cases since the foundation of the government." And there the matter rested.

While in Washington on this visit La Barge was summoned before the Senate Committee on Pacific railroads and questioned by B. Gratz Brown upon his knowledge of the Western country and his opinion upon the availability of certain routes for a transcontinental line.

Before he left Washington the Captain was the central figure in an amusing little incident that occurred at Ford's Theater. *Harper's Weekly* had published a story of La Barge's steamboating experiences which ran something like this: On one of his trips up the river in the earlier part of his career there were several Englishmen aboard. They had a map and applied themselves industriously for the first day or two in trying to identify the various places upon it with those along their route. They were in the pilot-house a good deal, and one of them questioned La Barge rather officiously about the geography of the country. LOOK AT YOUR MAP.345,

"What place is this that we are approaching, Mr. Pilot?" he asked.

"St. Charles, sir," La Barge replied.

"You are mistaken, sir; according to the map it

La Barge made no reply. He stopped as usual at St. Charles and then went on his way. Presently they came to another village.

"What place, Captain?" inquired the Englishman.

"Washington, Mo., sir."

"Wrong again. The map gives this place as."

This experience was gone through several times, the Captain's temper becoming more ruffled with each repetition, though no one would have suspected it from his unruffled exterior. Presently a flock of wild geese passed over the river and drew the attention of the passengers and crew. The Englishmen were standing on the hurricane roof immediately in front of the pilot-house.

"What kind of birds are those, Captain?" asked one of them in eager haste.

The Captain, whose language still smacked somewhat of the French idiom, replied:

"Look at your map; he tell you."

The printed programme of the evening at the theater happened to have this story under the heading of "Old Joe La Barge." The Captain and some friends occupied a box, and as there were several persons in the audience who knew him, the fact that the hero of the story was in the box soon spread itself about. At one of the pauses in the performance someone called out for La Barge to stand up, and cries of "La Barge" soon came from all parts of the house. The modest steamboat pilot was panic-stricken at the occurrence and clung desperately to his seat, whereupon the audience called for him the more; but nothing would induce him to stir.

We may here properly refer to Captain La Barge's extensive acquaintance with public men of the West. His prominence in the carrying trade of Western rivers, when travel was largely done by boat, brought him into contact with distinguished characters from all parts of the country. There were few public men in the West whom he did not know, and his personal estimate of their character as they appeared to him is not without interest and value. We have already noted his acquaintance with Audubon, General Warren, Dr. Hayden, Brigham Young, and others.

The Captain knew General Lee when the latter was stationed in St. Louis as an officer of engineers in charge of river and harbor works on the Mississippi and the Missouri rivers.

He knew both of the Johnstons,—Albert Sidney and Joseph E.,— and at the time of the Mormon War transported much of the supplies and munitions of war used by Albert Sidney Johnston on his arduous and perilous campaign.

He saw Grant for the first time during the Mexican War, and frequently in later years when he lived near St. Louis. In Grant's visits to town La Barge became well acquainted with him. He saw him in the early part of the war, while Fremont was in command at St. Louis. He was trying to get an interview with the General, but that officer was harder to reach than a king or the Pope. He would keep people waiting for hours, and then as like as not refuse them an audience. In the winter of 1864-65 La Barge saw Grant in Washington. The head of the armies of the Union spoke to the steamboat pilot in as equal and friendly a way as when he was unloading wood in St. Louis. He asked the Captain if there was anything that he could do for him, and expressed his desire to serve him if he could.

La Barge saw a great deal at one time and another of General Fremont. He first met him when he went up the river as the assistant to the distinguished geographer and scientist, Jean I. Nicollet. Nicollet's party traveled on the boat which La Barge was piloting. At Leavenworth there was an extremely rapid current, and La Barge expressed a curiosity to know what its velocity was. Nicollet at once sent Fremont to measure it. It was found to be eleven miles per hour in the swiftest place. La Barge's opinion of Fremont was that which seems to have universally prevailed in St. Louis—that he was a greatly overrated man, and that his success was due more to his fortunate marriage [to Jessie Benton] than to his own merit. We must dissent, in a measure, from this view. In his proper niche, Fremont was a great man. He found that niche in the work of exploring the unknown West. In the faculty of making the unknown known, of doing work in such a way as to make its results popular with the public, in spreading. a knowledge of the Great West throughout his country and throughout the world, he stood without a peer among the explorers of that region. In the broader field of national politics or great military responsibility, he was wading beyond his depth.

Thomas H. Benton, Fremont's father-in-law, and Missouri's greatest statesman, was an intimate acquaintance of Captain La Barge, the two men having known each other from La Barge's childhood until Benton's death. Captain La Barge had a great admiration for the bluff old Senator, although he did not like the way in which he used his powerful influence in shielding the American Fur Company on so many occasions from the just consequences of their illegal acts. Benton was a frequent passenger on the Missouri River boats, and La Barge saw a great deal of him there. He recalled particularly a trip which the Senator made as far up as Kansas City, where he went to meet Fremont, who was returning from the West. It was a very interesting voyage. The people all along the river wanted to see him, and calls for "Old Bullion" compelled him to appear at every landing place. He made numerous addresses, and the boat was frequently delayed to permit this interchange of greetings between the people and their distinguished servant. Benton was in the pilot-house a great deal,— as every traveler in those days liked to be,—and La Barge never forgot his expression of deep faith in the future of the West, so unlike that of most of his Congressional associates from east of the Mississippi. He said once to Captain La Barge: "You will live to see railroads across to the Pacific, and up the Missouri beyond the Great Falls." La Barge, a much younger man, replied that he scarcely expected to see that in his lifetime. "But I have," said the Captain, in telling of this conversation, "and I have seen far more than even Senator Benton dared to hope for." In the same line of thought the Senator once said, as he pointed to the west, which was overspread with the marvelous glow of evening: "That is the East"—for he felt that we should yet go in that direction to reach the treasures of the Orient.

The interesting notes of Captain La Barge's observations of public men with whom he was thrown in contact would fill a volume. His acquaintance with the army was very extensive, owing to the Indian wars along the Missouri, and he personally knew nearly all the principal officers from General Sherman down. The same was true of the Indian agents, Territorial officers, and leading business men of the West. In a time when so much public travel went by steamboat he enjoyed exceptional opportunities of seeing and knowing the men who made the history of the Western country.

CHAPTER XXX.
THE INDIANS OF THE MISSOURI VALLEY.

The course of this narrative has shown that a large portion of the business of the Missouri River steamboats pertained to the Indians who dwelt on the banks of that stream. The great valley had been their home for unknown generations. The tribes were distributed along its course or those of its tributaries, from its mouth to their sources. First came the Missouris, whose name the river still bears— a tribe long since extinct as a separate organization. The Osages and the Kansas likewise bequeathed their names to the rivers in whose valleys they dwelt. The Omahas have lived, since the white man knew them, a short distance above the city which perpetuates their name, while a hundred miles to the westward in the valley of the Loup Fork of the Platte dwelt the four tribes of the Pawnees. From the point where Sioux City now stands, northward nearly to the British line, the great nation of the Sioux held a wide tract of country on both sides of the river. Within their territory dwelt the treacherous Aricaras, near the mouth of the Grand River, and the stalwart Cheyennes at the eastern base of the Black Hills. The unhappy tribe of the Mandans lived near the river some distance north of the modern town of Bismarck, and near them were the Minnetarees, or Grosventres of the Missouri. Along the northern shore of the river from the Mandans to Milk River, and northward far into British territory, roamed the numerous bands of the Assiniboines, one of the most populous of the plains tribes. From Milk River to the sources of the Missouri was the land of the hostile Blackfeet, where dwelt the Piegan, Blood, and Blackfoot bands and the Grosventres of the Prairies. Finally, in the valley of the Yellowstone and its great tributary the Bighorn, was Absaroka, the home of the proud tribe of the Crows.

All of these tribes gravitated toward the great watercourses, as man, in every stage of his history has done. It was not in this case the use of the stream as a transportation route that made it attractive. The Missouri Valley tribes, unlike those of the Great Lakes, or the Coast, or the northern rivers, were not good navigators. The stream was a treacherous one, and its shores did not yield a timber suitable to the crude workmanship of the Indian. Skin boats were used to a limited extent, but as a rule the horse and -not the boat was the means of travel and transportation. The great importance of the river arose from other considerations. In a region where streams are scarce and where most of them dry up in the summer, this river furnished a never-failing supply of as healthy a drinking water as flows on the surface of the globe. Then its valley was the only timbered region of consequence for hundreds of miles on either side. Groves of cottonwood, walnut, cedar, and willow lined its banks, and the Indian here found all the wood that his simple order of life required. The abundant groves along the bottoms gave splendid shelter from the heat of summer and the cold of winter.

The entire watershed of the river was thus originally occupied by Indians. Considering its extensive area, their numbers were very few—scarcely one to ten square miles. But as they mostly dwelt near the rivers, the country seemed to the early navigators more densely populated than it really was. Into this primeval domain there came, more than two centuries ago, strange visitors who never went away. They were welcomed at first; but every foot of ground they gained was held, farther and farther up the river to its source among the mountains, thence to the River of the West, and down its rugged valleys to the western sea. It was a sad day to the tribes of the Missouri Valley, as to every other, when the white man came, but a far sadder day when the emigrant and settler came. Between these two epochs there was a long interval in which the paleface and his red brother lived in comparative harmony together. It was the era of the trader. Under the fur-trade regime the Indian might have continued his native mode of life indefinitely. The trader never sought to change it. He introduced but few innovations; had no desire to introduce any; and looked with as jealous an eye as the Indian himself upon the approach of civilization. This relation of the two races was ideal, and during its continuance the Indian is seen at his best.

All this was changed when the emigrant came. The traders were few in number and made no permanent settlements. The emigrants came by the thousand and spread themselves all over the country. They made roads, discovered rich mines, laid out cities, and declared their purpose to send the "fire-horse" across the plains, as they had sent the "fire canoe" up the great river. Before this ever-increasing host the game wasted away. It was estimated that in the single year 1853 four hundred thousand buffalo were slain. As the buffalo was the very life of the plains tribes, its extermination meant inevitable starvation or hopeless dependence upon the government.

All this the Indian foresaw with unerring vision, and it affected him just as it would any other independent people. A state of unrest ensued. Depredations and outrages occurred—for the Indian understood no other way of expressing his displeasure,— and the government was forced to interfere. The era of the fur trade came to an end, and that of the treaty, the agent, and the annuity, began—an era whose history will bring the blush of shame to its readers to the latest generations. And yet it would be wholly unjust to charge the flagrant wrongs which followed to this or that particular cause. History will exonerate the government from any but the purest motives in its dealings with the Indians. It may have been unwise in some of its measures; it was certainly weak in carrying its purposes into effect; but it always sought, with the light it possessed, the highest good of the Indian. The problem, unfortunately, was beyond human wisdom to solve. The ablest minds of this country and century have grappled with it in vain. It was the problem of how to commit a great wrong without doing any wrong—how to deprive the Indian of his birthright in such a way that he should feel that no injustice had been done him. It was the decree of destiny that the European should displace the native American upon his own soil. No earthly power could prevent it. *This* was the wrong; all else was purely incidental; and whatever consideration or generosity might attend the details of the change, nothing could alter the stern and fundamental fact.

With this impossible problem our law-givers wrestled for a century in vain. They sought to deal with the Indian on a basis of political equality, where such equality did not and could not exist. The treaty system was the outgrowth of this attempt. Perhaps it was impossible to deal with the Indians except by treaty, but it is difficult at this day to see the wisdom of that method. It only deferred the inevitable. It made promises which, in the nature of things, could not be kept. Made to be broken, they served no other purpose than to lull the natives into temporary quiet while the paleface was fastening his grip ever more tightly upon their country. It was throughout a policy of insincerity; the fostering of a spirit of independent sovereignty when in fact the tribes were only vassals. Like all insincerity, it bred endless wrong. The loss of his lands would not have been so bad to him if he had understood it from the start; but as it was, he had not only to bear this loss, but the ever-increasing evidence of the white man's bad faith; and he thus came to hate the whites and distrust their government.

This, if we were to venture a criticism, has been the government's one great mistake in dealing with the Indians. A firm attitude of authority toward the tribes, with an unqualified claim to sovereignty of the soil, and an assertion of the right to reduce it and them to a condition of ultimate civilization, would have eliminated the element of bad faith which has always characterized the treaty system. But instead of this the government continued to foster to the last the notion of tribal sovereignty over the lands of the West. Under the farce of obtaining these lands by treaty it saved itself from the charge of wresting them by force from the Indian. It was a distinction without a difference, and in its effort to save its honor in one direction, it hopelessly sacrificed it in another.

—"What consideration will induce you to give up war and remain at peace?" is the hypothetical question of a certain Indian agent to a tribe of the Sioux in 1867. And the hypothetical answer, based upon his many talks with them, was this: "Stop the white man from traveling across our lands; give us the country which is ours by right of conquest and inheritance, to live in and enjoy unmolested by his encroachments, and we will be at peace with all the world."

—Gruff old General Harney had his own views upon this treaty business. When Commissioner Cummings came down the river from the council with the Blackfeet, and, having lost his mules at Fort Pierre, besought the General to give him some others to complete his journey with, the General replied: " Yes, Colonel, I have plenty of mules, but you can't have one; and I only regret that when the Indians got your mules they didn't get your scalp also. Here all summer I and my men have suffered and boiled to chastise these wretches, while you have been patching up another of your sham treaties to be broken to-morrow and give us more work."

—"It is beyond question that such a system of treaty-making is, of all others, the most unpolitic, whether negotiated with savage or civilized peoples, and aside from its effect in encouraging and stimulating breaches of treaties of peace, is always attended with fraud upon the government and upon the Indian."—*General John Pope, Report of August 3, 1864.*

—"Send me one man who will tell the truth and I will talk with him," was the laconic reply of a celebrated chief who had been asked to meet a government commission in council.

The first general treaty with the tribes of the upper Missouri was held at Fort Laramie in September, 1851. It included nearly every tribe in the valley from the Omahas up, except the Blackfeet. The Indians came from far and near and pitched their separate camps on the council ground. Tribes that had never met before here made each other's acquaintance. Others, who had met only on the battlefield, encamped side by side in peace. The government was represented by men of experience and dignity. In particular, Superintendent D. D. Mitchell and Father P. J. De Smet were men in whom the Indians felt the most implicit trust. The council was convened for the purpose of coming to some understanding among the tribes themselves and between them and the whites as to their immediate future relations. It was hoped to put an end to inter-tribal wars and to outrages upon the emigrants, and to secure the right of way for roads and railroads across the Indian lands. The several tribes showed the greatest interest in the work of the council. The deliberations were conducted with solemnity and evident sincerity on both sides. The presents from the government were munificent and well chosen, and were received with deep satisfaction. When the work of the council was completed, the tribes bade each other farewell, and departed for their several homes with every appearance of mutual trust and friendship. To all outward appearances the council had been a complete success. Treaties were made with all the tribes present. The gifts received were to be in full compensation for all previous losses caused by the white man, and the Indians were to receive goods annually to the aggregate amount of fifty thousand dollars. The treaties, as amended in Washington, were to remain in force for fifteen years. Four years later a similar treaty was made near Fort Benton with the several bands of the Blackfeet by a commission consisting of Governor I. I. Stevens and Alfred Cummings, Superintendent of Indian Affairs.

It was thus that the annuity system came into extensive vogue among the tribes of the upper Missouri. It probably gave rise to more abuses than any other one thing in the conduct of Indian affairs. The temptations for fraud were as great as the opportunities for its commission were numerous and excellent, and it required more than average public virtue to resist them. The Indian could not go to the market and help select his goods; he had no hand in awarding the contracts for their transportation to his country; nor any means of seeing that he received what he was entitled to. His only function was to accept what the agent saw fit to give him. During the Civil War, when the currency depreciated to such an enormous extent, the annuities shrank in quantity as prices went up, and the Indian was a heavy loser from causes that he could not comprehend. The annuities were always sent up the river in the boats of the traders, generally in those of the American Fur Company. The agents were given no escort and no separate residence or warehouse, and were compelled to throw themselves upon the hospitality of the traders. In this way the annuity goods became mixed with those of the traders, and the Indian paid in furs for what he was entitled to as a free gift. This abuse was a grave one and very difficult to correct, for all that the Department required in evidence of the delivery was the signature of the chiefs, witnessed in the usual manner. It is easy to see how wide open the door was in this business for the commission of almost unlimited fraud.

It is doubtful if, during the period from 1850 to 1870, the Indian tribes along the Missouri River received more than half the bounty which was promised them by the government.

"*The government appropriations are supposed to be liberal; but it so happens that by the time they reach their destination, they have, and not mysteriously either, dwindled down into a paltry present.*"—Henry A. Boiler, in "Among the Indians."

"*This system of issuing annuity goods is one grand humbug.*" —Report of Gen. Alfred Sully, August 18, 1864.

In the early days of the Republic the conduct of Indian affairs was in the hands of the military authorities, and it has always been a mooted question whether it ought not to have remained there. The verdict of history will undoubtedly be that it should. The spoils system came into absolute control of the agencies, and fitness and experience received scant consideration. There was more or less friction between the agents and the military, for the latter always had to be called in when the former could no longer control their flocks. But the greatest defect of the system was the total absence of anything like a fixed and recognized procedure. The annual reports of the agents show how utterly lacking in all the elements of practical business was their haphazard management. Every new agent felt called upon, as a necessary preliminary to his own work, to criticise the conduct of his predecessor. He put forth new schemes and tried new experiments, until finally he himself made way for a successor who in turn deplored the failures of those who had gone before him.

Probably the majority of the agents were men of average integrity, but there were many who sought the business solely for "what there was in it." The whole atmosphere of the Indian trade was so against an honest conduct of the business that an agent who should undertake to enforce strict integrity in his official work was regarded as a fit subject for an asylum of the feeble-minded. At one time the experiment was tried of appointing only clergymen to the agencies. But the scheme was a visionary one. What these agents made up in honesty they lacked in experience, and were pliant tools in the hands of the shrewd trader. Their saintly character, moreover, was not always a sure panoply against the attacks of worldly temptation. To more than one of them, in the words of Captain La Barge, "a dollar looked bigger than a cart wheel," and they, like the rest, learned how to connive at the crookedness of the traders. But whatever their virtues or intentions, they were powerless to accomplish any good work. The fault was in the system, which was inherently vicious, and mere honesty in the individual could not eliminate its defects.

The actual results of the treaty-annuity-agency system in the conduct of Indian affairs are now matters of history. No treaty that it was possible to devise could stand. The encroachment of settlement continually increased. It led to resistance on the part of the Indians, and resistance to chastisement and to new treaties, and these invariably to loss of territory and abridgment of rights. At last it led to war, and the final transition of nearly all the tribes to their present situation was accompanied by scenes of blood.

It is not possible to follow here the intricate pathway of the treaty system through the quarter century after 1850, for it is a long story. There were treaty after treaty, commission after commission, and a constant exercise of its best offices on the part of the government to reach some satisfactory result; but in vain. The life of a people, like that of an individual, cannot be extinguished without a struggle. Whether in this case the inevitable struggle was intensified by the procrastinating policy of the government may be an open question. It probably was, for it was preceded by years of bad faith, broken pledges, and cruel wrongs, until the hearts of this unhappy people were embittered, and they drew the sword in a spirit of hatred and revenge.

Throughout the painful annals of the river tribes during the past century there was no more attractive feature of their relations with the whites than the means of transportation by which the paleface came to their country. The keelboat and the steamboat are a part of their life history. The steamboat in particular came to be what the buffalo had been—their principal resource for the necessities of life. It was a difficult role that it had to fill. To the Indian it was friend and foe, truth and falsehood, honor and shame, alike. It brought the early traders with their welcome merchandise, and alas! with their liquor and the smallpox. It brought the Commissioners to make treaties, and the annuities which those treaties guaranteed. It brought the Indian agent and the evils that followed in his train, and finally it brought the sword. When the Indian at last gave up the fight he and the steamboat abandoned the river together, and both are now strangers where once they made the entire valley teem with life.

CHAPTER XXXI.
THE ARMY ON THE MISSOURI.

The role which the army was called upon to fill in the history of our Indian affairs was a most unpleasant one. It began while the proud spirit of the tribes was as yet unbroken, but had been aroused by ever-increasing aggression to the point of active resistance. It then became necessary to subdue them by force to absolute subordination to the government, and to remove them from their larger hunting grounds to small reservations. This thankless task devolved upon the army. It was not merely a thankless task, but a most arduous and formidable one. Compared with service in the Indian campaigns, that in the South during the Civil War was a holiday pastime. What tragedy in all our national wars can compare with the battle of the Little Big Horn? What record of retreat and pursuit is there like that of the Nez Perce campaign of 1877? Napoleon's retreat from Moscow had no terrors for the individual soldier like those of the winter campaign of Crook in the Powder River country in March, 1876, when it was so cold that the men were not permitted to go to sleep at night for fear they would never wake up.

In the course of twenty years after 1855 military posts sprang up all over the West. There was scarcely an Indian trail in that entire region that did not witness the passage of government troops. From one haunt to another his relentless pursuers tracked the desperate Indian. Ambushes and massacres were met with crushing defeats in battle, but the general drift of the conflict was uniformly one way. The Indian was learning the weight of that dread power which had so far tolerated his independence, but was now to extinguish it forever. The struggle lasted in its main features about sixteen years, or from 1862 to 1877; but its extreme limits were the Grattan Massacre of August 19, 1854, and the battle of Wounded Knee, December 29, 1890.

For some years the Indians who were parties to the treaty of Laramie observed its conditions fairly well; but in 1854 an unfortunate affair occurred which temporarily interrupted the general peace. Some fifteen hundred Indians of three different Sioux bands were encamped in the Platte Valley, about six miles below Fort Laramie, in August of that year. One of the Indians drove off and killed a stray cow belonging to an emigrant train. The owner complained of the theft to the officer in command at Laramie, and Lieutenant Grattan, with about twenty men, was sent to bring in the thief. He probably did not show very much tact in performing his delicate task, and made the mistake of attempting to take the culprit by force in the presence of nearly ten times his number of Indians. The result was the massacre of his entire party. The Indians then went to the American Fur Company warehouse, where their annuity goods were in waiting, broke open the building, and carried off the annuities.

Thereupon the government ordered General Harney to take the field with a military force, establish convenient bases of supplies, protect the frontier and the emigrant routes, and to deal a heavy blow upon the offending Indians. On September 3, 1855, General Harney attacked a large force of Indians who had taken part in the Grattan massacre, completely routed them, killed and captured upward of two hundred, and destroyed nearly all their property. This affair took place across the Platte River from Ash Hollow, a noted situation on the emigrant trail, from which the battle has taken its name.

General Harney next moved his force to the Missouri River, where the old trading post of Fort Pierre had been lately acquired by the government, and there held councils with various tribes, which again resulted in general pacification. In the following year the important military post of Fort Randall was built, and Fort Pierre was abandoned because of its undesirable situation. General Harney discharged his task in a manner highly creditable to himself and satisfactory both to the Indians and the government; and seven years were to elapse before any further difficulty of a serious character should occur.

But while the severe lesson of Ash Hollow, the frank counsel of General Harney, and the presence of a military force at Fort Randall, kept the tribes in comparative peace, the wrongs from which they suffered continually increased, and their temper grew constantly worse. The discovery of gold in Montana brought a multitude of emigrants to and through this country, with the consequent destruction of game and threats of roads and railroads and loss of lands. Events were fast developing into a crisis, when the outbreak of the Civil War in the United States gave the tribes their desired opportunity. The frontier garrisons were depleted in order that the regular troops might be sent south. New levies made up of the able-bodied citizens went away to the war. The Indian was quick to see how this movement weakened the frontier settlements. He was made to believe, by gross exaggeration, that the situation of the Great Father in Washington was a desperate one, that his capital was about to be taken and his power destroyed. It has been asserted that the Confederates had emissaries among the Indians, but there is no proof of any direct intrigue of this character. Indirectly, however, they exercised a powerful influence upon them. The people of the British possessions, like those of the mother country, sympathized ardently with the South, and this sympathy found effective expression in the intercourse of the British half-breeds north of the boundary with the Indians south. These half-breeds knew the border tribes perfectly, and had greater influence with them than the whites, who were strangers to their customs and the authors of their many wrongs. Selfish motives of trade combined with national prejudice to stir up strife against the Americans and to provide means for making that strife effective. The half breeds circulated freely south of the border, and the tracks of their carts could be seen everywhere from the Red River of the North to the Missouri River. They brought powder and balls, guns, rum, and regular merchandise of trade, and their influence at this particular time was decisive. Their territory, moreover, offered a sure asylum from punishment for any outrages which the Indians might commit.

"I saw, while at Sioux City, Captain La Barge, who had just returned with his boat from the upper Missouri. Captain La Barge has been in the American Fur Company employment for twenty-five years, and says that never before this trip have the Indians been unusually hostile. He says that now the whole Sioux nation is bound for a war of extermination against the frontier,

Trouble first broke out in 1862 among the Minnesota Indians, where the evil conditions from which the tribes had been suffering had reached an acute stage. Under the leadership of a noted Sioux chief, Little Crow, the Indians in the valley of the Minnesota River above Mankato attacked the settlement of New Ulm and others in that vicinity, on the 18th of August, murdering and taking captive the inhabitants, destroying property, and spreading consternation in every direction. In the course of three days nearly a thousand persons were killed and two million dollars' worth of property destroyed.

The State and national governments sent instant relief; the outrages were checked; the Indians were driven up the Minnesota Valley and beaten in several battles; the captive whites were mostly released, and a large number of hostiles engaged in the massacre were taken prisoners. This work was done under the immediate leadership of General H. H. Sibley, first Governor of Minnesota. The captured Indians were tried by court martial, and a great number were condemned to death, but this penalty was commuted by President Lincoln except in the cases of thirty-eight, who were hanged at Mankato, December 26, 1862.

In the meanwhile the Indians under Little Crow, though checked and driven back, were not conquered or discouraged. Their emissaries were active among the tribes of the Missouri, who were aroused almost to' the point of war. The execution of the Indians at Mankato exasperated Little Crow to a desperate pitch, and he vowed extermination of the whites. It was clear that an Indian war was at hand, and the government at once prepared for it. Its conduct was placed in the hands of General John Pope, who had been relieved from his command of the Army of the Potomac after the second Bull Run, and was now in command of the Department of the Northwest, with headquarters at Milwaukee. General Pope organized two expeditions, one under General Sibley, to move west from Mankato against the Indians and drive them toward the Missouri, and the other under General Sully, to move from Sioux City up the Missouri and cut off their retreat. The plan was well conceived, but the extreme low water in the Missouri in 1863 prevented General Sully from receiving his supplies in time to carry out his part of the programme. Sibley's expedition left Camp Pope in the Minnesota Valley June 16, 1863, and two days later that of General Sully left Sioux City. Sibley's route lay up the Minnesota to its source, thence by way of Lake Traverse to the Cheyenne River of North Dakota, and up that stream toward Devil's Lake, where the Indians were supposed to be. Learning that they had left that region and had gone toward the Missouri, General Sibley changed his march to the southwest, and pursued the retreating enemy with great vigor. He came upon them and fought three battles within a week— Big Mound, July 24; Dead Buffalo Lake, July 26; and Stony Lake, July 28. The Indians were defeated in all three fights, and then crossed the Missouri River just below where Bismarck, N. D., now stands. General Sibley reached that stream on July 29, and here his expedition ended. Two days later his command set out on its homeward march.

At this time General Sully was at Fort Pierre. The transportation of his supplies had delayed him, and it was not until the 14th of August that he started from that point on his march north. He went up the east bank of the Missouri, with a great deal of vexatious delay, and finally reached the scene of Sibley's third fight just a month after it had taken place. The Indians, meanwhile, far from being conquered or dispirited, had recrossed the river and were on their way back to the grazing grounds on the Coteau of the Missouri. Some of them harassed the homeward-bound column of General Sibley. Sully pursued them to the northeast and overtook and fought them at Whitestone Hill, some thirty miles south and slightly west of Jamestown, N. D. The Indians were badly defeated, many of them were killed, and a large amount of their property was destroyed. Sully then returned to the Missouri and built a new post, Fort Sully, on the left bank of the river, opposite the head of Farm Island, midway between Fort Pierre and Fort George. With this work the campaign of 1863 came to an end.

The movements of troops in this campaign and the force of Indians engaged were the largest yet known in the history of the United States. The number of warriors was estimated at over six thousand, while the troops under Sibley and Sully numbered about four thousand. The campaign, however, was not conclusive. Although the Indians had been defeated with severe loss in every engagement, they were still unsubdued, and retained their defiant attitude during the following winter. Accordingly another campaign was planned for the summer of 1864. General Sully was placed in charge with a cavalry force of about 2500 men.

General Sully's first move was to build a post near the mouth of the Cannon Ball River—Fort Rice, forty miles below where Bismarck now stands, and on the other side of the river. The Indians being reported as near the source of Heart River, General Sully concluded to continue his march in search of them, whether found or not, until he should reach the Yellowstone River. He took with him only the necessary rations for the march and sent his steamboats with supplies and materials for a new post around to meet him at the Brasseau Houses on the Yellowstone, fifty miles above the mouth of that stream. Accompanying Sully's march to the Yellowstone was an emigrant train of about 125 people bound for the mines of Montana.

Sully's route lay up the Cannon Ball River nearly to its source, and thence across to the head waters of Heart River. Here the General packed his train and left it with the emigrants under a strong guard, and himself and command, in light marching order, struck out for Knife River, where the Indians were reported encamped. He found them as expected. They were defiant and eager for battle, and an engagement immediately followed. The Indians were badly defeated, a large number being killed, and all of their property destroyed. This was the battle of Tahkahokuty, or Killdeer Mountain, and was fought July 28, 1864.

Sully then returned to his camp on Heart River, and, under the guidance of a single Indian, who, of all those with him, professed to know a passable route, started on the perilous undertaking of carrying a wagon train through the Bad Lands to the Yellowstone River. The route was west to the Little Missouri, where it turned sharply to the northwest and struck the Yellowstone about fifteen miles below the Brasseau Houses. This point was reached on the 12th of August, and fortunately the supply steamers were close at hand to relieve the necessities of the troops. This was the first expedition across the Bad Lands of North Dakota, and was accomplished at the cost of great labor and suffering.

The command crossed the Yellowstone and then marched to the Missouri River opposite Fort Union. This stream was forded with much peril, and the troops then returned to Fort Rice along the north shore. Garrisons were left at Forts Union and Berthold, but the contemplated post on the Yellowstone could not be built, owing to the wrecking of one of the steamers with most of the material on board.

Thus the military forces of the United States were advanced in permanent occupation to the mouth of the Yellowstone River. Only twice before had the uniform of the American soldier been so far up the Missouri—in 1805-06, when the Lewis and Clark expedition passed this point, and in 1825, when General Atkinson took his command to a point about a hundred miles farther up. Neither of these earlier visits contemplated permanent occupation.

By this time the Indians began to realize the magnitude of the power they were contending with, and to show signs of weakening. No extensive campaign was found necessary along the river for a number of years, although many of the Indians continued hostile and committed numerous depredations. The termination of the Civil War, with complete victory for the government, and the release of so many soldiers from Southern fields who could now be sent to the frontier, all tended to make the Indians proceed in their schemes of war with greater caution and hesitation. Could the evils of our Indian system have been corrected the tribes might readily have been brought to terms of "lasting peace," which was so confidently predicted at the time by Indian agents and even by some military officers.

In this matter of the military conquest of the Missouri Valley, as in that treated in the last chapter, it is not possible, with our present space, to follow in detail the course of events during the next twelve years. The army made some new advances every year, not only in the Missouri Valley, but throughout the entire West. Campaigns, battles, and some appalling massacres occurred, and the soldiers became as familiar with the country and as expert in savage methods of warfare as the Indian himself. Finally, in 1875-77, came the last act in the great tragedy, by which the power of the Sioux nation was broken and their career as an independent people brought to an end.

Great efforts had been made for several years to reduce the Sioux tribes, by peaceable methods, to life on the reservations. Several government commissions were sent to them, and one in particular, of which General Sherman was a member, went into the whole matter with the greatest possible care. Most of the Sioux were finally located on the reservations and appeared to be peaceably disposed. But there were some exceptions, estimated to number not more than six or eight hundred warriors, who had persistently refused from the first to recognize in any way the treaties or other arrangements with the government. The agents had failed to get them to quiet down on the reservations, and they continued to roam over the country as of old, subsisting upon the fruits of the chase. They were uncompromisingly hostile to the whites and their Indian allies, and committed outrages without number upon both. Finally the Indian Department served notice upon them that unless they settled down on the reservations before January 31, 1876, they would be turned over to the military authorities and be dealt with by force. The Indians paid no attention to this ultimatum, and their case was accordingly placed in the hands of the army.

An effort was made to reach these Indians by a winter campaign, but after one attempt, which ended in a battle of no decisive results, the scheme was abandoned, because the excessive cold made it impossible to conduct operations in that shelterless country. General Sheridan, who was charged with the conduct of this important business, thereupon planned a campaign which was to be carried out as soon as the season would permit. He determined upon a concentric movement by which bodies of troops from widely separated localities should move upon a given section where it was believed that the hostile band would be found. General Crook was to start from Fort Fetterman, on the Platte, and move north; General Terry from Fort Abraham Lincoln, on the Missouri, and move west;

and General Gibbon from Fort Ellis, in western Montana, and move east. The point of rendezvous was to be in the Yellowstone Valley near the mouth of the Powder River, or wherever in that vicinity further development might indicate. General Crook left Fort Fetterman May 29 with about 1000 men; General Terry left Fort Lincoln May 17 with about 1000 men, sending his supplies around into the Yellowstone by steamboat. General Gibbon, with 450 men, left Fort Ellis on the 1st of April, crossed over to the Yellowstone, and marched down the left bank of that stream.

Up to this time all obtainable evidence indicated that the hostile Indians did not number more than 800 warriors. As a matter of fact, discontented Indians from nearly all the surrounding Sioux and Cheyenne agencies had for some time past been leaving the reservations and going to the hostiles, until the latter had gathered a force of not less than 2500 men. It was against this force, more than three times as large as was supposed, that the joint movement of Generals Terry, Crook, and Gibbon was directed.

General Crook was the first to encounter the Indians. He met and fought them on the head of the Rosebud River June 17, and although the Indians withdrew, the battle was indecisive, and the great number of the Indians, as disclosed by the fight, induced General Crook not to take the risk of going further. He withdrew to the valley of Goose Creek and sent for re-enforcements.

Generals Terry and Gibbon met about fifteen miles below the mouth of the Tongue River on the 9th of June, and their combined forces formed a junction at the mouth of the Rosebud on the 21st of that month. Here the plan of operations against the Indians was agreed upon. Nothing was known of Crook's whereabouts, nor of his recent fight, but it was pretty well established, from various scouting parties, that the Indian village was in the valley of the Little Big Horn, from seventy-five to ninety miles distant. It was decided that General Custer, with the 7th Cavalry, should proceed up the Rosebud until he should strike a large Indian trail which had been discovered a few days before, and should then follow it to the Little Big Horn, feeling well to the south to prevent the escape of the Indians. General Gibbon, whose column General Terry accompanied, was to ascend the Yellowstone to the mouth of the Big Horn, and that stream to the mouth of the Little Big Horn, where it was expected to arrive not later than the 26th, and where it should come into touch with Custer.

In carrying out his part of the programme, General Custer moved more rapidly than his instructions contemplated, so rapidly, in fact, that he would have arrived at the appointed rendezvous, had his march not been interrupted, an entire day in advance of that fixed for the arrival of General Gibbon. The result was that his command came upon the Indian village on the morning of the 25th while advancing in three separate columns not within supporting distance of each other. Custer's column was surrounded and annihilated to a man. The other two detachments, under Major Reno and Captain Benteen, effected a junction and intrenched themselves on the river bluff of the Little Big Horn, where they withstood for nearly thirty hours the terrific siege by the Indians, who were confident and exultant from their late victory over Custer. The total loss to Custer's command was about 270 men. General Gibbon's column reached the scene of the battle on the 27th, the Indians withdrawing upon their approach.

This was the crowning tragedy of the long Sioux wars, which had been waged at intervals for upward of twenty years. Although a great disaster to the whites, it marked the downfall of the Indian power. The various bands into which the hostile force scattered after the Custer massacre were relentlessly pursued until all were driven into the reservations or beyond the British line. Once on the reservations they were disarmed and dismounted, so as to cripple them from further resistance. Another year was consumed in this work, and the military posts were further extended into the Indian country; but by the end of 1877 the military problem in our Indian affairs was practically solved.

CHAPTER XXXII.

THE STEAMBOAT IN THE INDIAN WARS.

Throughout the Indian wars of the Missouri Valley the steamboat played a part of the very highest importance. It was almost the exclusive means of transporting men and supplies along the river, except when in active campaign work in the interior. Its use in the military service dates from the very beginning of steamboat navigation on the river, as well as from the first important step toward the military occupation of the valley. When the first steamboat entered the Missouri, in 1819, arrangements were being perfected to transport by steam to the mouth of the Yellowstone a large body of troops designed to establish a post there. Five boats were brought into requisition for this purpose, and a sixth, the *Western Engineer*, was built by the government to transport a party of scientists who were to accompany the expedition. Owing to the entire absence of experience in navigating the Missouri with steamboats, this attempt proved a failure. None of the boats except the *Western Engineer* got as far as to the old Council

Bluffs, and the troops, after marching a part of the distance, went into winter quarters at that point.

Four years later the first Indian campaign west of the Mississippi River took place, when Colonel Leavenworth, with a considerable body of troops, went up the river from Fort Atkinson (old Council Bluffs) to chastise the Aricaras, who had attacked a fur-trading party under General Ashley and killed a number of men. Keelboats were used on this expedition.

Two years later, 1825, General Atkinson took a large body of troops from Fort Atkinson to a point about one hundred miles above the mouth of the Yellowstone and return. His purpose was to make treaties with the Indian tribes along the valley and acquaint them with the power of the United States. Keelboats were used, and a novel feature was introduced in propelling them—a wheel, or wheels, which were operated by hand power, the soldiers being used for this purpose.

No further use of steamboats in the military service except at Forts Leavenworth, Kearney, and Croghan, and in connection with the Mexican War, occurred until Harney's campaign of 1855. All the troops that went up the river at that time were transported in steamboats. The transfer of ownership of Fort Pierre from the American Fur Company to the army, and the movement of material connected therewith, were also done by steam. The establishment of Fort Randall and the subsequent maintenance of that post were mainly accomplished by the aid of the steamboat.

The outbreak of the Sioux War in 1863 and the campaigns of 1863-64 called the steamboat again into extensive use. A remarkable instance of this use was the transportation of the Winnebago Indians from their home near Mankato, Minn., to their new home on the Missouri River. The feeling against the Indians after the Minnesota massacre was so bitter that it was taken advantage of to move them all from the State. It does not appear that the Winnebagos were active participants in the outbreak, but the hand of vengeance fell upon them as upon the others. They were moved westward several hundred miles, and in exchange for the fertile lands of the Minnesota Valley were given a home on the sterile wastes of the Missouri. In making this transfer the Indians were not taken directly across the country, which was perfectly practicable for wagons all the way, but were transported by *steamboat*. They were put on board the *Favorite* and other boats at Mankato on the Minnesota River, taken down that stream to the Mississippi at Fort Snelling, down the Mississippi to the Missouri, and up the Missouri to the mouth of Crow Creek, twenty miles above the present site of Chamberlain, S. D. The distance around was 1900 miles, against about 300 miles across. The Indians arrived at Crow Creek on May 30, 1863. A reservation was laid off, the necessary agency buildings were erected in a stockaded inclosure, and the place was named Fort Thompson, in honor of Clark W. Thompson, the Superintendent of Indian Affairs for the Northern Superintendency. Mr. Thompson personally supervised the work of locating the Indians on this new reservation.

In the campaign of General Sully in 1863 he relied entirely upon steamboats for transporting his supplies from Sioux City to the field of operations, and one boat accompanied him from Fort Pierre well on his way to the scene of actual hostilities. It was on this campaign that General Sully impressed Captain La Barge's boat, the *Shreveport,* into his service for a time.

The campaign of 1864 from Fort Rice to the Yellowstone River was conducted in connection with steamboats. Three boats were sent around into the Yellowstone to meet the troops at the Brasseau Houses. They were loaded with rations, forage, and material for a new post which it was proposed to build on the Yellowstone River near the mouth of Powder River. These boats were the *Chippezva Falls,* the *Alone,* and the *Island City.* The last-mentioned boat had all the forage for the animals on board and was unfortunately wrecked just below the mouth of the Yellowstone River. This occurrence caused General Sully to abandon for the time his contemplated establishment on the Yellowstone.

During the next twelve years steamboats were constantly in the service of the government in transporting troops and supplies along the river. It is impossible to estimate the great value in the military operations of the valley of this important line of communication. Forts and cantonments were strung all along the river from Fort Randall to Fort Benton, and all of them, as well as the troops in the field, depended for their support upon the river boats. The conquest of the Missouri Valley would have been a very different matter had the government been deprived of this important aid in its operations.

In the Sioux campaign of 1876 steamboats bore a prominent part, one of the very highest importance, and one which had its full share of the thrilling incidents of that tragic conflict. A considerable fleet of boats was sent up the river from Fort Abraham Lincoln to co-operate with the troops under Terry, who marched across the country to the Yellowstone. They not only carried supplies, but assisted in patrolling the river to prevent the Indians from crossing, and moved the troops from point to point as their services were needed. One boat in particular, the *Far West,* Captain Grant Marsh, master, performed a service which will go down in the history of the campaign as one of its most thrilling episodes.

The *Far West* was for a few days used by General Terry as his headquarters boat while his command was moving up the Yellowstone to the mouth of the Big Horn. The boat, after ferrying General Gibbon's command to the north bank of the Yellowstone, was directed to proceed up the Big Horn, and, if possible, to reach the mouth of the Little Big Horn. General Gibbon, being ill at the time, remained on the boat with a company of infantry a part of the way, when he joined Terry's column and resumed command of his own troops. The *Far West* ascended the Big Horn fifteen miles above the mouth of the Little Big Horn and then dropped down to that tributary. It remained there until the 30th, by which time all the wounded from Reno's fight had been placed on board, and it then moved down to the Yellowstone, where it arrived on the same day. Three days later it started down the river for Fort Abraham Lincoln with all the wounded, and a volume of dispatches, official and private, relating to the terrible tragedy of which the world had but just been informed. The very nature of its mission made the voyage of the *Far West* one of romantic interest. Its cargo of wounded men, its greater burden of news to anxious friends and an impatient public, all mark it as one of the historic incidents of our Indian wars. The *Far West* arrived at Fort Lincoln July 5, about midnight.

The *Far West* returned from Fort Abraham Lincoln immediately after she had discharged her cargo, and remained with other boats on the Yellowstone until the subsiding waters made it impossible to navigate that stream. Among these boats was another, well known to the army for many years, and the only one of the old fleet that still survives. This was the *Josephine,* which is now in the service of the government as a snagboat in the work of keeping the upper river free from obstructions.

It has been asserted that the *Far West* bore the first news of the Custer massacre to the world; but this is not so. General Terry's dispatch to General Sheridan, written in camp on the Little Big Horn June 27, was sent by courier to Fort Ellis, 240 miles distant, and there put on the wire.

The following graphic account of the voyage of the *Far West* is well worth preserving in spite of its many errors of fact. As a word picture of what was really a notable performance, it is a fine example of journalistic writing. It is from the pen of M. E. Terry, and was published in the *Pioneer Press* of St. Paul in May, 1878:

"The steamer *Far West* was moored at the mouth of the Little Big Horn. The wounded were carried on board the steamer and Dr. Porter was detailed to go down with them. Terry's adjutant general, Colonel Ed Smith, was sent along with the official dispatches and a hundred other messages. He had a traveling-bag full of telegrams for the Bismarck office. Captain Grant Marsh, of Yankton, was in command of the *Far West*. He put everything in the completest order and took on a large amount of fuel. He received orders to reach Bismarck as soon as possible. He understood his instructions literally, and never did a river man obey them more conscientiously. On the evening of the 3d of July the steamer weighed anchor. In a few minutes the *Far West,* so fittingly named, was under full head of steam. It was a strange land and an unknown river. What a cargo on that steamer! What a story to carry to the government, to Fort Lincoln, to the widows!

"It was running from a field of havoc to a station of mourners. The steamer *Far West* never received the credit due her. Neither has the gallant Marsh; nor the pilots, David Campbell and John Johnson. Marsh, too, acted as pilot. It required all their endurance and skill. They proved the men for the emergency. The engineer, whose name is not known to me, did his duty. Every one of the crew is entitled to the same acknowledgment. They felt no sacrifice was too great upon that journey, and in behalf of the wounded heroes. The Big Horn is full of islands, and a successful passage, even on the bosom of a 'June rise,' is not an easy feat. The *Far West* would take a shoot on this or that side of an island, as the quick judgment of the pilot would dictate. It is no river, in the Eastern sense of that word. It is only a creek. A steamboat moving as fast as a railway train in a narrow, winding stream is not a pleasure. It was no pleasant sensation to be dashing straight at a headland, and the pilot the only power to save. Occasionally the bank would be touched and the men would topple over like ten-pins. It was a reminder of what the result would be if a snag was struck. Down the Big Horn the heroine went, missing islands, snags, and shore. It was a thrilling voyage. The rate of speed was unrivaled in the annals of boating. Into the Yellowstone the stanch craft shot, and down that sealed river to pilots she made over twenty miles an hour. The bold Captain was taking chances, but he scarcely thought of them. He was under flying orders. Lives were at stake. His engineer was instructed to keep up steam at the highest pitch. Once the gauge marked a pressure that turned his cool head and made every nerve in his powerful frame quiver. The crisis passed and the *Far West* escaped a fate more terrible than Custer's. Once a stop was made, and a shallow grave explained the reason. He still rests in that lone spot. Down the swift Yellowstone, like shooting the Lachine Rapids, every mile a repetition of the former. From the Yellowstone she sped into the broad Missouri, and then there was clear sailing. There was a deeper channel and more confidence. A few minutes were lost at Buford. Everybody at the fort was beside himself. The boat was crowded with inquirers, and their inquiries were not half answered when the steamer was away. At Berthold a wounded scout was put off, and at Fort Stevenson a brief stop to tell in a word what had happened. There was no difference in the speed from Stevenson to Bismarck. The same desperate rate was kept up to the end. They were approaching home with something of that feeling which always moves the human heart. At eleven o'clock on the night of the 5th of July they reached Bismarck and Fort A. Lincoln. One thousand miles in fifty-four hours was the proud record."

Captain La Barge also saw service in the Custer campaign. The need of a light-draft boat for use in the latter part of the season led the authorities to engage his boat, the *John M. Chambers,* to carry supplies to Fort Buford. The boat left St. Louis August 5 and reached Buford September n. The commissary stores were at once unloaded, with the assistance of soldiers detailed for the purpose. General Terry and staff, with a company of troops and a piece of artillery, were then taken on board, and the boat started for Wolf Point in the hope of heading off the Indians, who were reported to be in that vicinity. The boat started early on the morning of the 12th. She proceeded about thirty miles that day, having made a stop at Fort Union to put off General Hazen and take on a supply of meat for the troops. Owing to the low water she made only about twenty miles on the 13th. On the 14th the party stopped to examine a broken-down ambulance on the shore. It was found to have belonged to Reno's troops, who were in pursuit of the Indians. A little farther they came upon a party of seven men on their way down the river from Montana, and through them news of Reno and the Indians was received. These men had been terribly frightened the night before. The boat had laid up near their camp and had thrown a shell into a grove of cottonwoods to search for Indians. It struck near their bivouac and almost paralyzed them with fright. They came on board next day and went down by the boat on its return home.

On the 15th the boat reached Reno's camp. The Indians had already crossed, and Captain La Barge immediately commenced ferrying Reno's command over. This work was accomplished before night, and the boat left for Buford the following morning, with General Terry and staff and 270 men. Buford was reached on the 17th, and the boat was discharged.

She at once started on her return to St. Louis, where she arrived October 8.

Strange as it may seem, considering the nature of a campaign like that of 1877 against the Nez Perce Indians, the Missouri River steamboat played an important, and perhaps a decisive, part in its operations. Chief Joseph, in his long march from Idaho, had crossed the Yellowstone National Park, and finding himself pursued and harried in every direction, struck north for the British line. The pursuing troops, whom he had so far eluded, he felt confident would not overtake him; but he did not count on a danger which arose in a quite unexpected quarter. General Miles, with about 350 men, was encamped on the Yellowstone at the mouth of the Tongue River, where the news reached him that Indians had crossed the Yellowstone farther up and were making for the British line. He at once put his command in motion to intercept them. His first objective was the Missouri River at the mouth of the Musselshell. As soon as he came in sight of the river, scouts were sent on ahead to stop any steamer that might happen along. By the greatest good fortune the scouts reached the bank just as the last boat of the season was passing down. Fifteen minutes later and she would have been gone.

The troops were brought down to the river and ten days' rations were put on the boat and taken to the mouth of the Musselshell. The officers of the boat stated that the Indians had not yet crossed the Missouri, and General Miles accordingly decided to march up the valley of the Musselshell to intercept them. The boat was discharged and dropped downstream, stopping about a mile below to take on some wood. While there, two men came down the river in a mackinaw and reported that the Indians *had* crossed the river, some eighty miles above, and were making for the British line. General Miles instantly ordered some cannon shots fired in the direction of the steamboat. A Captain Baldwin, who had been sent down on account of sickness, was on board. He at once understood that the boat was wanted, and caused her to be brought back. The command was ferried over, and on the following morning, September 27, set out to the northwest after the Indians. They were overtaken on Snake Creek, where Chief Joseph was defeated in battle, and the greater part of his people captured. This point was within fifty miles of the boundary, and about one hundred of the Indians actually got across the line. But for the timely aid of the steamboat it is probable that the whole band would have escaped.

CHAPTER XXXIII.

THE PEACE COMMISSION OF 1866.

We left Captain La Barge in 1865 just as he had returned from Montana on his second journey by way of Great Salt Lake. His boat, the *Effie Deans,* had reached St. Louis some time before he did. The boat was still owned in partnership with John S. McCune and Eugene Jaccard. La Barge tried to get full possession of her, offering, however, either to buy or sell. Not being able to negotiate a purchase, he demanded a dissolution of the partnership, and bought the boat in. He then put six thousand dollars' worth of repairs on her, and in the spring advertised for a trip to Benton. He secured a full cargo, and had every prospect of a profitable trip, when one of those sudden accidents overtook him which were so common in the hazardous business he was carrying on. He had hesitated a good deal about insuring the boat, and finally, upon McCune's advice, concluded not to do so. He felt safe if he could get out of port, the greatest danger being from fire there. The insurance rates were so high that it was a great object to avoid them, if possible. It was on Friday that he had his talk with McCune and decided not to insure. He was to start next morning. He mentioned to his wife what he had done, and she, with a woman's intuition, remonstrated strongly, saying she knew he would repent it. About one o'clock next morning the doorbell rang. La Barge raised the window and asked who it was. "Watchman of the *Effie Deans,"* was the reply. "What is the matter?" asked the Captain. "The *Effie Deans* is burned up."

"The loss to me," said Captain La Barge, "was difficult to reconcile, from the fact of my having rejected insurance the day before, as well as an offer of forty thousand dollars for the boat the same day. The fire had been communicated to the boat from one of the neighboring vessels, the *Nevada,* and was in no sense the fault of my crew. Next morning Robert Campbell came down to the levee and said he understood I had no insurance on the boat. I replied that such was the case. He said that he had always put me down as a prudent man, but that such a course showed great recklessness. I replied that I thought not; that the loss was the fault of my neighbors, and not my own. 'Well, if that is any consolation, I have nothing more to say,' he replied, and walked away. His apparent indifference surprised me. I had done business with him for many years, and had paid him as high as sixty thousand dollars commissions. Now, in my misfortune, he did not as much as offer the least assistance.

"Very different was the conduct of John S. McCune. He also came down soon after Campbell left. He looked at the wreck, said it was most unfortunate, talked very little, but told me to be early at his office Monday morning. I called according to appointment. McCune said, 'You have got to have a new boat. Let us go down to the Marine Railway Ways in Carondelet and see what we can do. We went down, saw the superintendent, told him what we wanted, and asked him if he could undertake the construction of a boat. He replied that he could, and McCune told him to go ahead on my plans, and he would back me with his credit. I drew the entire plans and specifications for the boat, machinery and all, and she was built that summer accordingly. Before I got back in the fall McCune had named her for me, but I renamed her *Octavia,* for my second daughter. She cost fifty-seven thousand dollars, and was a splendid boat. I paid for her partly in cash and gave my notes for the balance."

In the meantime a commission had been appointed. to go up the river and make treaties with certain tribes of Indians in regard to the right of way for railroads across their lands. It was officially known as the Northwestern Treaty Commission, but was popularly referred to as the Peace Commission of 1866. It was composed of Newton Edmunds, Governor of Dakota Territory; General S. R. Curtis, a well-known officer of the Iowa Volunteers; Orrin Guernsey, and the Rev. Henry W. Reed, who so long figured as an Indian agent on the upper river. The Commission were well provided with presents and proposed to travel in becoming state. Captain La Barge had secured for the summer, while the *Octavia* was building, another boat, a fine new one, the *Ben Johnson.* The Commission contracted with the Captain to carry them up the river and back at three hundred dollars per day. One of the Commissioners wanted the Captain to hire his son as clerk, or in some other capacity, at five dollars per day. The Captain had made up his crew and did not care to go to this extra and unnecessary expense. But as the Commissioner rather insisted, the charter price was raised to $305 per day, and the young man enjoyed a fat sinecure during the trip— an instance of the kind of corruption which was almost universal in the period following the war.

To Captain La Barge the voyage seemed more like a pleasure excursion than a business enterprise. The boat moved by very leisurely stages, always tying up early in the evening and starting late in the morning. Whist and other games were the order of the day. Long stops were made at all interesting points, and the party enjoyed exceptional opportunities of seeing Indian life in all its wildness. As a means of accomplishing any good, the Commission was looked upon from the first by the people of the Missouri Valley as little more than a farce. No end of ridicule was poured upon it, and it was held up to the general contempt by those who had any definite acquaintance with the situation. The Indians were generally loath to negotiate, fearing that the Commission "would want them to sign some paper that would take from them their lands and houses and oblige them to seek new ones farther west." It cannot be said that any good came from this Commission—certainly nothing to justify its great expense. It did without doubt create new complications, lead to increased dissatisfaction on the part of the Indians, and, on the whole, aggravate an already serious situation.

Some of the incidents on this trip had a flavor of danger about them, and we shall narrate one as given us by Captain La Barge. It related to an interview of the Commissioners with the Yanktonais, who were well known as the most relentlessly hostile of any of the Sioux tribes.

"Some twenty miles below the mouth of White Earth River," said Captain La Barge, "I saw two Indian hunters on the hills. I hailed them, landed the steamer, asked them on board, and after feasting them (an indispensable preliminary to the transaction of any business), inquired if they were Yanktonais, and if so where were the rest of the tribe. They replied in the affirmative, and said that their camp was about ten miles off, on the White Earth River. The Chairman of the Commission asked them to go to camp and tell the chiefs to move their whole village down to the mouth of the White Earth and there await the arrival of the boat for the purpose of holding a council. He inquired the size of the village, and found it to be six hundred tepees, which meant about three thousand Indians.

"I remonstrated at this proposition, strongly urging that only the chiefs be invited. Should so powerful a band of these hostile Indians get any advantage of us they would certainly use it. We had no power of resisting them, having only thirty people in all, and they were poorly armed. The Indians would, I feared, make a rush and attempt to capture the steamer as soon as we landed. Our interpreter, Zephyr Rencontre, seconded me in this opinion. I had been in the power of these Indians once before, and, thanks to Rencontre, I was wearingmy hair on this occasion.

"The Chairman of the Commission said he perceived that I was afraid of the Indians, but not to be alarmed; he would answer for all harm. The Indians would never dare molest a government officer. To me, who had spent all my life among the Indians, this gratuitous insinuation from a mere novice in Indian experience cut me to the quick, and I replied: Very well, I will land as you say, but before we get through we shall see who is afraid of Indians.'

"This was another instance of the mistakes made by our government in the selection, to treat with the Indians, of men without knowledge of the native character. It was a universal rule that such men would treat with contempt the cautious bearing of those who knew the Indians; and this ignorant bravado has many times led to disastrous consequences. It is very unpleasant to act with such men, who ridicule one's honest knowledge of peril, and are powerless to help when they get you into danger. It was also a common observation with me that the volunteer officers of the war were always more haughty and overbearing than those bred to the profession. They loved to assume, assert, and display authority, where the trained soldier would see no occasion to do so.

"I said to Curtis on this occasion, This course is contrary to my judgment, General; and in order not to be responsible for the consequences I desire a positive order from you before I adopt it.' He gave me the order. The Indians arrived just as we were tying up the boat. The women immediately commenced setting up the lodges and the men began to rush on board. They were all armed. Curtis had said, when I foretold this: 'We will keep them off, only letting on those we want.' I replied, 'You will see, General. It will be impossible to keep them off.'

"As already stated, the Indians at once rushed on board, and unfortunately did not congregate in one place, but scattered themselves in every direction. Matters at once became serious. I was thoroughly alarmed for the safety of the boat and her passengers, but remained perfectly cool and indifferent in outward appearance, and did not permit myself to resent the actions of the Indians. An act of that sort might have precipitated difficulty. We were over a powder mine, and a spark was liable to fall at any moment. The Indians became insolent, would elbow us around, sneer at us, display their muscular arms, and try in every way to provoke us to action. One Indian, an ugly fellow and noted villain, Crazy Wolf, followed me everywhere I went, armed with gun, pistol, and bow and arrows. He tried in every way to get me to notice him. At this time I consulted with Zephyr on the situation, saying that I feared trouble was brewing. He replied that he thought so too, and that I had better prepare for prompt measures. I had steam kept up. Pilot and engineer remained at their posts, and the mate was kept forward. He had been instructed to cut the line whenever he should hear a single tap of the bell.

"Meanwhile the Commissioners had been attempting negotiations, but to little purpose. In front, on the boiler deck, there were a table and seats for the principal Indians. Curtis tried to call them to order, but without success. He then summoned Rencontre and tried to talk to them. He told them he was about to roll some bales of goods on shore and requested that they would withdraw and distribute them. They answered to roll them on shore; the women would take care of them; for their part they would remain on the boat.

"Nothing whatever could be done. Matters became dubious. One by one the Commissioners slipped away and locked themselves in their staterooms. General Curtis was finally left alone, and after a while he also withdrew, and told me to get out of the scrape as best I could. He fully realized the gravity of the blunder he had made, and his own inability to cope with the situation.

"The Indians as yet had made no attempt on the staterooms, but they were incensed at the withdrawal of the Commissioners and might do so at any moment. Rencontre said to me, 'The Indians don't like this, and will give us trouble. We had better do something right away.' 'Is it time to cut loose?' I asked. 1 think so,' he replied. I gave the signal, the line was cut, the wheels began to turn backward and the boat slid quickly from the bank. The sudden move astounded the Indians. Those on shore seized the line and began pulling before they discovered that it was cut. I knew they would not dare to fire, for fear of shooting their own people. Those on the boat were panic-stricken and began to leap overboard. I caused the nose of the boat to be held close to shore so that they could get to land without drowning, and in a few minutes the boat was clear of them. Then, reversing the engines, we steered for the opposite shore and made the boat fast. The danger being over, I went to Curtis' room and told him it was safe for him to come out. When he appeared I said: 'Who is afraid of Indians now, General Curtis?' His only reply was: 'Who would have thought that the rascals would dare molest a government officer?' They cared a good deal about a government officer, indeed, and the remark showed how little he knew of the Indian character. I asked the General if he wanted to make another trial, but he replied that he had had enough.

"No further attempt was made to treat with these Indians, and we went on up the river. As on a previous occasion, the Indians followed us. Durfee & Peck at this time had a post on the site where Fort Buford later stood. The Indians made a signal from the opposite side of the river that they had robes to sell, and the agent at the post wanted to borrow our yawl to go across and get them. I consented, but advised against it. They crossed and actually bought several hundred robes, but just as the boat was about to put back, the Indians jumped upon the crew, killed one, severely wounded another, and would have killed all, had I not promptly crossed over with the steamboat to their assistance. Mr. Durfee afterward thanked me very heartily for this action."

The Commissioners then went on to old Fort Union, where they remained for a time treating with the Assiniboines, Crows, and Grosventres. The Crows and the Grosventres came down by the steamboat *Miner*, under promise that they should be taken back to their camp on the Musselshell by boat. The river being too low to take so large a boat as the *Ben Johnson* farther up in safety, the Commission impressed into their service, for the purpose of taking these Indians back, a small boat, the *Amanda,* which was in the employ of the War Department. She was then on her way up the river to meet Colonel Reeve, who was expected back from the Judith, where he had just established a post. The Crows and Grosventres, with their presents and with copies of the new treaties, got on board and started up the river. The agent for the Blackfeet, George B. Wright, was also on board on his way to Fort Benton.

At the mouth of the Milk River the *Amanda,* met Colonel Reeve, who promptly took the boat into his own charge, put the Indians ashore with their presents and other property, and left them to walk home. The anger of the Crows was fired to a desperate pitch by this action. They refused to take the presents, tore up some of the treaties, and sent others back to the Commissioners, and declared that they would henceforth fire upon every boat going up the river. Agent Wright thought the situation too critical for him to attempt to go on overland to Benton, so he returned with the boat and went to his station by way of Omaha, Salt Lake, and Helena. The Commissioners criticised him severely for this action, and he, on the other hand, charged them with positive misrepresentation in regard to their work. They had already prepared a report setting forth in glowing terms their success in treating with the various tribes. Agent Wright had likewise written a report of his experiences at the mouth of Milk River and the action of the Crows in repudiating the treaties. As the two reports conflicted in important matters the Commission requested, and finally prevailed upon, Agent Wright to modify his report, so as to be in harmony with their own.

After the business was completed at Fort Union the *Ben Johnson* turned her prow downstream and proceeded homeward by leisurely stages, stopping at the various camps, agencies, and military posts.

The property remaining on the boat was put off partly at Yankton, partly at Sioux City, and partly at Omaha. At Sioux City it was put off at night. Captain La Barge knew nothing of it. Hearing the noise of unloading he arose and went to see what was going on, and found the crew unloading freight. He asked by whose orders they were doing this, and they replied, those of the Commission. He said no more. It was clearly the intention to conceal this move from him, and again he saw how mercenary was the patriotism of many of our government officials. The boat pursued her way safely to St. Louis, where she arrived late in August.

Captain La Barge turned over the steamer to her owners and took possession of his new boat, the *Octavia,* brought her to the wharf, finished her construction, and left on her first trip October 1. He ran in the lower river the rest of the season, and then on the Mississippi until ice closed in. He laid up the boat for the winter at Kimmswick, twenty miles below St. Louis.

CHAPTER XXXIV.

THE MURDER OF CAPTAIN SPEAR.

The voyage of the *Octavia* in the summer of 1867 was one of the most successful and important in all Captain La Barge's career on the river. It was unhappily marred by a most revolting crime, committed on board, but in other respects passed off without any untoward incident. Its narrative will be presented in the Captain's own words.

"Early in the spring of 1867 I started in the Weston and St. Joseph trade, and about April I advertised for a trip to Benton. Business on the river seemed rather dull at this time, and people ridiculed me for attempting a trip. But within two weeks my boat was filled; in fact it was the largest trip I ever had up the river. I remember that one morning, about two days prior to our departure, Captain Walker S. Carter, a merchant of St. Louis, who was on the levee, said to me, 'Have you got a trip?' I replied, 'More than I can carry.' It is astonishing/ said he. ' Anybody else than you could not have got half a trip.' 'That shows the value of a reputation,' I replied.

"This trip of the *Octavia* was a very profitable one. The cargo was composed entirely of private freight, Mr. W. M. McPherson having been the successful bidder for government contracts. I had freight for nearly every firm in Helena, besides a good list of passengers, among whom was Green Clay Smith, newly appointed Governor of Montana, and also the Surveyor General for the same Territory, Thomas E. Tutt, now of the Third National of St. Louis, and Robert Donnell, now a New York banker.

"An interesting incident took place just before the departure of the boat in which no less a personage than General Sherman was concerned. Colonel Thomas, Sherman's Quartermaster, had contracted with W. M. McPherson, as I have said, for all the season's business up the Missouri River. The *Octavia* was to leave port on Tuesday, and on the Saturday previous General Smith came on board and said to me, 'Did I not understand you to say that you had no government freight or troops to transport this year?' I answered in the affirmative—that McPherson had the contract, and I would not carry for him.

'Well,' returned General Smith, 'I am just from General Sherman, where I went to apply for an escort. I was told by the General that I would not need one, for he was going to send a hundred men by the *Octavia* to Camp Cook, near the mouth of the Judith River, under Lieutenant Horrigan.' To confirm his statement he showed me a dispatch that he had just sent to Omaha to have the men all ready, so as not to detain the boat beyond a few minutes. This was a good deal of a surprise to me, as I had had no intimation of such action, and had my boat about full. I told Smith I would go and see Sherman about it, and did so at once. I found the General in his office, and before I could tell him my business he said, 'I know what you want' and he took down his dispatch book to show me that he had taken all precautions not to cause me any delay. 'But that is not the question, General/ I said; 'I cannot take the troops.' 'Ah! that alters the case. Haven't you room?' I replied that I could probably make room, but understood that this shipment was under the McPherson contract. The General said it was. Well then' I said, 'I will not carry them, for I will not work for McPherson.' The General asked my reasons. 'Because McPherson will not pay enough for the work' I said. 'He gets a good price from the government, but the poor steamboat man who does the work gets nothing for it. For example, he gets fifty dollars per man to haul the troops to Camp Cook. He will pay me fifteen and pocket thirty-five, and do no work nor take any risk. I will not work for him on such terms.' 'I think you are perfectly right,' said the General. 'In your place I would do the same thing. But you will carry the troops up for General Sherman?' I replied that I would if he would contract with me individually and directly and pay me the McPherson rates. 'That's fair,' said he, and he called in Thomas and told him to draw up a contract. 'Well,' said Thomas, 'this work is for McPherson to do under our contract with him. If you pay La Barge you will also have to pay McPherson.' Thomas wanted to argue the matter, but Sherman shut him off by saying, 'It's no use, Thomas; you just draw up that contract as I tell you to.' And he did.

"The *Octavia* left St. Louis Tuesday, May 7, 1867, on the most important trip I ever made up the river. There were no incidents of note until the boat reached Omaha, where the troops were taken on board. We also received at this point a passenger in the person of a Captain W. D. Spear, 79th Royal Rifles, an officer of the British Army, on furlough from India. He was on his way to Salt Lake *via* the Missouri River, and was going thence to California. He seemed to be a man of means. This embarkation of the troops and of this officer was the prelude to one of the most distressing tragedies that ever occurred on the Missouri River. The troops were mostly Irish Fenians, and the Lieutenant in charge was an Irishman, all intensely hostile to the English. This fact may in part explain what subsequently transpired. Spear himself felt doubts for his safety, and one day remarked to me that he would be lucky if he got out of this scrape without accident. I did not know what he meant, for he was a very fearless man, going on shore frequently in spite of danger from the Indians. Just after midnight of the 7th of June, or more precisely about 12.30 A. M. June 8, as Captain Spear and Joseph C. La Barge, my son, were going up the steps to the hurricane deck, Captain Spear being a little ahead, a sentinel, William Barry, stationed near there, fired at Captain Spear, the bullet passing through his head at the base of the brain and killing him instantly. The following day an inquest was held by a committee of the passengers consisting of Thomas E. Tutt, Green Clay Smith, Sam McLean, Richard Leach, T. H. Eastman, Geo. W. McLean, and W. J. McCormick, Secretary. Several of the passengers and crew were sworn and their testimony taken. No motive could be discovered for the deed. The sentinel's orders required him to challenge only parties approaching the boat from the shore, and it was expressly agreed with me, by Lieutenant Horrigan, as a condition of permitting sentinels to be posted on the hurricane deck, that they should not interfere in any way with the passengers. The finding of the committee was that "the shooting was not in accordance with any instructions given to said sentinel, and that he deserves the most rigid punishment known to the law." There was indeed a strong sentiment among the passengers in favor of lynching him, but the military could easily have prevented it, and everyone believed that he would meet with due punishment in regular order. The sentinel was of course at once relieved from duty and placed under arrest.

"Our trip up the river was a dangerous one, owing to the intense hostility of the Indians, but by taking great precautions no accidents happened. I put off the remains of Captain Spear at Fort Buford to await my return. I asked the commanding officer if he could suggest any way of embalming the body. He advised the construction of a large box and the filling of it with green cottonwood sawdust. The experiment seemed to work well, although I had never heard of such a thing before. The post commander refused to receive the prisoner, who was taken on to Camp Cook. The commanding officer there refused to try him on the ground that the crime had been committed in Dakota. He held him for us to take back to Yankton.

"The troops were left at Camp Cook and the boat went on to Benton. I found many passengers for the down trip and great quantities of gold dust. I filled the office safe and every other available receptacle with it. There were no incidents of especial importance on the return trip. The soldier, Barry, was taken down to Yankton and there turned over to the United States marshal, who held him until orders came from Washington for his release, when he was sent back to his company.

"I took Captain Spear's remains back to St. Louis, where I found telegrams directing the shipment of them to Europe. A Lieutenant Terry of Spear's company came to St. Louis to get full particulars of the affair. I was then living with my family on the *Octavia,* and invited him to stay there with me. He did so, and I gave him as full an account as possible of Captain Spear's death. When the news reached England that the assassin had been released without trial, the government promptly took up the matter and I understood that a demand was made upon our government through Minister Thornton for a civil trial of the soldier. This demand was complied with, and the man was tried before Judge Kidder at Vermillion, Dak. Myself and several others went up as witnesses. The evidence seemed to me overwhelmingly against the accused, there being nothing in his favor except his own statement that he acted in the line of his duty. The jury returned a verdict of not guilty, upon instructions from the judge that the man had simply obeyed his orders. They were given a verdict to sign written out by the judge, and thus the culprit escaped.

"To us who knew the facts, this travesty upon justice seemed the crowning outrage of the whole deplorable affair. Here was as deliberate, coldblooded, and unprovoked a murder as the annals of crime afford, actuated unquestionably by the national hate of the murderer for the country of the victim. The crime was considered by the passengers as meriting the severest penalty of the law. The pretense that the sentinel acted under orders had not the remotest foundation, or if it had, it only made the officer *particeps criminis*. The final outcome was the grossest miscarriage of justice which even frontier annals afford, and it was unquestionably a justifiable ground for reprisal on the part of the British government. Let those who lament British obduracy in the case of Mrs. Maybrick ponder upon this far more lamentable case of the unavenged death of Captain Spear.

"Upon my return to St. Louis I called upon McCune, who advised me to attend promptly to my obligations for the construction of the boat, which had now about matured. He offered to help me get them renewed. I told him it was unnecessary, as I should take them all up and clear the debt off. He was greatly surprised and delighted at the success of my trip, which was indeed almost phenomenal. I made a clear profit of forty-five thousand dollars between May 7, the date of leaving St. Louis, and the date of my return. Yet it was a hard trip. The responsibility was very great. I was heavily in debt for my boat. I had on board three hundred passengers and three hundred tons of cargo. The difficulties of Missouri River navigation, the dangers from the Indians, and the many other contingencies of such a trip made it wearing in the extreme. Many boats that had set out weeks before us were passed on the way. On the trip I was awake the greater part of the time night and day. I kept up all right and stood the strain so long as the excitement was on, but the moment we landed at Benton and I knew the danger was over, I went to sleep and instructed my wife not to awaken me even for meals. I slept almost continuously for twenty-four hours."

The *Montana Post* is authority for the statement that this voyage of the *Octavia* was the quickest ever made from St. Louis to Fort Benton.

CHAPTER XXXV.

THE BATTLE WITH THE RAILROADS.

The great enemy of the Missouri River steamboat was the railroad. The impression now exists that the river has ceased to be a navigable stream. It has ceased to be a navigated stream, but it is as navigable as it ever was. Let it be known that all railroads in its valley will cease running for a period of five years and there will be a thousand boats on the river in less than six months. It is not a change in the stream, but in methods of transportation, that has ruined the commerce of the river.

The struggle between the steamboat and the railroad lasted just about twenty-eight years, or from 1859—when the Hannibal and St. Joseph railroad reached St. Joseph, Mo.—to 1887, when the Great Northern reached Helena, Mont. The influence of the railroads had been felt to some extent before this on the lower river. The Missouri Pacific railroad, which parallels the river from St. Louis to Kansas City, was opened to Jefferson City, March 13, 1856, but did not reach Kansas City until ten years later. This road did not have much effect upon the steamboat business of the river. Most of the boats ran far beyond the points reached by the road, and would have kept on the river whether the railroad were there or not. Being there, they secured a large part of the freight, even along the line of the railroad.

When the Hannibal and St. Joseph railroad reached the Missouri River at St. Joseph in 1859, that town became an important terminus for river commerce connected with the railroad. A line of packets including three boats ran south to Kansas City and north to Sioux City, with an occasional trip to Fort Randall. The first service of Captain La Barge's boat, the *Emilie,* was in this trade, in which he remained for two years.

The next point on the river reached by the railroads was at Council Bluffs and Omaha. On the 15th of March, 1867, the Chicago and Northwestern railroad reached the former place and on March 15, 1872, the Union Pacific bridge was opened across the river. Omaha largely supplanted St. Joseph in the upper river trade, and still further restricted the business from St. Louis.

The Sioux City and Pacific railroad entered Sioux City in 1868 from Missouri Valley, thus connecting with Omaha and Chicago. In 1870 the Illinois Central reached the same place 'directly across the State. Sioux City became, and for a long time remained, a more important river port than either St. Joseph or Omaha. All during the period of the Indian wars, in the decade from 1870 to 1880 it was the great shipping point for the army in all its work on the upper river. Even the trade to Fort Benton was in great part transferred to this point, and the St. Louis trade with that port suffered another severe falling off.

And now its bold antagonist attacked the steamboat business on every side. The Union Pacific railroad was opened to Ogden in 1869, and a freight line was at once established through to Helena, thus diverting south a large part of the business which had before gone to the river. In 1872 the Northern Pacific reached Bismarck, and cut off nearly all the upper river trade from Sioux City. In 1880 the Utah Northern entered Montana from Ogden and captured a large share of the trade of that Territory. In 1883 the Northern Pacific reached the valley of the Upper Missouri, and virtually controlled all the business that had hitherto gone to the Missouri River except the small proportion which originated at Fort Benton and below to Bismarck. The final blow was delivered to the river trade in 1887, when the Great Northern reached Helena.

This was practically the end of the steamboat business on the Missouri River, and the doom of old Fort Benton. A new town arose at the Great Falls, under the fostering care of the railroad, absorbed most of the former trade of Fort Benton, and grew into one of the largest towns of the State. Fort Benton dropped rapidly into a condition of decadence from which it has never recovered. In the meanwhile all the regular steamboat owners withdrew from the river except the Benton Transportation Company, which has maintained to the present day a very small fleet of boats at Bismarck, N. D. It was a sad day for the marine insurance companies when the fate of the river commerce was settled by the railroads. Accidents occurred with astonishing certainty whenever it was found that boats were no longer needed; and it was left to the underwriters to close up the final account of this record of disaster.

The last commercial boat that ever arrived at Fort Benton left that port in 1890. The victory of the railroads was complete, and every year since they have extended their lines still further into the valley and along the shores of the river, gradually cutting off the small local trade to points not yet reached by rail. The boat was never able to compete with the locomotive. The river did not run in the right direction. Mile for mile the transportation of freight upon it cost more than by rail. As to passenger traffic —what could forty miles a day do against four hundred! Nothing but the absolute exclusion of railroads could save the steamboat, and the development of the country made this as undesirable as it was impossible.

In this long and hopeless struggle the steamboats found a strenuous ally in the government of the United States, which cheerfully undertook to alter the course of events and maintain a freight traffic along the river. The history of government improvement work upon the Missouri River is an instructive one. For many years it consisted solely in the removal of snags and obstructions, and to this extent was a great and unquestionable benefit. Of the hundreds of steamboats lost on the river about seventy per cent, were lost from striking snags, and the removal of these obstructions was therefore an obvious step of good policy. Appropriations began to be made for the Missouri River jointly with the Mississippi and the Ohio as early as 1832, but the first actual work seems to have been done in 1838. In that year two snagboats, the *Heliopolis* and the *Archimedes,* ran up the river 325 miles and 385 miles respectively, removing altogether 2245 snags and cutting 1710 overhanging trees from the banks, at a total cost of twenty thousand dollars. In this same year the river was examined as far up as Westport (Kansas City), with a view of taking up the question of its general improvement. The officer of Engineers who made this examination was Captain Robert E. Lee.

From this time on to 1879 appropriations continued to be made jointly for the Mississippi, Missouri, Ohio, and Arkansas rivers, with occasional lapses of one or more years. The work done under these appropriations was exclusively the removal of snags, and was undoubtedly of great value. It was done when the traffic on the river was at its height, and it was therefore applied when and where needed. There can be little doubt that the property saved by this work many times repaid its cost.

In 1879 the government began a general improvement of the river by contracting its channel, so as to produce a greater depth at low water and make navigation possible at all stages. It was a doubtful policy at best, in view of the rapid and inevitable decline of traffic, but this consideration seems only to have increased the determination to keep boats on the river whether the interests of the public required them there or not. The policy was kept up in ever-increasing measure, and in 1884 Congress created a Commission of five members to take the matter in charge and conduct the work in a systematic way. A more fatuitous course has rarely been adopted by any government than this attempt to reverse the decrees of destiny and accomplish the impossible. Even at that time the fate of Missouri River navigation was to most men as clear as the flash of light in the night. It was dead beyond the hope of resurrection, at least within another century. The desultory traffic which existed here and there would not amount, in the total value of the freight carried, to the appropriations made for facilitating its transportation.

Nevertheless, in face of this inevitable march of events, the problem was taken up in earnest. Millions of dollars were appropriated, a vast accumulation of plant was made, and an astonishing amount of actual work accomplished. The result? So far as its influence upon the commerce of the valley is concerned the same as if this money had been used to build a railroad in Greenland. Not a boat more has followed the river than if the work had not been done. From that point of view it has all been wasted effort. From another viewpoint, however, it has been of great benefit. It has protected many miles of river front, saved from destruction thousands of acres of valuable bottom lands, and millions of property on city fronts and along the lines of railroads. It has developed some of the most effective methods known to engineering for the control of alluvial rivers, and has made a solid contribution to the advancement of science. From a purely engineering point of view and its great value in the protection of property, the work may be considered a success; from its influence upon the commerce of the country, something very different.

For seventeen years the Missouri River Commission dragged out an unnecessary existence, and was finally abolished by Act of Congress, June 13, 1902. But the lesson, if a costly one, has been well learned. So far as government work on the Missouri River is concerned, it will, in the near future at least, be confined to two purposes. On the lower stretches of the river it will be devoted to the protection of property along the banks; in the upper course to the building of reservoirs and canals, for the utilization of its waters in irrigation.

Thus the battle between the railroads on the one hand and the steamboats, with their government ally, on the other, has resulted in overwhelming victory for the former. It is a victory not to be regretted. It is in line with progress. The country has passed beyond any use that can come from transportation methods like those of the Missouri River steamboat. It served its purpose and served it well. It filled a great place in the early development of the Western country. But its day has passed, and henceforth it will be of interest only to lovers of history.

CHAPTER XXXVI.

LAST VOYAGES TO BENTON.

As soon as the ice broke up in the spring of 1868 Captain La Barge commenced work on the river, and after two trips to St. Joseph advertised for a trip to Benton. He received a good cargo and had a fairly profitable voyage, but in no sense so satisfactory as the year before. After his return in the fall to St. Louis he received a proposition for the charter of the boat in the government river work. Terms were arranged with General McComb of Cincinnati, through Captain Charles R. Suter, who was later for many years in charge of the government work on the Missouri River. Captain La Barge remained on the boat, working for the government, during the rest of the season, when he sold the boat to the Engineer Department for $40,000.

"And here," said the Captain, "I have to record another of the great mistakes of my life. I was now well 'fixed,' as the world goes. I had the $40,000 which I had received for my boat. I had about $50,000 in the bank. My home, forty acres in Cabanne place, was easily worth $40,000 even at that itime; and I was entirely out of debt. I had thought much of retiring from the river and ought to have done so. It was only too evident that the steamboat business on the Missouri had seen its day. It had passed its meridian in the middle of the sixties, and henceforth it was sure to decline. The reluctance of an active man, still in the prime of life (I was fifty-three), to lay aside the pursuits of a thrifty career, may have blinded my eyes to the certain and early fate of the business I had been engaged in, and have led me to hope that it would continue to be what it had been in the past. I had no desire to go on any other river. The Missouri was my home. I had grown up on it from childhood. I liked it, and knew I could not feel at home on any other.

"And so I unwisely concluded to continue at my old business, and went into it on a larger scale than ever before. I built the *Emilie La Barge,* a larger and finer boat even than the *Octavia,* costing me $60,000. The hull was built on the Ohio and brought to St. Louis for completion. This was in the winter of 1868-69."

Government business up the river was still very good, but competition for it was getting closer, as other lines of steamboat trade declined, and Captain La Barge failed to secure a contract. He went to work, however, for the successful bidder and did a paying business during the summer. He returned to St. Louis in September and made two trips to New Orleans, when the boat was laid up until the spring of 1870. He then entered into a contract with the government to transport Colonel Gilbert and 480 men with over 400 tons of freight to Fort Buford. It was a low-water season and the trip was slow and tedious; but the boat got through all right. After his return Captain La Barge ran in the lower river the balance of the season. But the profits were small, for the railroads had thoroughly gotten the upper hand. There was no longer any money in the lower river trade.

"I recall a little incident that amused me somewhat while on this summer's trip," said the Captain. "Colonel Gilbert was a strict disciplinarian, yet withal much liked by his men. When he came on board he told me that I need not close the bar on the boat unless I chose to do so. If any of his men wanted a drink and had money to pay for it, let them have it. 'That's something very unusual,' said I, for generally when troops were in transport I had to close the bar. All right, I'll take my chances,' he replied. 'If any of them get drunk, they will not get drunk again.' I noted throughout the trip that there was not a single drunken soldier, although the bar was open all the time.

"It was customary whenever we stopped to have a guard posted near the gangway, and this was done on our arrival at Fort Randall. A guard from the post was also ordered down, presumably to prevent the post soldiers from getting on the boat. The young lieutenant in charge made his way on board past Colonel Gilbert's guard, on telling who he was. He inquired of me for Colonel Gilbert, and I took him up and introduced him. After a few minutes' conversation he noticed the open bar on the boat and some soldiers there, drinking. He said to Colonel Gilbert that he would like to have the bar closed, as such were his orders. 'Why don't you have it closed, then?' said Colonel Gilbert bluntly. 'Well, I don't like to order it when you are aboard with troops.' 'It suits me to have it open,' returned the Colonel. The lieutenant explained that they were afraid that some of the post soldiers would get aboard and get drunk. 'You have a guard out there, haven't you?' asked the Colonel. 'Yes, sir.' 'Well, if they get past your guard they won't mine,' and he turned and walked off, leaving the lieutenant quite crestfallen at the encounter.

"It was while we were here at Randall that I was subpoenaed by a United States marshal to appear at the trial of the murderer of Captain Spear. I had the greatest difficulty in getting permission to continue my trip, although the trial was not to come off for several months. I had to give $20,000 bonds for my appearance.

"After my return to St. Louis that fall I made several Mississippi River trips and laid the boat up late in the season. In the summer of 1871 I ran in what is called the Omaha line all the season. In the fall I sold the boat for $30,000. She had paid me just about what she cost. I remained at home all the winter of 1871-72, when I again got tired of doing nothing; and being bred to the steamboat business, and not daring to turn my hand to anything else, commenced building another boat. She was completed by the middle of the summer, and named *De Smet,* in honor of the distinguished Jesuit missionary. I at once took a contract to transport freight from St. Louis to Shreveport, La., for the construction of the Southern Pacific railroad. This enterprise was disastrous in the extreme. I found the Red River without water enough at the mouth for me to enter, all of it going down the Bayou Atchafalaya. I did not get away from there until January, having had to import one hundred mules at my own expense to get the freight through. The enterprise was so disastrous that I was released from the contract. I secured fifteen hundred bales of cotton for my return trip to St. Louis, but the winter was severe and I was stopped by ice at Helena, Ark., and had to send the freight on by rail. Take it all in all, the season's venture was a most ruinous one." While engaged in this work Captain La Barge found it necessary to run down to New Orleans with his boat. He went to transact some business with Jesse K. Bell, a man closely connected with Mississippi River business and a capitalist well known throughout the valley. While in his office someone came in and asked to see Dave McCann. "What McCann is that?" asked La Barge. "Dave McCann." "Dave McCann?" "Yes. Do you know him?" "I used to know a Dave McCann over forty years ago." "Well, I guess it's the same man. Let's see if he knows you," and Bell sent his servant to call McCann in. When La Barge was on the *Warrior* during the Blackhawk war in 1832 McCann was second engineer on the boat. The two young men became intimately acquainted and very fond of each other. They were together for a time during the cholera scourge and promised to take care of each other if either were taken sick. Finally their ways parted and neither had seen or heard of the other since. McCann quickly appeared in Mr. Bell's office and glanced at where La Barge was sitting. "Well, if here isn't Joe La Barge!" he exclaimed, grasping his old associate by the hand. "And if this isn't

Dave McCann!" was the Captain's warm rejoinder. McCann was at the time president of the Cotton: Compress Company and of the New Orleans Foundry Company.

Captain La Barge did not reach St. Louis until February, 1873. He remained there for a while and made a second, and this time profitable, trip to Shreveport. He then advertised for Benton, secured a good cargo, and made a successful trip.

"An incident occurred on this voyage at Fort Rice," said the Captain, "which illustrates some traits of General Custer's military character. Custer was daily expected to arrive opposite Fort Rice, and General Stanley, who was commanding there, wanted me to delay a day or two and ferry him over. I made an arrangement with him to do this, and when Custer arrived I crossed the river with an order from Stanley to bring him over. I cleared the deck of the *De Smet* entirely, and rigged stages so that the horses and wagons could be driven directly on board. As the command approached, I saw an officer come riding down, clad in buckskin trousers from the seams of which a large fringe was fluttering, red-topped boots, broad sombrero, large gauntlets, flowing hair, and mounted on a spirited animal. I had never seen Custer, but of course had heard a great deal of him, and there was no mistaking this picture. I went out on the bank to meet him. He stopped his horse, but did not get off. I said,

'General Custer, I suppose?' He nodded assent. I showed him my order for the transportation of the command and told him that if he would have the wagons brought down I would see to their proper disposition on the boat. 'Stand aside, sir,' he replied; 'my wagon-master will take charge of the boat and see to ferrying the command over.' 'Not if I know myself,' I replied, and started for the boat. Custer sent for a guard to arrest me, but I took time by the forelock, drew in the stage, and steamed across the river and reported to General Stanley. Stanley immediately sent me back with an officer and guard, who arrested Custer and brought him to his headquarters.

"Custer seemed to me to be generally unpopular, that is, I rarely heard him well spoken of. Stanley, on the other hand, always appeared to be a gentleman of rare qualities, one who never forgot to treat a civilian as a man—something that many officers were little disposed to do."

While at Benton awaiting passengers for a return trip Captain La Barge had some new experiences of the character of men who were delegated by the government to do its business with the Indians. He was one day arrested by Mr. C. D. Hard, deputy U.S. marshal, sub-Indian agent, and special Indian detective at this point, on charge of selling and trading whisky on Indian reservations. The second day afterward Captain La Barge was brought up for examination, but not being allowed to introduce any evidence in his own behalf, made no effort to clear himself. The agent then seized his boat in the following words: "I seize the boat as sub-Indian agent, and turn her over to myself as deputy marshal for safe keeping." Being requested to produce papers for such a proceeding, he replied that verbal seizure was sufficient for him, and others would have to accommodate themselves accordingly. He immediately placed a fellow criminal over the boat and applied to Captain Kirtland, the military officer in charge, for a squad of soldiers to aid him in his rascality. This request was peremptorily refused. Hard became very insolent and abusive after the seizure, and it was soon evident that the object of himself and his confederates was to levy blackmail upon the Captain. Being determined to defeat this outrageous scheme, he left for Helena to consult legal authorities.

When Captain La Barge reached Helena he had no difficulty in securing a telegraphic order from Chief Justice Wade, of the Territory, directing the release of the boat, and he returned to Benton and resumed possession of her, much to the chagrin of the authors of this high-handed proceeding. This virtuous public officer had endeavored to work a similar game on another boat the same season, but was defeated by some of the passengers.

The boat had been detained by this incident upward of two weeks, and it was not until the middle of July that she set out on her return trip. Among the passengers was the family of Colonel Wilbur F. Sanders, already known in these pages as counsel for the plaintiffs in the case against La Barge, Harkness & Co. The Captain and he were always on good terms, however, and their former relations had nothing to do with their subsequent friendship.

On the way up the river this season two Catholic Sisters came on board on a begging visit in the interest of the Chicopee Mission in Minnesota. The Captain gave them passage to Benton and back. They visited Helena and Virginia City, and were very successful. They came back from Helena with the Sanders family and returned to Sioux City. About a month later Captain La Barge received by express a beautiful specimen of needlework handsomely framed, representing St. Joseph. It is still in the possession of the La Barge family.

After Captain La Barge's return to St. Louis he entered the Alton trade, and made daily trips in opposition to the Eagle Packet Company. He entered the same trade again in 1874 under an arrangement with John S. McCune, who had long controlled the trade on this part of the river. But in March of this year, while Mr. McCune was in Jefferson City to settle some details in regard to the sale of lands constituting the present Forest Park of the City of St. Louis, he was taken sick with pneumonia and died one day after his return to St. Louis. This broke up all the Captain's plans, and as he was not able, unaided, to compete with the Eagle Packet Company, he sold his boat to them.

Captain La Barge spent the remainder of the season in St. Louis, and in the fall commenced building a new boat, which he christened the *John M. Chambers,* in honor of the infant son of B. M. Chambers, President of the Butchers' and Drovers' Bank. The boat was ready for use in the spring of 1877. Captain La Barge made a trip as far as to Fort Rice, loaded mainly with quartermaster stores. He then entered the Yankton trade, that being at the time an important terminus for the declining river business. Certain defects in the boat's machinery, which could not be remedied at Yankton, compelled an early return to St. Louis and the loss of some important work. Captain La Barge remained in St. Louis until the following spring. He then returned to Yankton under a government contract to transport goods from that point. He finished this work early, but had scarcely returned to St. Louis when he was called upon to go up the river again, as we have elsewhere related, for service in the Custer campaign.

In 1877 La Barge took the *Chambers* as far up the Missouri as to the mouth of the Yellowstone, and up the latter stream to the mouth of Tongue River. In the following year he made a trip to Benton, arriving there on the 4th day of June. This is believed to have been the last commercial trip from St. Louis to Fort Benton. Upon his return to St. Louis he sold his boat and retired permanently from the business of boat owner and builder. He served as pilot on the lower river during the summer of 1879, and then finally withdrew from connection with commercial boating on the Missouri.

From 1880 to 1885 Captain La Barge was in the service of the government as pilot of the steamer *Missouri,* which was then engaged in making a survey of the river valley. This duty was little enough like the active business of his better days. It was filled with reminiscences of his past career which could not but bring regretful reflections. His intimate knowledge of the river was of great help in recovering the proper geographical nomenclature of the valley, and might have been of far greater value had the surveyor under whose charge he worked possessed an ordinary appreciation of the mine of knowledge which lay at his disposal. In 1885 the boat was taken from St. Louis to Fort Benton, this being the very last through trip ever made. The year 1885 closed Captain La Barge's career on the Missouri River, and he took his hand from the wheel after a record of service unequaled by any other pilot in its history. Three years more than half a century had elapsed since he made his first voyage up the river.

CHAPTER XXXVII.

DECLINING YEARS.

It is a sad reflection that, after a life of hard and useful work and the prominent part he took in upbuilding the great West, Captain La Barge should have closed his career in comparative want. But such were the vicissitudes of the business to which his life had been devoted. That business had passed away, and like a sinking ship it dragged down all who clung to it. Captain La Barge struggled bravely against these adverse conditions, but it was impossible to withstand the downward tendency.

From 1890 to 1894 Captain La Barge held a position under the city government of St. Louis. His very last remunerative work of any kind was for the United States Government, under the direction of the author of this work, whom he helped compile a list of the steamboat wrecks which have occurred on the Missouri River. This work was done in the year 1897, and was published as a part of the report of the Missouri River Commission for that year. Although the number of these wrecks lacks but five of three hundred, the Captain's memory embraced them nearly all, and most of them with great accuracy of detail.

Truly a mournful task was this to the veteran pilot. What reminiscences of a strange and wonderful past did it bring to mind! He lived over again his river life of fifty years, saw the old keelboat, the mackinaw, and the canoe, dodged again the bullets of the treacherous savages, killed the wild buffalo, sparred his boat over sandbars or warped it up the rapids, beheld again the wild rush to the gold fields, heard the tramp of the army going to battle on the plains, and mused upon a thousand other features of a life that existed no more. And as he recalled one by one these wrecks of a once flourishing business, he could not but reflect that the greatest wreck of all was the business itself. It was gone—buried so deep in the sands of commercial competition that not even the pennant staff or smokestack caused a ripple on the surface—passengers, cargo, and all that clung to her a total loss.

Captain La Barge survived most of his associates in the river business, and in his later years was frequently consulted by those who had occasion to recover facts concerning the early history of the river. He lived only about two years after the completion of his work for the government. He had grown visibly feebler during this time, and it was apparent to those who knew him that the end of his life was near. It came at last, however, quite unexpectedly. He was taken suddenly ill on the 2d of April, 1899, d at 3. P. M. of the following day breathed his last.

The funeral of Captain La Barge was from the St. Xavier Cathedral in St. Louis, and was largely attended. The Jesuits were under a deep debt of gratitude to the Captain, who, throughout his career, had extended to their missionaries the freedom of his boats. Through mistaken information they had often credited this generosity to the American Fur Company, for which Captain La Barge worked so much. Upon discovering their error they made due acknowledgment of it, and upon this occasion made a particular point to correct it and to acknowledge their lasting debt to the great pilot. It was probably in line with this purpose that the Church paid to the deceased its very highest honors. On Thursday morning, April 6, solemn high mass was celebrated at the Cathedral for the repose of the soul. Archbishop Kain, assisted by eight priests, officiated at the mass. Six grandsons of the deceased acted as pall bearers. Father Walter H. Hill, a lifelong friend of Captain La Barge, preached the funeral sermon. In the course of his remarks he said: "Captain La Barge led an honorable life. In the eyes of the Church to which he belonged he led a good life. There was no stigma upon his name. No vice marred his character to bring the blush of shame to his children. His life was an example of which they might well be proud."

The speaker drew an interesting picture of the changes that had taken place in the city of St. Louis and in the great West within the span of this man's life. In his infancy he had actually been in peril from the Indians in what are now the outskirts of the city. Then luxury and plenty, as we now know them, had no existence. The mother cared for her children and did the work of the house. The candle and not the incandescent furnished light at night. Water was pumped from the well and people did not ride to and from their business in swift electric cars. In the words of a local paper, commenting upon the Captain's career, "He passed through all the gradations and progressive steps of the century until in its very last year the sun of his life set forever, and his expiring gaze beheld a little village grown to a great metropolis, enmeshed in a perfect tangle of railways, factories, and furnaces, teeming with busy activity, converting the crude material into every possible contrivance imaginable for the use of man; palatial mansions where, in his youth, was a wilderness; in short, every improvement that the brain of man had wrought." Father Hill illustrated this marvelous growth by a reference to the growth of his own Church in St. Louis: "As I stand here to-day," he said, "to pay the last sad tribute of respect to the memory of the friend of my early youth, I cannot help thinking of the marvelous changes that have been wrought in the last eighty-four years. On the evening of October 22, 1815, a mother entered a little frame church on the banks of the Mississippi, bearing an infant in her arms. The parent had come to have the child baptized. Tallow candles lighted her way through the aisle to the rude altar where the ceremony was to be performed. To-day the remains of that babe, grown to manhood's estate and full of years, lie before me. The spirit now dwells in his Father's house. At the christening were only the most primitive conveniences; at the burial services his remains rest in a magnificent granite structure; hundreds of electric lights glare upon the dead; hundreds of heads are bowed in silent prayer. Which of us can ponder for an instant upon the span of this life and not be bewildered at the contemplation?"

Captain La Barge was buried in the beautiful Calvary Cemetery, which lies adjacent to the even more beautiful Bellefontaine Cemetery in the northern part of the City of St. Louis. His grave is within a short distance of where he spent his earliest infancy, and is in all respects a peculiarly appropriate resting place after a life like his. To the eastward, in full view where not cut off by the foliage, flows the mighty Mississippi. To the northward the impetuous Missouri brings down its flood from the dim and shadowy distance.

How often had this individual guided his intrepid bark up the channels of these two streams, headed for remote and almost unknown ports, and anon, gliding swiftly on his homeward journey, sped eastward into the Mississippi and south to the port to which he always returned. Standing by his grave and overlooking the valleys of these streams, their history through the past two centuries thrills the mind like a romance of the past.

In personal appearance Captain La Barge was one of the most distinguished-looking men of the West in his time. He stood five feet ten, was well proportioned, weighed about 180 pounds, was erect, muscular, and alert, with a sharp, quick eye and a quiet energy in all his movements. He always wore a beard after reaching manhood's estate, and in later years bore a striking resemblance to General Grant. Colonel Thomas of the army, long stationed in St. Louis, always addressed him by the name, Grant; and only a few years before his death a gentleman met him on the street and said, "Well, if I did not know Grant is dead, I should say there he comes."

Captain La Barge's manner in social intercourse was mild and agreeable, and his accent pleasant to a degree. It was a satisfaction to hear him talk. Although almost invariably soft and unobtrusive, his voice would occasionally swell, under the influence of emotion, until it possessed all the power of command. It is said that this characteristic marked his entire career. His men were not deceived by it. They never dared to take undue advantage of the sunshine of his manner, lest they call down upon them the thunder of the tempest.

Captain La Barge was a lifelong, consistent Catholic in religion, and in politics a lifelong, consistent Democrat.

CHAPTER XXXVIII.

DESTINY OF THE MISSOURI RIVER.

What of the future? Is the useful purpose of the Missouri River in the up-building of the West already fulfilled? Is its great history a closed book? Such, it must be admitted, is the general view. In popular estimation that river to-day is little more than a vast sewer, whose seething, eddying waters bear down the sands and clay and debris from the far upper country, scattering them along its course, swelling the floods of the Mississippi, and pushing ever seaward the delta of that mighty stream. To the railroads it is a million dollar obstacle wherever they want to cross it. As a competitive route of commerce it has sunk beneath their notice. To the husbandman along its borders it is a perpetual nightmare, for he knows not what morning he may awake to find his worldly possessions ruthlessly swept away. From all points of view it now seems like one of those things in the economy of nature which could be dispensed with and the world be none the worse for its absence.

Nevertheless the river is still there—a fact, a thing to be reckoned with in some way or other. It will not let its presence be forgotten. In its old-time fashion it carves up the lands, but with vastly greater destructiveness now that they have become so valuable. Its terrible ice gorges pile up as of yore, but are now more dreaded than they used to be on account of the property along the banks. In other respects as well it is the same peculiar stream that it has ever been. The weird sandstorms drive over its illimitable bars, the willows bend to the blast, and the swift-rolling waters are lashed into foam by the prairie gale. In periods of calm its silvery sheen stretches away under the morning and evening sun as when the pilot followed its interminable windings through the prairies; and its resistless tide rushes on, as in the blithe steamboat days, when it carried upon its bosom the commerce of the valley.

But here the likeness between the past and present ends. No aboriginal savage now roams upon its borders. The buffalo does not come to its shore to quench his thirst, or to swim its current, or to cross upon its ice. The lonely dwellers of the valley have long since ceased to watch the eastern horizon where the river runs into the sky, for the curling smoke no longer tells them of the approach of those white-winged messengers of civilization, the Missouri River steamboats. They are gone, its greatness and glory, never, in their ancient form, to return.

But the river itself is still there, and those who dwell on its shores refuse to believe that its power for good has passed away. For years they have wistfully looked upon its waters, flowing by in absolute waste, and then upon the rich lands on either side, parching in a rainless climate. A vague hope of what the river *may* be already possesses their minds. Does it not hold the secret germ of a mighty future empire? Twenty-five millions of people these wasted waters could sustain, if only they could be scattered upon the neighboring lands. With great canals to divert them from the river, with great reservoirs to keep them from going to waste, there would follow the necessary millions of money and men to turn them to proper account.

This is the dream. Can it be realized, or must it always remain nothing more than a dream? It is an engineering problem purely. The grand desideratum would be that everywhere, whether upon the main stream or its tributaries, the water could be saved and used in irrigation. But the obstacles in the way of so complete a result seem at present almost insurmountable. The higher tributaries can doubtless all be utilized, but the main streams, in their lower courses, have so little fall that it will be very difficult to build canals of sufficient length to get the water upon the higher ground. Whether the water will ever have a value that will justify pumping it to the necessary elevation it would be unwise at present to hazard a conjecture. But even if not more than half can be utilized, it will still be enough to maintain a population equal to that at present existing in the entire arid region of the West.

Here, then, is the answer to our question—What of the future? Turn this river out upon the lands. Unlock its imprisoned power. Where the rains do not fall let it supply the need. Then the new and greater history of the Missouri River will begin. Utility will take the place of romance. The buffalo, the Indian, the steamboat, the gold-seeker, the soldier, will be seen in its valley no more, but in their stead the culture and comfort, and the thousand blessings that come with civilization. Such, let us hope, in drawing the curtain over a mighty past, will be the consummation of a still more mighty future.

On the 13th of June, 1902, Congress passed an Act abolishing the Missouri River Commission, and virtually abandoning the river as a commercial highway.

On the 17th of the same month it passed an act inaugurating a government policy of reclamation of the arid lands. This policy will eventually result in an extensive use of the waters of the Missouri in irrigation.

THE END.

BIG BYTE BOOKS is your source for great lost history!

Made in the USA
Lexington, KY
09 May 2017